Charles Edgar Prather

**Winning Orations of the Inter-state Oratorical Contests**

And Biographies of Contestants

Charles Edgar Prather

**Winning Orations of the Inter-state Oratorical Contests**
*And Biographies of Contestants*

ISBN/EAN: 9783337009892

Printed in Europe, USA, Canada, Australia, Japan

Cover: Foto ©ninafisch / pixelio.de

More available books at **www.hansebooks.com**

OF THE

# INTER-STATE ORATORICAL CONTESTS,

AND

# BIOGRAPHIES OF CONTESTANTS.

---

COMPILED AND EDITED BY
## CHARLES EDGAR PRATHER.

---

TOPEKA, KANSAS.
1891.

Copyright, 1891, by
CHARLES EDGAR PRATHER.

# A SOUVENIR.

This volume has been compiled as a Souvenir of the Inter-State Oratorical Association, inasmuch as this association was the first formed for the advancement of the study of oratory. These pages contain the grand and superior productions delivered on the annual events of this association, rendered in competition among college students since its origin, in the year of 1874. And deem this association worthy that has aided the science of oratory whereby it has become a powerful branch of knowledge.

# PREFACE.

AFTER much delay and long continuous labor I take great pleasure in now presenting this Souvenir of the Inter-State Oratorical Association to the public. The work deserves much favor. It is worthy to be studied for its history, its philosophy, and its precepts. The orations are the exquisite productions of the best minds in college circles delivered annually in contest before the association. So, to the young orator whose victory in the arena of debate has contributed to the world such specimens of learning and eloquence, to say nothing of its marvelous influence, retribute your grateful admiration. In this work I have introduced the successful orators— one after another according as they took their respective positions in the succeeding reign— with brief biographical sketches and excellent engraved likenesses, which increase the interest and value of the book. The chapters on "Oratory and Orators," and "Plagiarism," written in a brilliant manner by prominent educators of the day, are highly appropriate and instructive, and merit the popular praise of the public as well as the student. Accordingly from the desire to meet the frequent applications made for these prize orations became the purpose of compiling this volume, which I kindly dedicate to the orators and their relatives and friends.            CHAS. E. PRATHER.

TOPEKA, KAN., January, 1891.

# CONTENTS.

|  | PAGE |
|---|---|
| Historical Introduction | 7 |
| Constitution of the Inter State Oratorical Association | 11 |
| The Heart, the Source of Power | 15 |
| British Rule in India | 21 |
| Culture, a Basis of Brotherhood | 31 |
| The Two Races in Ireland | 37 |
| The World's Conquerors | 42 |
| Beatrice and Margaret | 48 |
| Satan and Mephistopheles | 53 |
| Faith and Doubt as Motors of Action | 58 |
| The Loneliness of Genius | 66 |
| Dante | 72 |
| Iago | 78 |
| Mahometanism and its Enemies | 87 |
| Poe | 94 |
| The Evolution of Government | 99 |
| The Philosophy of Scepticism | 105 |
| Progress, its Sources and its Laws | 111 |
| The Old and the New Civilizations | 117 |
| The Cause of the Gracchi | 122 |
| The Political Mission of Puritanism | 128 |
| The Saxon Element in Civilization | 134 |
| Judas Iscariot | 141 |
| The Unity of Science and Religion | 145 |
| The Conflict of Labor and Capital | 150 |
| Schiller and Germany | 157 |
| Conservatism, an Essential Element of Progress | 164 |
| Mob and Law | 171 |
| John Brown | 177 |
| The Man and the State | 183 |
| Principles of Political Parties | 190 |
| The Defender of the Constitution | 197 |
| The Philosophy of Inequality | 202 |
| Riot and Revolution | 208 |
| The Puritan and the Cavalier in Our National Life | 215 |
| Our English Language | 221 |
| Orators and Oratory | 231 |
| Plagiarism | 237 |

# HISTORICAL INTRODUCTION.

THERE always exists in ambitious natures an inborn desire to excel, and never does this desire become more prominent than during the years spent in college. And since this rivalry has existed in nearly every educational institution, there has been arranged some method of testing the much-desired superiority. This has been in nearly if not all cases a contest of physical power and endurance. It is now an open question as to the beneficial results from inter-collegiate contests in boating, ball games and similar sports.

It remained for the Adelphi Society, of Knox College-Galesburg, Illinois, to crown all former efforts in conceiving another outlet for this restless and impetuous spirit of rivalry, by testing intellectual merit through the eloquence of oratory; and to this society should be given the honor of our present Inter-State Oratorical Association.

Invitations from the members of the Adelphi Society were sent to the following institutions to join a contest in oratory: Illinois State Industrial University, and Chicago University, of Illinois; Iowa State University, and Iowa College, of Iowa; Wisconsin State University, and Beloit College, of Wisconsin. These invitations were accepted by all except the Wisconsin State University, whose faculty refused, and Monmouth College, of Illinois, was substituted. The following is the invitation *verbatim:*

GALESBURG, November 4, 1873.
**To the Honorable and Students:**

SIRS—The Adelphi Literary Society, of Knox College, feeling that it would be for the mutual benefit of "Western colleges" to engage in friendly rivalry, and preferring the culture of the rostrum to the oar, desires to submit for your consideration the following proposition:

1st. The Adelphi Society offers two prizes in oratory, to consist of one hundred dollars and seventy-five dollars respectively, to be open for competition to the following-named universities and colleges, each institution furnishing one orator: Illinois State Industrial University, of Illinois; Iowa

State University, and Iowa College, of Iowa; and Wisconsin State University, and Beloit College, of Wisconsin.

2d. The contest will be held under the auspices of the Adelphi Literary Society, of Knox College, in the Galesburg Opera House, on the evening of February 27, 1874.

3d. The Governors of the three States represented shall each select one man, and these three men so appointed shall appoint the awarding committee.

4th. In marking the contestants the judges shall take into consideration excellence of thought, style of composition, and delivery, marking each on a scale of ten. The person receiving the highest average mark shall be entitled to first prize, and the one receiving the next highest, to the second prize.

5th. At the close of the contest the committee of award shall place their marks, in sealed envelopes, in the hands of the chairman, without any confering together or comparing of marks.

6th. A committee of three, selected from the audience by the contestants, shall receive the marks from the chairman, take their sums, and announce the successful contestants.

7th. The Adelphi Society further agrees to pay the railroad fare of the contestants to and from Galesburg.

8th. As soon as the names of the contestants are reported to the Adelphi Committee they will cast lots for positions on the programme, and report the positions, as drawn, to each of the contestants.

By order of the society.

F. I. MOULTON,
HENRY W. READ,
GEO. A. LAWRENCE,
Committee.

The contemplation of this event gave birth to the idea of forming an association for the purpose of continuing contests in oratory. Accordingly other invitations were issued to the same institutions, requesting each to send a delegation to a convention, to be held in Galesburg, at 2 o'clock P. M., of the 27th of February. These invitations were also accepted, and the convention was held at the appointed time in the handsome parlors of the Union Hotel.

Mr. Geo. Sutherland, of Chicago University, was chosen president, and Mr. F. I. Moulton, of Knox College, secretary. After some discussion and mature deliberation it was decided to make the association an Inter-State Oratorical Association, in the following manner: The chief colleges in each of the several States, namely, Wisconsin, Illinois, Iowa, Michigan, Indiana, and Ohio, were to form themselves into separate State associations, and hold contests between the colleges of their State.

The successful orator in each of the State contests should be the contestant at an inter-State contest. The State associations and contests to be distinct organizations from the inter-State association.

A constitution was then drawn up for an association of the colleges represented, which was to serve as a preliminary to the inter-State organization, thereby giving the representative colleges a temporary organization. As officers of the same the following were elected: President, H. C. Adams, of Iowa College; vice president, J. B. Dimond, of Illinois State Industrial University; Secretary, A. R. Sprague, of Beloit College; treasurer, R. T. Wilson, of Iowa State University. The formation of an inter-State association could not be realized, as Michigan, Indiana and Ohio were not represented. The convention decided by ballot that the next inter-collegiate contest should be held at Iowa City, under the auspices of the Iowa State University; and the making of necessary arrangements for the coming occasion was left in the hands of an executive committee. Thus a temporary organization being effected the convention adjourned to a further time.

The first contest in oratory took place in the evening of the 27th of February, 1874, in the City Opera House of Galesburg. The meeting was marked by the largest audience ever congregated in the city. The programme opened with an overture by the Grand Orchestra.

F. I. Moulton, president of the Adelphi Society, then introduced Mr. H. C. Adams, of Iowa College, Grinnell, Iowa. Subject: "The Student and the Mysterious," which the speaker rendered with true grace and eloquence. Mr. A. G. McCoy, of Monmouth College, Monmouth, Ill., followed Mr. Adams. His subject, "Conservatism," was of a political nature, and the speaker's style was energetic.

Mrs. Chas. G. Hurd rendered the "Cavatima from Lucia di Lammermoor," an operatic solo that was highly appreciated, after which Mr. T. Edward Egbert, of Chicago University, Chicago, Ill., appeared. His theme, "The Heart, the Source of Power," won for him the first prize. Mr. Frank E. Brush, of Iowa State University, Iowa City, Iowa, next addressed the audience on the subject of "Ideas: their Power and Permanence." It was an erudite production, and Mr. Brush a natural orator.

The "Blue Danube Waltzes," by the Grand Orchestra, was given next place on the programme, at the conclusion of which Mr. Geo. T. Foster, of Beloit College, Beloit, Wis., discoursed "The British Rule in India," which was pronounced the second best oration. The last orator, Mr. W. W. Wharry, of the Illinois State Industrial University, Champaign, Ill., came forward with the subject of "Labor and Liberty; or, the Mission of America," which he delivered in an easy manner, and retired amid applause.

While the judges who had been appointed, according to agreement, by the Governors of the three States represented in the contest, withdrew for decision, Mrs. Hurd sang the favorite ballad, "Five O'clock in the Morning." The judges appointed were: Dr. A. Burns, president of Simpson Centenary College, Indianola, Iowa; Prof. A. Stetson, of Normal University, Bloomington, Ill.; and Judge A. A. Smith, of Galesburg, Ill. The prizes were awarded to Messrs. T. Edward Egbert and Geo. T. Foster.

Thus closed one of the greatest events in college history, the result of which is to-day an honor to our educational institutions.

A meeting called to convene in Chicago, June 9, 1874, was largely attended, and the plans for the permanent organization of the Inter-State Oratorical Association were completed and perfected. It now includes sixty-three colleges, comprising the States of Ohio, Indiana, Illinois, Wisconsin, Minnesota, Iowa, Missouri, Kansas, Nebraska, and Colorado.

# CONSTITUTION

OF THE

## INTER-STATE ORATORICAL ASSOCIATION.

### ARTICLE I.

This organization shall be known as the "Inter-State Oratorical Association," and shall consist of the Collegiate Associations of Illinois, Iowa, Wisconsin, Ohio, Indiana, Minnesota, Kansas, Nebraska, Colorado, and such other State associations as shall be admitted by a two-thirds vote of the delegates present at any annual convention.

### ARTICLE II.

SECTION 1. The object of this association shall be to hold contests in oratory, and such other literary contests, at such times and places as shall be decided upon by the association at its annual convention.

SEC. 2. In the contests of this association each State shall be represented by the successful contestant at its annual contest: PROVIDED, He be an undergraduate of the collegiate course at the time of such State contest.

### ARTICLE III.

SECTION 1. The officers of this association shall consist of a president, vice president, and secretary, (who shall also be treasurer,) who shall constitute the executive committee of the association. All nominations of officers of the association shall be by informal ballot, and an election shall follow by ballot upon the three names receiving the highest number of votes, a majority of all votes being necessary for a choice.

SEC. 2. The officers of the association on their retirement from office, and ex-orators, shall be honorary members of the association.

### ARTICLE IV.

SECTION 1. It shall be the duty of the president to preside at all meetings. In case of a tie in voting, he shall cast the deciding vote. He shall also have power to call a special meeting at the written request of four State associations, giving at least thirty days' notice to each State association of such meeting.

SEC. 2. The duties of the secretary shall be such as are common to that office, and any other duties that the association may authorize. He shall have printed yearly one thousand (1,000) copies of the constitution, and shall send one hundred (100) copies to the secretary of each State association. As treasurer, he shall keep the accounts of the association, and pay all bills audited and allowed by the executive committee. He shall be required to deposit with the president of the association a bond for $1,000. He shall receive as remuneration for his services the sum of $25.

SEC. 3. The contests of the association shall be under the control of the executive committee. It shall be the duty of the executive committee to audit all accounts before they are presented to the association.

### ARTICLE V.

SECTION 1. Six persons shall be chosen each year by the executive committee, to act as judges of the literary contest of that year; and each State association shall be notified of their appointment at least six weeks before the contest.

SEC. 2. The judges shall not in any way be connected with the institutions represented in the contest, nor shall any two judges be selected from the same State. Nor shall any judge on delivery be selected from the State in which the contest is held, except in case of extreme emergency.

SEC. 3. Any judge shall be removed upon the protest of any State association made in writing, within thirty days after his appointment, the reason for such protest being given in writing; PROVIDED, No State shall be allowed more than two protests.

SEC. 4. The judges selected shall be divided into two equal sections, A and B: the judges of section A to grade on the merits of thought and composition, and the judges of section B to grade on delivery, without consultation, each judge giving one grade, which shall be on the scale of 100.

SEC. 5. The secretary of the association, at least two weeks before the contest, shall forward a copy of each oration to each of the judges in section A, who shall grade them, and send sealed copies of their grades to the vice president and secretary of the association, so as to reach them at least two days before the contest; said marks to remain sealed until after delivery to the secretary of the marks of the judges of section B. But neither the names of the authors of the orations, nor the institution represented, shall be known by the judges of section A.

SEC. 6. At the close of the contest, the president and secretary shall take the grades of all the judges for each contestant. The grades of each judge shall be ranked 1, 2, 3, 4, etc. The orator ranked first by four or more of the judges shall be awarded first prize. If no orator is thus ranked first, the orator, the sum of whose ranks is least, shall be awarded first prize. In case of a tie, the orator receiving the highest grand average shall receive the first prize. The first prize having been awarded, the grades of the remaining orators shall be again ranked 1, 2, 3, 4, etc., and the second prize determined in the same manner as the first. The president shall then announce the result. The markings of the judges shall be published in at least one daily paper.

### ARTICLE VI.

SECTION 1. In the contests of this association no oration shall contain more than two thousand (2,000) words, and it shall be the duty of the secretary to construe this article strictly to the letter, and to return any orations exceeding the above limit to the secretary of the State from which such oration is sent.

Sec. 2. Any outline, synopsis, analysis or explanation attached to an oration shall be considered and counted as a part thereof.

Sec. 3. The several contestants shall send one hundred (100) printed copies of their orations to the secretary of this association, so they shall reach the secretary at least three weeks before the contest. One (1) copy shall be sent to each of the judges of section A, as directed in article V. section 5 of this constitution. The remaining copies shall be distributed by the secretary of the Inter-State Association to the secretaries of the various State associations, in sufficient number that each local association composing the State association may receive a copy of all the inter-State orations.

Sec. 4. The orations for the inter-State contest shall be printed by the State association according to the following uniform standard: They shall be set in brevier type, the body of each page being four (4) inches wide and six (6) inches long, with a margin one and one-half (1½) inches in width. Ninety (90) copies of the orations shall contain the name and college of the author, and ten (10) copies shall be printed with name and college omitted.

## ARTICLE VII.

Section 1. The annual convention shall meet in the afternoon of the day on which the contest is held, and the following day in the forenoon, in which convention each State shall be entitled to three (3) votes.

Sec. 2. No delegate shall be entitled to a seat in the convention whose credentials shall not have been signed by the president and secretary of his State association.

## ARTICLE VIII.

Any State in this association failing to send a representative to any annual contest without furnishing a satisfactory reason shall be excluded from the association.

## ARTICLE IX.

The names of the orators engaged in the contest, and copies of the orations, also the names and markings of the judges, shall be kept on record by the secretary.

## ARTICLE X.

Section 1. The association shall pay all necessary expenses connected with the contest, including prizes, and all necessary expenses of judges, the president and secretary, and vice president when acting as president.

Sec. 2. Such an admittance fee to the oratorical contest shall be charged as the executive committee shall deem proper.

Sec. 3. Each State association shall, at least thirty days before the inter-State contest, deposit with the treasurer of the Inter-State Association the sum of twenty-five (25) dollars, which shall be subject to use by the executive committee in case of a deficit at the inter-State contest. Any State association failing to comply with this provision, without sufficient reason being given, shall be denied representation in the next contest and convention.

Sec. 4. Within ten days succeeding each annual contest all surplus funds exceeding twenty-five (25) dollars, which shall remain in the inter-State treasury, shall be divided equally among the State associations, and be deposited with their respective treasurers. Should there be any deficit it shall be met by an equal tax upon the State associations.

SEC. 5. As testimonials of success in the contests of this association there shall be awarded as first honor SEVENTY-FIVE DOLLARS; as second honor, FIFTY DOLLARS.

### ARTICLE XI.

SECTION 1. This constitution may be amended at an annual meeting of the association by a two-thirds vote.

SEC. 2. The organ of this association, in the future, shall be annually a college newspaper published where the next contest is held, and it shall be the duty of the secretary to keep standing in that paper each year the list of officers of the Inter-State Association and the secretaries of the several State associations. Any bulletin or correspondence in reference to the inter-State contest shall be sent to the editors of that paper.

SEC. 3. All questions involving parliamentary forms, not provided for by the constitution, shall be referred to "Roberts' Rules of Order."

## AMENDMENTS TO THE CONSTITUTION.

### ARTICLE I.

SECTION 1. The State whose orator appears first on the programme shall be entitled to the presidency.

SEC. 2. The State whose orator appears fourth on the programme shall be entitled to the vice presidency, and shall have the location of the next contest.

SEC. 3. The State whose orator appears seventh on the programme shall be entitled to the secretary and treasurership.

# THE HEART, THE SOURCE OF POWER.

By T. EDWARD EGBERT, of Chicago University.

### BIOGRAPHICAL.

The subject of this sketch, T. Edward Egbert, was born near Georgetown, Ohio, March 26, 1848. When eight years of age his parents moved to Woodford County, Illinois, and settled on the prairie to make a farm. Here he attended school but fourteen weeks in nine years. Truly it may be said his advantages were very meager in his youthful days. However, life on a farm secured to him a sturdy physique, and such principles of independence and economy as are necessary in life. In the fall of 1865 he prepared to take a college course. At the end of five weeks his father's sudden death called him home. This sad experience compelled Mr. Egbert to remain on the farm three additional years. In September, 1868, he returned to the preparatory department, taking up the studies one year in advance of his former studies. The next year, at the age of twenty-two, he entered the freshman class of the Chicago University, and graduated in four years as bachelor of arts. He was the first member of the freshman class initiated in the Chicago chapter of the D. K. E. fraternity, and is still an enthusiastic member. He was unusually active in his literary societies, never declining an appointment, either regular or impromptu. In June, 1873, while a student, he delivered an oration entitled "The Voice and the Pen," and later one on the subject of "The Hercules of Civilization," and received very flattering comments from the press. His most notable oration, "The Heart, the Source of Power," he delivered at the inter-State oratorical contest at Galesburg, Illinois, where he attracted great admiration, and was considered foremost among them all. Mr. Egbert possesses by nature the elements of an orator—an imposing figure, a ready utterance, and a full-toned melodious voice. At the organization of the Illinois Oratorical Association he was elected chairman, and likewise of the meeting at the Tremont House, in Chicago, when the Inter-State Oratorical Association was formed. Immediately upon leaving college he entered the Union Theological Seminary, at Chicago, graduating in May, 1877, thereafter devoting five years to the ministry of the gospel in the Baptist denomination. In 1881 he resigned the pastorate of the second largest church in Indiana, because of financial embarrassment resulting from the failure of a business in which he was interested. Although a severe blow he has ever since been laboring to re-establish his former possessions. He married Miss Maggie Baker, one of Chicago's accomplished ladies, in June, 1875. Mr. Egbert has lost none of his interest in oratorical days in the colleges. His oration, on the following pages, has never before appeared in print, and is worthy of careful perusal.

## THE ORATION.

Delivered at the Inter-State Oratorical Contest, at Galesburg, Illinois, February, 1874, taking first prize. Judges: Dr. A. BURNS, Prof. A. STETSON, Judge A. A. SMITH.

Orpheus, poet, philosopher, master of the lyre, is a name immortal in classic song. The skill with which he struck the tensile chords is fabled to have been such, that the unconscious rocks and trees left their places and moved to the time of the air he played; and the beasts of the mountains, bewitched of their ferocity and charmed to friendship, gathered lovingly at his feet at the sound of those chords, the sweet harmonies of whose notes beneath the touch of the divinely ingenius artist were like the chanting of the gods.

Heart-bruised and disconsolate at the loss of his bride, Eurydice, fatally stung by a venemous serpent, he resolved on descent into the under world, that if possible he might oppose the cruel rulers there, and obtain permission for the return of his nymph-spouse to their mountain home.

Armed with his lyre, strung with tedious care, he trustfully entered the realm of hades and essayed entrance to the palace of Pluto.

At the thrice-guarded gates further advance was denied.

The prayer from the depths of his hungry soul he poured over the sensitive strings of his second love, the lyre. At the first note from the "golden shell" the chariot wheels of the gods stood fast, Tantalus forgot the infernal torment of his insatiable thirst, the vulture ceased to tear the constantly reproduced vitals of Titios, the palace gates turned upon their golden hinges, and Pluto, melted into sympathy with the bereft soul that sobbed out the story of its lonely sorrow on the harp strings, granted the prayer. Eurydice was released.

This scrap of mythology reveals to us, that according to the judgment of men of that far-away day of its authorship, the power of perfect art was unlimited. Was that conception unwarranted? May it not be that the only limit of the ministry of art is the attainment of the artist. The principal realm of the ministry of art is the affections, the emotions, the passions. Art is not primarily a teacher. Its concern is not to instruct in fundamental truths or radical principles. It does not engage in intellectual controversies, or go to war. It forever appeals to what is already known and freely granted, or by the winsomeness of its appeals disarms the contentiously disposed. Its ministry is invariably to its friends; toward the unfriendly it is speechless forever. It silences the opposer, or remains silent toward him.

The ministry of music to man is through a single sense; painting and sculpture through another. The art of arts, that art of which all others are part expressions, appeals to the *whole* man, to head and heart, reason, affections and emotions, calling into highest and holiest activity the choicest qualities and noblest power of his being.

This is the art of oratory.

Books—the vaults in which have been accumulated the gains of the intellectual toilers of the ages—have contributed immensely to the progress of mankind. Teachers, too, often like nature's forces, have wrought in silence, but in might, in the world's advancement. But in the long march from cannibalism to civilization, from barbarism to Christianity; from the Egypt of slavery of body to masters, and of mind to priests, to the Canaan of liberty—both the pillar of cloud and fire, that has been both guidance and cheer to the leaden-hearted and heavy-footed multitudes in the weary ages that lay between the start toward the better state and the attainment of it, has been the oratory of those ages.

The trumpet that has aroused the sluggish from lethargy to activity, the faint-hearted from submission to oppression, to resistance of it, that has cheered the slave of appetite on in the struggle for kingship over self, has been the voice of the orator.

This art, without the possibility of aid of strings, or mallet and chisel, or paints and canvas, with truth its subject, the soul of man its immediate object, has been the herculean force in the world among men. What is the secret of its power? Masters in the sciences tell us that the source of energy in the natural world is heat. In the realm of the arts it is true beyond dispute that the deeper the pathos, the sweeter the poem. The sobs of a wounded heart awaken the tenderest responses, and stir the deepest emotions. The more impassioned the song, the greater the enchantment. The intenser the passion portrayed, the more captivating the picture. The fire burning in the soul of painter or sculptor glows from the canvas, or radiates from the marble to which the artist tried to transfer the picture carried in his soul. In poems, paintings and statuary are registered, as upon a thermometer, the temperature of the passion of their artist creators at the hour of the transfer of the picture from soul to material. As the field of the orator's art is wider, its sphere broader, so are its obstacles more, its difficulties greater. Its range is the whole gamut of man's nature. Sight, the avenue through which the painter and sculptor reach the soul; hearing, the gateway of the musician to the temple within, are at the orator's disposal, as well as every element of the intellectual and moral nature, every emotion of the soul. Every fibre of man's being recognizes his touch, and responds to his call.

But truth cannot often be painted, nor principles chiseled. Herein lies one of the difficulties. In oratory the soul charged with a great thought, or a truth, must ordinarily discard all *media*, and express itself immediately. Mind in immediate contact with mind, and soul to soul, is the attitude in oratory. In the material world, we observe again, heat is the source of energy. In the arts, in general, heart intensity is the measure of effectiveness. In this particular art it is pre-eminently true that triumphs in it are where one soul on fire with truth sets others aflame by immediately communicating that truth to them. The results of the communication are usually in proportion to the grasp of the truth upon the soul of the orator, and the intensity of his earnestness in delivering it to others. Highly emotional states, that spring from deep and clear convictions of truth that are well expressed, are followed by action in the direction dictated by the truth-giving origin to the emotional state. No harp string, or chord of lyre, is so exquisitely sensitive and responsive to a master's touch as the emotions of man.

Horace, that old master of human nature, long ago wrote in substance:

"Answeringly the face of man laughs
To those that laugh indeed, and weep to those that weep."

Thoughts are expressed by words. The emotions have their own peculiar unworded language of mystical signs. Each emotion, every shade of emotion, each passion, every mood of mind, has its own peculiar dialect of symbolical signs, which express even the most delicate shades of quality and intensity of feeling. It is by these that the emotions and passions communicate themselves from orator to auditors, definitely expressed, and thoroughly understood. However much the thought of the orator may be misunderstood, misinterpreted, and misapplied, the emotions never are. Genuine feeling expresses itself accurately, and is understood definitely. So is pretended feeling at once detected, and instantly condemned. We need not look at a thermometer to see whether the temperature is ninety above or thirty below. We feel, and so know the difference. So does an audience intuitively and unconsciously take the temperature of an orator accurately. The string of the piano is deaf and mute to all tones except the one to which it is strung.

The emotions make no answer to arguments directed to the head, but heart does answer heart in the same pitch as that in which it is addressed. The breeze against the sails propels the ship, and the pressure of steam in the chest gives motion to the engine; so do the emotions acting upon the will beget action in the direction in which they impel. The flight of the ship and the speed of the engine show the velocity of the wind and pressure of the steam. So does the disposition of an audience to act responsively to the persuasions of an orator furnish the infallible test of the effectiveness of the oration.

Higher compliment was never paid an orator than the cry of the Athenians at the close of one of Demosthenes's harangues, "Let us march against Philip." The dissatisfaction among the American colonists at the injustice and oppression of the mother country was general, but the indignities were endured without protest till those whirlwinds of fiery indignation burst from the breasts of the Otises and the Henrys, who in holy recklessness dared denounce tyranny in their own king. It was the manly courage, the sublime heroism, the lofty patriotism of these forest Demostheneses, ringing out across the colonies, that lighted the fires of liberty on the hearth-stones in the cabins of the people throughout the land. With courage aroused, and determination fixed, with patriotism aflame, the rallying of the people through those long years of privation was to the standards which those "master spirits of storm had lifted on high." From these few souls issued streams of patriotic fire, which spread from hearth to hearth, till the homes of the New World felt its influence, and every patriot was aglow with its holy warmth. These few outspoken haters of tyranny; the few whose petition was "give me liberty or give me death" became the inspiration of millions. The earnest-hearted few, ardently desiring liberty for the colonies, dominated by the single purpose of having it whatever might be the cost, by virtue of that desire and that determination became leaders of millions of others.

In all those weary years from Bunker Hill to Yorktown, in the uncomplaining sufferings of hunger and cold, in the quiet endurance of anguish in the hospitals of painful suffering, who can not read the impress and hear the echo of that sublime sentiment, "give me liberty or give me death." So has it always been, and while human nature remains what it is, it will always be, that he who leads the way from the worse to the better, that he who charms, sweetens, thrills, and betters other's lives, carries in his heart the source of power.

# BRITISH RULE IN INDIA.

By GEORGE T. FOSTER, of Beloit College.

## BIOGRAPHICAL.

George T. Foster, the successful competitor for the second prize of the first inter-State oratorical contest, in 1874, was born August 3, 1852, at Lancaster, Grant County, Wisconsin. At an early age his parents sent him to the Lancaster Institute, a private academy founded under the management of Sherman Page, the man who subsequently as circuit judge in Mower County, Minnesota, gained notoriety. His next experience was as a student at Beloit College. In the preparatory department of this institution he was under John P. Fisk as master. During his college course for two years he was a roommate of E. D. Eaton, D. D., now president of the college, and for three years a classmate of Chicago's famous criminal lawyer, Wm. S. Forrest. In 1873 he was offered an appointment to West Point by J. Allen Barber, then member of Congress, but declined, which action he has never regretted. After graduating in 1875 he was principal successively of the high schools at Potosi and New Lisbon, Wisconsin, and at Cherokee, Iowa. Three years later he was married to Miss Lizzie G. Eunor, of Potosi, Wisconsin, who graduated as valedictorian of the class of 1873 from Sinsinawa Mound College. Besides winning the second prize for oratory at the inter-State oratorical contest of 1874, he also received the freshman prize for declamation in 1872, at Beloit College. He delivered the master's oration in 1878, and will return this year to deliver the alumni oration. Mr. Foster has of late years delivered a great number of orations and lectures, and is known as a popular and eloquent speaker. His voice is full, and remarkably flexible. During a portion of his time from 1875 to 1878 he read law in the office of Barber & Clementson, Lancaster, Wisconsin, and at this writing he is successfully engaged in the profession of law at Cherokee, Iowa, where he is universally respected, and it is hoped many more years of successful life are yet before him. The oration which follows is admitted to be his masterpiece.

## THE ORATION.

Delivered at the Inter-State Oratorical Contest, at Galesburg, Illinois, February, 1874, taking second prize. Judges: Dr. A. BURNS, Prof. A. STETSON, Judge A. A. SMITH.

Mystery has peculiar charms. India has ever been mantled with blank mysteries. Her earlier history is lost in imaginative stories and romantic fables. The legend that antiquity's greatest woman, Semiramis, invaded India, and the fact that Alexander subdued a part of the country, stand out against the remaining gloom like rockets against the blackness of night. In some unknown way the nations of remote antiquity were supplied from India with the precious metals, the rarest gems, "purple and fine linen." The knights of the Middle Ages obtained their "Damascus" blades from beyond the Indus. Nowadays India sends forth her troops of unsurpassed jugglers, who apparently have revived the old black arts of magic, and the American belles sport their camel's hair shawls, woven in the sunny vales of Cashmere.

Not merely for curiosity does India possess charms and interest. Beneath her mysteries the scholar and the student discover matter for the deepest study. For the consideration of the scholar, India presents the oldest language of which we have any records, the Sanskrit, whose origin points back to a time near the confusion of tongues at the tower of Babel. To the student, she offers the study of her history, graven upon her ruined temples, upon the fallen columns and broken arches of her ancient royalty. Europe, having long possessed the trade of all the Orient, has grown familiar with questions connected with Asia. Until quite recently Americans have had little reason to allow their attention to wander across the Pacific Ocean, and for us, therefore, these questions at least possess the charm of novelty. Since the completion of the Union Pacific Railroad, the most direct route from eastern Asia to Europe lies directly through the heart of our country from San Francisco to New York. Trade and travel are already forming a beaten track in this direction. The spices and silks of the East are finding their way to Europe along this route. There is thus held before America the dazzling prize of controlling the intercourse between Europe on the one hand, and India, China, Japan, and the East Indies on the other. If the United States can *acquire* and *hold* this trade, the merchant fleets of the world will flock to our marts of commerce on the Atlantic and Pacific coasts, and our multiplied canals and railways "bearing the commerce of nations," will make our country the emporium of the world.

As we are thus drawn toward India, we feel a greater interest in the questions of her history. We cannot help thinking that she is destined to play a prominent part in the coming centuries. This seems reasonable, in view of her vast population, which is as great as that of all North America, all South America, Great Britain and Ireland, Spain, Russia, and all the islands of the world.

> "Know ye the land of the cedar and vine,
> Where the flowers ever blossom, the beams ever shine;
> Where the light wings of zephyr, oppressed with perfume,
> Wax faint o'er the gardens of Gul in her bloom;
> Where the citron and olive are fairest of fruit,
> And the voice of the nightingale never is mute;
> Where the tints of the earth, and the hues of the sky,
> In color, though varied, in beauty may vie? . . .
> 'T is the clime of the East; 't is the land of the Sun."

Nature, with lavish hand, has bestowed upon that country endowments susceptible of indefinite improvement. But have they been improved by the rule to which India is subject? Many people, from reading the great orations that were made on this subject about a hundred years ago, have almost concluded that it would have been better for the Hindoos had the British remained forever away. Yet, on contrasting their present with their past condition, there remains little room for doubt that, by England, India has been elevated to a position of rapid growth in civil institutions, mental acquirements, and moral strength. This is shown by facts more eloquent than words, by statistics more irresistible than arguments.

Two views may be taken of India. The first, previous to the British conquest. Five hundred years ago the clouds, which had shrouded India for fifty centuries began to rise. As they lifted they revealed a sight never witnessed elsewhere in history. The tyranny and superstition of man were here struggling against the overflowing bounties of nature. It was a country teeming with population, having within its power great wealth; but, sunk to the lowest depths of heathenism, the rites of human sacrifice, the burning of widows, the killing of children, self-torture, and suicide, were then practiced with the inflexible strictness of Pharisees. The distinctions of caste were far more rigidly observed than now. The whole country swarmed with robbers. There existed a large sect whose religion was murder; who killed strangers, friends, and relatives, as a religious duty.

In one respect, India, at that time, bore a striking resemblance to Persia. In both countries large districts of land had been tilled from time immemorial. As a consequence, the fertility of the soil had been much reduced. Successive generations had cleared the country of all timber. This affected the atmosphere, and produced a scarcity of rain. Droughts, in their turn, destroyed all remaining vegetation, and dried up all the productive power of the earth. Rains became unknown, famines became the regular occurrence, and the once fertile soil was rapidly becoming marked with somber hues of devouring deserts. As the inhabitants had no connection with the outside world, and thus could receive no assistance from abroad, so whenever their crop of rice failed devastating famines resulted, and there was nothing left for them but to lie down and die. Famine succeeded famine in rapid succession, attended in almost every case by pestilence in the form of Asiatic cholera. Persia, Northern India, were thus becoming an uninhabited, unproductive wilderness. The entire country was divided into innumerable petty districts, each governed by an absolute despotism, tyrannical and cruel as only an oriental despotism can be; nine-tenths of the population reduced to servitude by the oppression of the Eastern tax-gatherer. The history of these small governments is little else than an interminable series of revolutions. Seldom did a rule last a lifetime. Each division carried on a continual predatory warfare with each of its neighbors. All was rebellion, anarchy, and chaos. Internal wars were finishing up the work of famine, pestilence, oppression, and superstition. A country in this mutinous state presented an easy conquest to the fierce warrior-tribe north of the Himalayas, and west of the Indus. Hence we see them pouring down through the passes of the mountains. First came the Persian hordes; their ravages were followed by the long-continued invasions of the ferocious Afghans. After these succeeded the inroads of the Rajpoots, mercenary soldiers, Seiks, Jahrets, and Mahratos. Before these shaggy demons of the wilderness, the Indian peasants who escaped the sword fled to the wilder neighborhood of the hyena and tiger. Terrible as was this scourge for India, the worst was reserved until the last. Mohammedan kings had resolved on the conversion of the Hindoos to the faith of Islam. In this they failed. Exasperated with defeat, they determined to exterminate the Hindoos. In this they met with better success. With eastern devotion they girded themselves for the work. They swept the country as with the besom of destruction. A single king led twelve separate expeditions into India. Death seldom reaped such a harvest. The work of extermination seemed approaching its consummation, when the Mohammedans tired of their own bloody work. Scarcely had they retired, when, from the tableland of Asia, the home of the Huns, there came the cruel Tartars, led by Tamerlane Timoor. He was the conqueror who sought fame by erecting monuments of human bones; who seemed to have a passion for that style of architecture. Of him the historian says: "When Tamerlane had finished building his pyramid of seventy thousand human skulls, and was seen standing at the gates of Damascus, glittering in his steel, with his battle-ax on his shoulder, till his fierce hosts filed out to new victories and carnage in southern India, the pale looker-on might have fancied that nature was in her death-throes; for havoc and despair had taken possession of the earth, and the sun of manhood seem setting in a sea of blood." Thanks to the muse of history that she never permitted the details of those horrors to be chronicled. It is well that a career marked by columns and pyramids of human skulls should forever remain a mystery. The despotism thus founded, maintaining its strength until the British accession, filled out a period of three thousand years in which India made not a single step in advancement, and which presents not a single redeeming feature.  This is the first view which history gives of India.

The second view dates from the British accession.  The remedy which England applied to Indian degradation, though it has been effective, and though eventually it will prove complete, yet was not immediate in good results.  The atrocities of some of her rulers have sullied the honor of the English nation, and have left upon her records a stain so indelible that years of just rule have not been sufficient to wipe it out.  The world shudders at the stories of the Rohilla war, of the plundering of the Begums of Oude, of the hiring out of British soldiers to a heathen despot, and of the cruel punishment inflicted on captives taken in the Sepoy rebellion, when they were strapped to the mouths of cannons and blown to pieces. It is a matter of shame that the East India Company was permitted for so long a time to practice monopoly and extortion; it is a matter of shame that, for a short time, they prohibited Christian missionaries from their borders; and it is a matter of shame that they once decorated Hindoo temples, thus patronizing idolatry.  But when we reflect that Burke, Sheridan, and Fox lived to see redressed all the wrongs of India, and that country placed under as pure a rule as even those great critics could wish; when we consider that the opposition to missionaries aroused the Christians to such strenuous efforts as only that opposition could have aroused; when, through the vicissitudes of her history, there begins to gleam forth as in lines of fire "the tracing of God's finger," then the evils of British rule sink into nothingness compared with the untold horrors of the previous rule of Mohammedans and Tartars.  If the British have been guilty of some wrongs, they have overshadowed each one of them by huge mountains of benefits.

First, let us look at the civil and physical benefits which they have conferred on India.  That which they found necessary to accomplish at the outset was the establishment of a government sufficiently strong to quell internal rebellions, and to render the country safe from foreign invasion.  This was done thoroughly and completely.  The natives were trained to obedience to home-rule, and to self-defense against aggressive tribes.  The Decoits, the robber-bands, were disorganized, and their leaders transported to foreign lands.  The Thugs, the sect whose religion was murder, were exterminated. The rites of human sacrifice, of the suttee, and of infanticide, were suppressed by the most stringent laws. We hear no more of foreign invasions, and the country which so long had been turbulent with anarchy was now free to enjoy the blessing of peace.

England next turned her attention to the prevention of famines. To provide means of transportation she built canals all through the rainless regions of India. One of these is five times as large as the Erie canal. Year after year these great arteries were lined with canal boats laden with provisions for the starving millions of India. Year after year saw the silent progress of vegetation creeping up from the banks of the canals, and stealing silently over the surrounding country. Year after year found the British engaged in the work of irrigation, in cleaning out, repairing, enlarging old reservoirs, and building new ones. Year after year young trees were brought from distant forests, and planted on the banks of the canals, until at length these various influences combined to produce there what had hitherto been unknown—they produced rain. With astonishing success, England at once introduced from her island home, barley, oats, corn, and wheat. Large tracts of Hindoostan, which once were inhabited by a perishing population, and where were only the bleached and drifting sands of the desert, are now inhabited by an enlightened people, are covered with waving fields of golden grain, and blossom with perpetual harvests.

The critics of England estimate the number of natives killed in the wars of India, since the British conquest, at the extravagant figure of 3,000,000. The advocates of British rule can point to 30,000,000 Hindoos saved by England from the horrors of famine. We have seen that one hundred years ago Persia and India lay side by side in the physical condition of the country. Persia remained independent, and in 1872, 3,000,000 of her inhabitants perished from famine. India fell to Great Britian, and in 1872 her newly developed resources were employed in sending relief to the dying nation of Persia.

As yet it is not a foregone conclusion, that the rainfall in all parts of Hindoostan will be great enough to render abundant crops certain each year. It has sometimes happened there, as in our own land, that while in the greater part of the country there have been plenteous harvests, yet in a single district the crops have been an entire failure. The want of provisions, consequent upon drought, is felt at this very time in the district of Bengal. But we learn that breadstuffs and rice are going from the other parts of India into that needy province at the rate of 10,000 tons per week. A drought in that country can never again produce a depopulation famine.

These are some of the things which Englishmen have done for India. They have laid open to her the manufacture of India-rubber. They have checked the consuming of her forests for fuel, have taught the natives from the timber to build ships for European navies, and have gone down into the bowels of the earth to disclose to the wondering natives that they have an infinite wealth of coal. They have improved and enlarged the manufacture of indigo, silk, and opium. Opium! whose culture has, in some respects, largely benefited India. It is commonly supposed that it has not, but statistics show that, while the growth of the poppy has vastly increased, the actual consumption of opium in India has scarcely increased at all. The culture of the poppy supplies with employment great communities of idlers, and its sale to the Chinese has become a source of great revenue. The English have brought the tea-plant from China, the sugar-cane from the West Indies, and they have taught the naked savage to raise them both. They brought the cotton-plant from the West Indies, and they taught the natives its cultivation. They brought sheep from Australia; they brought looms from London; they have taught the natives from the cotton and the wool to weave cloth which they make into clothing, which they have taught the natives to wear. England has also improved the mental state of India. Vast sums of money are expended annually in the work of education. A system of free schools is maintained by the local governments and missionaries, and in aid of this the central government annually devotes over £500,000 sterling. There is scarcely a town in all India that is without its schools and its hospitals, as is shown by the fact that there are in operation there three universities, 300 colleges, and 25,000 schools, attended by nearly a million children. Some of the native Hindoos are among the best physicians and civil engineers in the world. Her scholars rank among the first. Take, for instance, the great Sheshadre, who is now visiting this country. She has a native press as free as ours, and as extensive as that of many European governments. In the City of Calcutta there are published between fifty and sixty periodicals, which sell at the low price of one-fourth of a cent per copy. Truly India is attaining the glory of what Carlyle would call "her writing period."

India has also been elevated morally. This work, however, has progressed slowly when compared with her civil and intellectual advancement. But we must remember that India was in bondage for 3,000 years, and that in a single century England could no more break down the barriers of superstition and the distinctions of caste than she could roll down the Himalayas into the Indian Ocean. But in spite of gigantic obstacles the work has advanced.

No one can estimate the influence which Western improvement has upon the Hindoo mind. We have an illustration of it in the effect produced by the introduction of railroads. The locomotive has traversed all India; it has thundered along the banks of the Ganges; its scream has been heard within the shadows of the Himalayas; it has been the means of an extended intercourse among the people; with its iron frame it has crushed right through superstition, and it has produced freedom of thought. It is the belief of the high caste Brahmins, that if they are brought in contact with those of a lower caste they will be shut out of heaven. With this for a plea, they petitioned the railroad managers to run *caste* cars. The railroads officials, who are quite as wise for their own interest in India as they are in Illinois, replied:

"REVEREND SIRS: We shall run not *caste* cars, but class cars. You pay your money, and you take your choice."

This was the severest blow that Brahminism ever received. At that reply thousands of idols fell from their pedestals like Dagon of old, and to-day are kicked about the streets of Bombay and Calcutta. Soon every night-owl of India shall have a discarded image to roost upon, and every mole a broken idol beneath which to burrow.

Yes, the awakening of India is near. The Himalayas no longer look down upon a land impotent in stagnation. The

Ganges no longer flows to the sea, drowning with its swift-rushing current the cries of the infant thrown to the crocodile, or the frantic shout of the devotee who flings himself from a precipice into its waters; but the mighty river moves on in majesty to the sacred chime of bells ringing from Christian churches, to the grand music of water-wheels, to the hum of factories, and to the thunders of the locomotive. The vast plains of Hindoostan are being peopled with the followers of the Cross. Haste! oh, haste! you who would have your name enrolled among those who have contributed to the regeneration of India, for soon, very soon the choirs in our churches shall have no cause to chant the thrilling hymn telling us that there comes a cry for help

"From Greenland's icy mountains
And India's coral strands."

From Cashmere to Cape Comorin the seeds of freedom are springing into vigorous life. The land of the sun is steadily rising to that place among modern nations which she held among the ancients while Abraham was sojourning in Egypt, and Semiramis was building Babylon. She already sends delegates to the Evangelical Alliance, and as the British Empire turns gradually into a grand republic, India will be prepared to send representatives to the British Parliament, or shall stand free, prepared to send representatives to the "Parliament of Man."

# CULTURE, A BASIS OF BROTHERHOOD.

By THOMAS I. COULTAS, of Illinois Wesleyan University.

## BIOGRAPHICAL.

Thomas Isaac Coultas was born in Scott County, Illinois, May 5, 1853, and is of English parentage. He is the youngest of seven children. When six years of age his father died, leaving the care of the farm and rearing of the children almost entirely upon his mother. Her force and nobleness of character had marked influence over her children, and she early led them into Christian lives. She thought Thomas was destined to the service of the ministry, and at an early age he conceived the same impression, ofttimes standing on a chair and preaching to the neighbors who came in, insisting, however, that the service was not complete without the collection. He first attended a country school, and at the age of fourteen he entered the Winchester High School, where in two years he finished the course. At sixteen years of age he was urged to accept license to preach, and the country school-houses and village churches were crowded to hear the boy-preacher. The success with which he met in this field of labor deterred his intention to enter college, but led him to enter the regular ministry, and in September, 1869, was admitted into the Illinois conference of the Methodist Episcopal Church. As a clergyman he served two years in Sangamon and Champaign counties. He then entered the Illinois Wesleyan University to complete his education, graduating in the classical course June 15, 1875, three years subsequently receiving the master's degree. In the fall of 1875 he was united in marriage with Miss Angie Morrison, daughter of Henry B and Caroline (Sears) Morrison, then residing in Bloomington, Illinois, now in Coin, Iowa. Three children now comprise the family. Mr. Coultas has ever since continued laboring in the ministry, occuping pulpits at Pittsfield, Quincy, Hillsboro, and Clinton, in Illinois. He was also pastor of the First Methodist Episcopal Church, Decatur, Illinois, for three years, and there was general regret when by limitation of church law his pastorate ceased. Thence he was sent to the Kimber Church, Danville, Illinois, and was just entering upon his third year as pastor of this church when he received an invitation from the First Church, St. Paul, Minnesota, to become their pastor. The presiding bishop made the appointment. But in a short period of time, finding the work was not congenial to him, and the effect of the severe winters on the health of his family, he requested the authorities to transfer him back into the territory he left, whereupon he was stationed at the Centenary Church, Terre Haute, Indiana, and was received with enthusiasm by the congregation. This is one of the largest and most prosperous churches in Indiana. Rev. Coultas is a preacher of great ability. As an orator he possesses marked characteristics. His sentences are ornate and vigorous; his thoughts are logical and closely connected, thus making it easy for his auditors to know his meaning, and quickly to recognize that he advocates what he believes. His oratory is of the Wendell Phillips style. He deals but seldom in pathos, rarely in wit, and does not rise to the dramatic, but is impassioned and earnest. Rev. Coultas is in the prime of manhood, and his physical strength and intellectual vigor foretell many years of influence and usefulness. The oration here given was delivered when a senior of the Illinois Wesleyan University, at the contest of 1875, held in Indianapolis, Indiana.

## THE ORATION.

Delivered at the Inter-State Oratorical Contest, at Indianapolis, Indiana, May, 1875, taking first prize. Judges: Prof. G. THAYER, Rev. C. C. BURNETT, D. D., Hon. EDWARD SEARLING, Gen. T. M. BROWNE.

The introduction of evil into the world brought countless woes, the dissolution of the human family following in their sad train. And viewing man through the medium of history, as it unfolds his cold seclusiveness, and exhibits wild, warring, struggling, surging humanity coming up the path of ages, we are prone to say, the family relations will never be restored. To him who reads, but pauses not to reason; to him who sees humanity only as delineated on history's page, but knows nothing of the principles unfolded by ethics and philosophy, how dark and foreboding the picture! Despair possesses him as he reads the first page of human career, for in the first family is a murder, and the first soul entering heaven's gates is driven from earth by the hand of violence. Here are seen whole empires torn and rent in pieces; whole armies mown down on a thousand bloody fields; thrones shaken to their foundations; hearts bleeding with sorrow; even the church, loaded with depravity's pestilential vapor, bearing the impress of evil; popes, prelates, and priests, led on by the powers of hell, grappling the secular sword until "the whole creation groaneth and travaileth in pain," under the dominion of human passion. Sad indeed is the picture; but we are not without hope. Culture —her garments yet wet with the dew of dawning day, her face luminous with the hopes of triumph, unveiling to our astonished vision the measure of human possibility, on the basis of mental and moral attainment — proclaims the brotherhood of man. Culture is bringing about a fraternity of minds. Cultured minds must commune with each other, for upon this depends the march of intellect. Miles and oceans cannot separate them, neither can centuries divide them. Thoughts expressed ages ago are thrilling the souls of millions to-day; and although the grave has long since opened to receive the speaker, he still lives, as human hearts beat in sympathy with his utterances, and human lips reiterate them again and again. In fighting the fierce battle of life, in walking up the same pathway, in entering into similar investigations, a harmony of sentiments, and identity of interests, have united the votaries of intellect in a brotherhood as sacred and consummate as the union of angels. Aristotle, in his scientific researches, investigated the wonders of animal life, unfolded many mysterious phenomena, gave us more enlarged ideas of man's relations to nature, more exalted conceptions of the plans of creation. All this, too, did Agassiz. Hence, through the medium of science these two men communed with each other, and across the chasms of centuries clasped the hand of brotherhood. Shakespeare, Milton, and Bryant walked up the same pathway, hand in hand with Virgil, Homer, and Isaiah; and, feeling the inspiration of the ancient muse, they soared to loftier themes. Blackstone and Kent breathed the spirit of liberty from the free hills of Greece; gathered greatness from the studied justice of Cicero and Justinian; received mightier animation from the inspired law of Moses, thus linking them together in sacred fraternity. The glorious hymn of victory which Moses sang and Miriam echoed back on the shores of the Red sea; the strains of Jeremiah, tear-steeped in the prophet's own sorrow; the heart-burst of grief from the trembling strings of David's harp; the rich melodies breaking forth from the lips of a Handel or Mozart, blending with a thousand voices from moorland and mountain sides, proclaim the brotherhood of song, and with mightier expression declare that impulses, wants, and woes of humanity are as the impulses, wants, and woes of one man. As culture advances, secrets unfolded from nature, powers delved from the earth, wisdom drawn from the skies, conspire to break down barriers of prejudice and unite mankind in enduring fraternity. The philosopher who reads in nature the hand-writing of Deity; the metaphysician who reduces chaotic thought to principles; the poet whose harp is the universe, and who plays on the strings of a million hearts; the artist who visits the spirit land and brings down to our grosser sense its archetypes of ideal beauty, sit together as one family, joined in one unity of purpose to elevate the race, and together are throwing open the portals of learning for the on-coming nations.

Science and religion, too, join hands standing upon a common level, not contradictory, but vindicative, one of the other; not by lowering religion to man's former misconception of science, but by lifting our conception of science to the plane of spiritual and divine truth. The final religion and the final science will own brotherhood. While religion will stand forth better understood, shining out in clearer lines, science will be heard saying, "The earth is the Lord's and the fullness thereof." Culture is uniting the nations, demolishing those barriers which ignorance and prejudice have reared; spurning that narrow-minded patriotism which confines its regards to a peculiar nation, with impartial benevolence culture embraces every man as kinsman and brother. However much the nations may have been at war with each other in the past, the signs of the times certainly indicate the near approach of that era when it will be recognized that "God hath made of one blood all nations of men." Profound and metaphysical Germany, artistic and imaginative France, practical and energetic America, bluff and sturdy old England, though distinct in customs and peculiarities are not divergent in thought and purpose. God is letting loose an army of thinkers in the world, and they are bringing the nations together. Science, commerce, religion, new facilities of intercourse, electricity converting the world into a whispering gallery, the abolition of slavery, the spirit of liberty bursting forth in both hemispheres, new friendships, new interests, are overcoming the old antipathy of nations, silently spreading the sentiment of human brotherhood, and the conviction that the welfare of each is the happiness of all. We as Americans are proud of our country. Justly so; we are the model government of earth. But a nation is not made in a day. We are more than one hundred years old. This model government is but the expansion and outgrowth of the past. One truth after another, slowly rising from the bosom of bygone centuries, has contributed to make for us this precious heritage. We have come up the pathway of generations, through toil and vicissitude, through the smoke of battle and the rage of passion, by the way of free Athens and free Rome and sacred Palestine. Noble men led us ages ago, who never breathed the free air of America or planted foot on our sacred soil. In view of this, we hail Asia as our birth-place; we grasp with firmer friendship the electric hand of Europe, beneath the foaming Atlantic, and forever severing the shackles of slavery, we open wide the doors for the admission of Africa into our sacred brotherhood. Culture is moral, and in the effulgence of its light the unity of Christianity is being recognized, and the churches are converging. It is here culture attains its highest dignity and its truest worth. The first and grand condition of true culture is an unselfish love of truth, which is the very soul of Christian virtue. Culture inspires love and faith, and these, centering in a common Lord, bind together the Christian world. It reveals a divine cause, and leads to a recognition of common origin. It opens the word of life, and brings the church to a common tribunal. Denominational distinction may exist as long as time, but sectarian prejudice is already becoming a thing of the past, and fraternal hands are being clasped across the crumbling walls of partition. The meeting of the Evangelical

Alliance in Brooklyn was the meeting of Christianity. Those men with cultured minds and cultured hearts were her worthy representatives; and as they came from Belgium and Greece, from Britain and France, it was no more our noble delegates who took them by the hand, and said to them, "Welcome," than it was Luther and Latimer, and Calvin and Wesley, who lived and worked together upon our free soil, through the rich results of their prayers and faith, as exhibited in a free religion, a free church, and a free nation. Above the platform in the Alliance hall was written Christianity's expressive motto: "*Unum corpus sumus in Christo*," while in every heart was felt, we are met—

"Where names and sects and parties fall,
And Jesus Christ is all in all."

Three of these noble men are gone. Two, from the decks of the *Ville du Havre*, sank beneath Atlantic's foaming billows, but "their works do follow them." Under the influence set in motion at that Alliance, the clash of religious sentiment is ceasing, Christians are uniting against a common foe, and the churches are converging. Love is mightier than logic, and as Christian hearts are being deluged with love they are becoming one, as "the Father and Son are one." Those of the ministry, too, with cultured minds and cultured hearts, are soaring above the narrow creed and catechism, and, as with the voice of one man, are crying out to humanity, "Behold, behold the Lamb!" From the banks of the Ganges; "from Greenland's icy mountains and India's coral strands;" from the shores of the Pacific, and where flow the waters of the Nile; from Alpine heights, and New England's palatial residences, comes the legitimate response, "I see, I see the star!" And over every barrier they are coming—they are coming to clasp hands around the cross of one common Redeemer, until soon in Heaven's courts will be heard the glad announcement, "The morning dawneth!" O Culture, noble is thy work! thy dignity is the brightest manifestation of divinity; yea, the symbol of God's infinity, for no limit can be set to thy unfolding. Humanity, as a unit, comes and bows at thy tribunal, acknowledging the sway of thy scepter, and marshaled under thy banner marches forward to conquer death and hell, and with thee to scale the battlements of glory.

# THE TWO RACES IN IRELAND.

By THOMAS W. GRAYDON, of Iowa State University.

### BIOGRAPHICAL.

Thomas W. Graydon is a native of Ireland. Naturally he was very scholastic, but through the advice of the eminent oculist, Sir William Wilde, of Dublin, Ireland, at the age of fifteen he was compelled to relinquish his studies and love of books to rescue his eyesight, which had become much impaired from excessive usage. This affliction has ever been one of the difficulties he has had to struggle with. At eighteen years of age he came to America, and settled on a farm in Illinois. Recovering sufficiently he entered Griswold College, Davenport, Iowa, in 1871, where he graduated. In 1872 he entered the Iowa State University, graduating there in 1875. It was while a student of this university he was the representative to the inter-State oratorical contest, and where he was admired in the many points of eloquence and oratory. The following year he located in Cincinnati, Ohio, where he began the practice of medicine. In 1885 he represented Hamilton County in the Legislature, declining the renomination in 1887. In 1888 he was appointed by Governor Foraker on the old board of public affairs, where he served until the board was abolished, in the spring of 1890. By a special session of the Ohio Legislature, in October, 1890, the mayor was given the appointing of a board of city affairs. Dr. Graydon was again assigned to that position. He is very active in political affairs, and quite influential in the municipal government of Cincinnati. Dr. Graydon has a large and lucrative medical practice, and is a man of excellent qualities. The following oration, delivered by him May 13, 1875, shows his original talent, and presents one of the most favorable specimens of college orations.

## THE ORATION.

Delivered at the Inter-State Oratorical Contest, at Indianapolis, Indiana, May, 1875, taking second prize. Judges: Prof. G. THAYER, Rev. C. C. BURNETT, D. D., Hon. EDWARD SEARLING, Gen. T. M. BROWNE.

Our attention was lately called to Ireland by the Froude-and-Burke discussion. Probably few think Mr. Froude has justified the English invasion of Ireland. But who has justified the Roman invasion of Britain, the Saxon, the Danish, the Norman; or the extermination of the Indians on this continent? History presents us terrible scenes — countries overrun, peoples enslaved, oppressions, annihilations. We cannot justify the inflicted wrongs, we *do* approve the results. The English historian and the Catholic priest judge history by different standards. The one, Carlyle's worthy disciple, comes saying: "The two civilizations conflicted — the stronger and higher — and the stronger, *because* the higher, prevailed." His opponent, the Dominican monk, tells us of penal laws and violated treaties, a proscribed priesthood and a degraded people, the peasant murdered in his burning cottage and the wail of his children in the midnight air, and asks our judgment. The standard by which Mr. Froude judges history is the Fatalist's, the Utilitarian's, and that of Mother Nature, who is always rejoiced to have the strong race crush out the weak. Father Burke's standard is more in harmony with the common notions of justice. The Englishman's defense of his country is a defense of the laws of progress; of the times, not past, when "might makes right." The priest's complaint is an indictment of "Specific Gravity," "The Persistence of Force," "The Survival of the Fittest;" England's justification — the right of the tiger to his evening meal; Ireland's plea — the claim of the poor victim to its life. When we shall have reconciled Fate and Free-will, and settled the respective rights of the wild beast and his prey, we shall have satisfactorily judged the English conquest and occupation of Ireland.

There are three periods of Ireland's history of peculiar interest to the student of political or social science. The first is that of Henry VIII. and Elizabeth, when the English colonists in Ireland adopted the Reformed faith, thus infusing a new element of discord, and making what was a war of races also a war of religions. The second period is the last quarter of the eighteenth century, when the Irish Parliament enjoyed a nominal independence. The third is the present, marked by Mr. Gladstone's Ballot Act. Briefly to consider these three periods is our task. When the Northern nations of Europe embraced Protestantism, hatred of her oppressors helped keep Ireland true to the church of the Middle Ages. Besides, Catholicism, appealing to our emotional nature, and cherishing an ideal of glowing faith, was intrinsically congenial to the Irish character. Only strong peoples assimilate strong creeds. The relentless logic of Calvin was for the Scotch, not the Irish race. The explanation, then, of Ireland's present state lies in the fact, that since the Reformation the colonists and the native Irish have been as clearly divided in religion as in race.

In the eighteenth century we find the original inhabitants deprived of their ancestral holdings, excluded from every office and voice in the government, disarmed, persecuted and outlawed, their religion proscribed, and their priests under ban, subject to the most odious penal laws, without the means, and almost without the will, to better themselves. On the other hand, the Protestant colonists, the ruling class, had been alternately caressed and taxed by England, as her fears or her avarice dictated. They were literally the "Irish garrison." They governed the country, and were themselves governed for England's aggrandizement. When, by their enterprise, any export or manufacture threatened England's interest, it was immediately suppressed. Their commerce with the American colonies had been prohibited, the exportation of cattle forbidden, and when they turned to the manufacture of woolen goods the trade in wool was completely annihilated. But these descendants of Cavalier, Roundhead, and Williamite—these colonists with their old Anglo-Saxon obstinacy—were not the men to endure such treatment. They had been trained in a severe school, one fitted to develop the virtues, as the vices, of a superior people. Justly, or unjustly, their fathers had won the land by the sword, and they had been compelled to hold it by the same means. Surrounded by numbers who were uniformly their enemies, and whom they considered their inferiors, they had maintained their position by superior intelligence, vigilance, and courage. No doubt they were arbitrary and somewhat despotic, yet generous, proud, and self-reliant. Such men the Irish Parliament of the eighteenth century represented, so far as it represented anything outside the British cabinet. In 1779-82 these men demanded the independence of their Parliament, and England, weakened by her American and European wars, graciously granted to 100,000 armed volunteers what she had ever denied to the claims of justice. Yes, England, in her weakness, granted the boon of independent legislation, to snatch it again by the so-called union of 1800 — a union conceived in the fine brain of that prince of moral prime ministers, William Pitt, warmed to life by the fanatical Tory reaction that followed the French Revolution, and ushered into the world by shameless intrigue and statecraft, by bravado and threats, by offers of safety to the Irish Protestant Church, and subtle promises of Catholic emancipation — promises which the subsequent action of king and ministers compels us to believe were never meant to be fulfilled.

In the past, the union of politics and religion has been the curse of Ireland. Mr. Gladstone, by the Ballot Act and the disestablishment of the Irish Church, did much to secularize Irish politics. By the ballot Act he rescued the voter from the power of both landlord and priest; by the disestablishment of the Irish Church he estranged England's warmest supporters, the ultra-Episcopalians, and united the liberal Protestants with the Catholics in the Home Rule party. The motto of the Home Rulers is "Home legislation in internal affairs." They claim an independence similar to that enjoyed by each State of the American Union. They have learned from the past. They remember that once the great heart of England was moved to pity Ireland, when, in 1782, she granted a nominally independent Parliament to the demands of an armed people; they remember, too, another occasion, when the British prime minister, the victor of Waterloo, presented the Catholic emancipation bill to George IV., and said: "Your Majesty, it is forced on you and me; you must sign the paper, or prepare for civil war and rebellion in Ireland." With these records the Home Rulers know what to expect from England's generosity.

Prejudices of Saxon descent may unfit me for judging, yet, from an intimate knowledge of the Celtic character, I must say that Ireland is not now fitted for self-government; that she will

be fitted for it when public opinion makes it possible, I hope
and believe. When that day of her independence comes, it
will have come, not through the sword, but through the voice
and the pen, through the burial of old jealousies and discords
of home, and the ultimate aid of English republicanism. Re-
lying on these means alone the reformers are hopefully laboring on—laboring for the time when religion shall no longer be
a factor in politics; when the two races shall be assimilated by
common interests; when with the rash enthusiasm of the Celt,
tempered by the steadiness of the more self-restrained Saxon,
the whole Irish people shall be a united, independent people—
a people with a secular political life. Visions of bygone times
cheer them in the noble struggle, as among the dying echoes
of the past century they hear the halls of the old Parliament
house ringing with the voices of the patriot leaders, with the
voices of the heroic Flood and the high-minded Grattan—men
whose spotless integrity was as well recognized by French and
English contemporaries as by their own countrymen—men,
the halo of whose genius sheds an immortal radiance o'er the
few short years of their country's independence, while even yet
their transcendent forms towering through the mists of British
corruption and treachery seem to point ever upward to those
clear heights, where calm, grand, over-arched and begirt with
the eternal sunlight sit the pure goddesses of their adoration—
Patriotism, Justice, Truth.

# THE WORLD'S CONQUERORS.

By CHARLES T. NOLAND, of Central College.

Delivered at the Inter-State Oratorical Contest, at Chicago, Illinois, May, 1876, taking first prize. Judges: Hon. THOS. A. HENDRICKS, Messrs. J. O. BRODHEAD, W. F. POSLE.

The leading characteristic of our times is a strong tendency to expansion and universality. We have turned from the narrowness and restrictions of the past; and instead of idolizing successful individuals, we praise the motives which actuated them, and crown as conquerors the principles which they have worked out to a successful result. The age of hero-worship is past, and we regard men merely as the creatures of circumstances; and, with Cicero, are ready, not to praise Regulus for his self-sacrifice, but to ascribe all credit to his times.

We admire Newton, who proclaimed and expounded the laws of gravitation; but we immediately account for his success by saying that preceding events and circumstances pointed directly to this conclusion; that, as the lofty mountain-peak first receives the beams of the morning sun, which after a time bathes even the deepest valleys with its life-giving light, so Newton, by his superior intellectual height, first caught the rays of that mighty scientific principle, whose light was sure soon to burst upon the minds of all. The discovery was bound to be made by some one, and Newton was that lucky one. Men live by believing something; and when we quit our belief in heroes, we but transfer it to those truths and principles in whose behalf the laboring and fighting, the dying and triumphing made these heroes what they were. The world's conquerors which we now worship are Science, Invention, and Religion.

When, in olden times, the Capuchin friar was about to speak to the multitude concerning the life of some saint, he held before the gaze of his hearers some relic of him—a lock of his hair, a shred of his garment, a drop of his blood. I have no

sympathetic souvenirs to present to you, but can only show you a few trophies of victory.

Science—how eventful is its history! How noble are its achievements! How comprehensive are its truths.

The founding of the Alexandrian Museum, at Alexandria in old Egypt, was the real birth of Science. From this humble origin, in a now darkened and depressed land, arose a power which has conquered time, annihilated space, given new beliefs for the present, new hopes for the future. Men have delved into the deep mysteries which shroud the past, and have disproved the old theory that the world was created just six thousand years ago—have found the site of ancient Troy, and once more allow mortal eyes to view the beauties of the palace of Priam. With rough and unfeeling hands they have destroyed the mighty legends of Rome's early days, torn to shreds the Spanish fictions concerning the new world, and tell the astonished people that Prescott's History of the Conquest of Mexico is but a petty story founded on the cunningly devised statements of Spanish priests and chroniclers. With wistful eyes they are peering into the future, and with tolerable accuracy are prognosticating the weather. They have discovered new worlds in the realms of space, and explained the laws which cause them to move in their silent and awful grandeur. They are driving dogmatism and intolerance from our midst, and recognize the existence of fanaticism in only one form — an enthusiastic search after the truth. Science has increased the longevity of our race. What, I am asked, live longer in this fast age than our sedate forefathers did in their quiet days of the past. Yes; the fastness of the age, deleterious as it may be, is more than counterbalanced by scientific discoveries in medicine and hygiene. Since the time of the Reformation, as is proven by statistics, the average length of human life has been nearly doubled. Such are a few of the victories of science; yet, how incomplete is the record! I have said nothing of the science of navigation and the discovery of a new continent; nothing of the advancement in the science of government and political economy, which has culminated in the grandest and best of governmental systems — the one under which we live; nothing of the great discoveries in chemistry, magnetism, and electricity; nothing of the laws of acoustics, and the great advantages arising from ventilation. In short, nearly everything bears the imprint of science. Nothing is so small as to escape its notice; nothing too great for it to undertake. Unfettered and free, as it now is, it will continue to bestow its blessings on humanity, and the bloodless victories already accomplished will shine with a cumulative radiance when the present, "like streaks of a morning cloud, shall have melted into the infinite azure of the past."

Perhaps, of all the world's conquerors, none possesses so many trophies of victory as Invention. The art of writing is the most miraculous of all the inventions which the cunning brain of man has yet devised. The soul of the whole past lies in books, and it may with truth be said that the writers of books are "the dead but sceptered sovereigns, who still rule our spirits from their urns." In former times learning was only obtained by traveling over the then known world; now you need but go to the nearest college. Truly the greatest university of modern times is a well-selected collection of books. Printing is but a mere form of writing, and from this invention newspapers are a necessary consequence. Who can estimate the power of the press? When the sands of the ocean are numbered, when space is measured, and the limits of eternity are defined, then may we attempt to compute the power of this mighty engine of civilization, this one achievement of the noble conqueror. Formerly parliaments and congresses decided what the people should do; but now, through the agency of the press, the people decide what parliaments and congresses shall do. This fact presents to us another great truth in regard to this mighty invention, *i. e.*, printing necessarily makes democracy. It is inevitable. History shows this. What is the tendency of the whole of Europe? The decay of monarchism. The people gradually are demanding liberty, equality, and justice, and sooner or later the demand will be met. I need not relate more of the many conquests of invention; the world knows them, for they exist all around us in such abundance that this has been very properly styled the age of mechanical invention. We use these inventions without knowing or caring for the originators of them. We care not whether Oersted invented the telegraph, and Morse gained the credit for it; we care not whether John Fitch first constructed a steamboat, and Robert Fulton acquired the fame—we have the *result*. The thousands of inventive geniuses who now sleep in secluded and unhonored graves, with their pallid faces turned toward the tips of daisies, and no epitaphs to mark their last resting-places, all bear witness to the great fact that the the world now worships principles and not men.

It is difficult to tell what religion has done for the world, because there has been no period when a religion of some kind has not existed. Every religion that has had any influence or met with any favor from the people, has had some truth in it, and that truth, small though it sometimes was, has always exerted a beneficial influence. But the principal form to which I wish to direct your attention is what is known as the Christian religion. The church has agitated all the problems of great interest to man—philosophical, historical, and political; hence has had great influence upon modern civilization. And the fact is evident that the moral and intellectual progress of Europe has been essentially theological. Religion being a friend to civil liberty, has supplied its place where that boon has been wanting. Legislative science owes its all to religion.

The first code of laws known to the world was the Mosaic. Since that time all branches of law, commercial, international, and civil, have been greatly modified and improved; but the fundamental principle—the great outlines of legislative science—are found in the civil polity of the Jews. Milman, one of the greatest historians, has well said in this connection, that "the Hebrew law-giver has exercised a more extensive and permanent influence over the destinies of mankind than any other individual in the annals of the world." Shall I speak of the ennobling spirit of Christianity, of the influences of its moral teachings, of its consolation to those in distress, of its admonitions to those in prosperity? Religion is to society what the sun is to the world. Once let that bright luminary be quenched and we could not by any artificial light or heat illuminate or fertilize the earth.

Let us now look at the relation existing between the conquerors, science and religion. Of late we hear much about the "inevitable conflict," "the conflict of the ages," "the warfare between science and religion." If there is an *antagonism* between them, we must choose sides, for in so important a struggle, one which so nearly concerns us, we cannot be neutral lookers-on. We cannot hug the quiet of the swamp—we must seek the current which will either bear us to the dreaded cataract or glide us into the peaceful harbor.

But these expressions are misnomers, or rather they are names for a thing that does not exist. How can there be a variance between two truths? The whole trouble is this: Some scientists have mistaken what religion is, and some religionists have mistaken what science is. There is a conflict, a strife between bigoted religionists and over-zealous scientists; but true religion and true science have nothing to do with it.

Religion is not your or my interpretation of certain passages in the Bible, for these interpretations may be wrong, as has been the case with a thousand others. What you or I may assert as a principle of science is not to be so received until it has been demonstrated beyond cavil by scientific men. So long as there is a dispute between scientists concerning a thing, it may or may not be a principle of science. You cannot build up a science from the Bible, and just as surely you cannot destroy one, for there is nothing there with which either to build or destroy. It is not a scientific book. Would that this discrimination had been made hundreds of years ago—the shrieks of many a martyr would never have been heard, much of the noble blood which has bathed our world would never have been shed, and thousands of illustrious names would shine in the bright galaxy of history which now are unknown and their fame unsung.

In conclusion let me say, that entering as we are now upon the Centennial Celebration of American Independence, while we sing loudly our pæons for the victories of arms which gave us our freedom, let us not forget the many conquests of peace which have given us our culture, our progress, our stability as a nation. Let science, invention, and religion spread their trophies, gathered from every part of this country, before the assembled nations. Let us harmonize all sectional differences and disputes, forget the dark cloud of fratricidal war which once hung loweringly o'er our fair land, and strike hands around our country's common altar of thanksgiving. Our nation *can* purge itself from its weaknesses, its follies, and its corruptions; so let it do, and with renewed youth and vigor spring forward to make the future as the past, and ever yet more glorious. Let the mighty conquerors of the first century go forth to yet grander triumphs; let Science and Invention subdue and subsidize to their purposes our forests and rivers, our mountains and prairies, and lakes; while Religion, untrammeled by civil laws or ecclesiastical bigotries, but bathed anew in the sunlight of its own pure heaven, and baptized with the spirit of the one Universal Father of us all, sheds its purifying and ennobling radiance over hill and valley, over mansion and cottage—then shall each successive year and age and century but mark the progress and perfect the triumphs so well begun.

# BEATRICE AND MARGARET.

By Miss Laura A. Kent, of Antioch College.

## INTRODUCTORY.

In 1876 Miss Laura A. Kent represented the State of Ohio, and Antioch College, Yellow Springs, Ohio, at the inter-State oratorical contest, and is the only lady in the history of the Inter-State Oratorical Association who received honors. Not to attain notoriety or even a recognition as an aspirant for personal honors did Miss Kent enter the contest, but for the sake of her college, and to her college her womanly modesty ascribes all the glory. The Chicago *Tribune*, referring to the contest, says: "Only one literary subject was chosen, and that, the relation between the first and second parts of Goethe's Faust, by the Antioch representative." Miss Kent married Lieut. H. S. Foster, who is now serving a three years' detail as professor of military science and tactics in the University of Vermont. The portrait here represented was taken three years subsequent to the contest.

## THE ORATION.

Delivered at the Inter-State Oratorical Contest, at Chicago, Illinois, May, 1876, taking second prize. Judges: Hon. Thos. A. Hendricks, Messrs. J. O. Brodhead, W. F. Poslè.

No writer, since the rise of the romantic schools of literature, when love became one of the chief themes of poetry and story-lore, have so reverently worshiped and so happily embodied the highest ideas of womanhood as Dante and Goethe - two of the *few* poets whom every nation and every age may claim as its own.

Beatrice and Margaret are, perhaps, the most exquisite delineations of womanhood to be found in the literature of the Christian centuries; and while so many fair divinities of

elder days are fading into myths, it is most pleasing to find that the critical method which has dared to lay irreverent hands upon the person of Jesus himself, concedes, almost without an exception, that these two characters are real flesh and blood: both are *essential facts*, while at the same time both are types of that intuitive wisdom that leads the soul from error to atonement and final rest.

With the precocious, romantic ardor of his age and his southern blood, Dante, in his boyhood, singled out a child of eight years as the "sole lady of his heart." Through the *Vita Nuova* we see the poet's mind and lover's heart growing together in beauty and power. It was the image of the gentle Beatrice that warmed and purified his soul, that inspired his genius until he became the "voice of ten silent centuries." Transfigured by years of memory and the idealizing light of imagination, she became a comforting, holy spirit, and illumined with intense joy the poet's heart, hitherto the saddest, perhaps, save one, in all Christendom.

Thus it was that Dante — hereafter to be known to the world as the noblest of all lovers, when Dante the statesman, the philosopher, the Guelphic leader, and the "Ghibelline turncoat" shall be forgotten — VOWED that, if it would "please Him by whom all things live," he would say that of her which had never yet been said of any lady." She became his Muse. It was a message from her which led him down through the Gate of Despair; across the Limbo that trembled with the sighs of hopeless longing; past horrid Minos, Judge of Hades; into the flaming City of Dis, garrisoned and guarded by demons and furies; past the "Hell of Violence," where murderers and tyrants are forever steeped in the boiling blood-waves of Phlegethon; through the increasing horrors of Circles and Evil-pits and Belts of Treachery; and then up the toilsome steps of Purgatory — until at last appeared, drawn in the bosom of a cloud of flowers thrown by angel hands, her form clad in in white, green, and red emblems of Faith, Hope, and Charity.

This sainted lady now became the poet's guide; more to him than the Madonna to the ancient worshiping hermit. By the subtle charm of spiritual beauty which shone from her eyes, she led him upward through the nine heavenly circles to the "Rose of the Blessed" and "Lake of Light." Beatrice is science, says one; philosophy, says another; reason, and a poet's dream of the Madonna, say others. Granting that she is either, or all, of these, she is yet more — she stands for spiritual insight, divine wisdom, and "love is the keeping of her law."

Dante, more than all others, has realized, not idealized, what the highest womanhood may and should become to all who keep in their hearts a sacred niche for its unspotted ideal. In turning to Margaret, the "crown jewel" of all Goethe's womanly creation, we find a mere child, delighting in all the dreams of girlish fancy and youthful affection, whose injured and defenseless innocence appeals to every heart, nor finds a thought of censure or a shade of reproach. Miranda's affection is scarcely more frank, Desdemona's not more self-forgetting, nor are Cordelia or Imogene more of the spirit of "*ewige weibliche.*" She is at once the ideal Gretchen of Goethe's first love, and the personation of Faust's own better nature. From her entrance into the cathedral to the darkly-draped dungeon scene, she holds all hearts to her great spiritual loveliness, her simple trust, and pure faith in God. Faust, prompted by Mephistopheles — the true devil of base impulse in every heart — appealed to Margaret's vanity and curiosity, the same passion that made the mother of the race offend in Eden.

Then, rejected and deserted, she tells her sorrow to her own heart in the deep love-melancholy of the spin-wheel song, which forebodes the dark tragedy of the sequel in its refrain:

> "Meine Ruh' ist hin,
> Mein Herz ist schwer —
> Ich find's sie nimmer,
> Und nimmermehr."

Tormented by the guilt that belonged to others, she sought refuge in the cathedral, where she used to pray when a child; but even here an evil spirit mocks and terrifies her. In the wild insanity of grief, and amid the gloom of a true modern epic, we see her at last in the dungeon, awaiting the stroke that is to free her spirit from its dark prison-house. She heeds not Faust's entreaty to escape, for it is not life that she asks, but the innocence and happiness of the past; and since they cannot be restored she gives herself up to the judgment of God. Though doomed in the flesh, the voice of infinite love whispers, "She is saved;" for hers is more the sorrow that purifies than the sin that condemns. Never was there such a perfect and exquisite idyl of love—the greatest theme of the poet and novelist. It is the very story-essence of all that is melting in pathos, thrilling in tragedy, and winning in simplicity.

Dear, beautiful Margaret! the purest ideal of womanhood in its chiefest joy and its deepest anguish. Thy sad, sweet story is the allegory of the human conscience—the true *mythos* of the higher life of duty and spiritual devotion. In the end thou wilt be avenged by subduing, yes, by *saving* thy betrayer! The victory of love is thine! Beatrice represents the finished harmony of a pure and noble soul, wherein all the best powers of mind and heart are ranged on the side of truth and goodness.

Margaret symbolizes the moral powers crushed and degraded by the baser elements of our nature. The gentle, holy spirit is sinned against, and takes its mournful departure, leaving our souls, like Faust's, in a Walpurgis night of dissipation and despair.

Yet, in themselves and their influence, these characters are not essentially unlike. It was the spirit or memory of a Margaret that led Faust of the second part away from his evil companionship to a life of noble self-sacrifice; while, on the other hand, the world-worn Dante was at first lost in a tangled forest, pursued by wild beasts, and seized with nameless fears. He, too, had learned that neither pleasure, nor knowledge, nor power can make man wholly unmindful of those truths—

> "Which, be they what they may,
> Are yet a fountain light of all our days,
> Are yet the master light of all our seeing.
> Upholds us, cherish, and have power to make
> Our noisy years seem moments, in the being
> Of the eternal silence."

Of these high, intuitive truths, Beatrice and Margaret, the crown-wearer and cross-bearer, were made types—symbols of duty and suffering, equally potent for good and conducive to perfection.

The haughty, cold-hearted Goethe was fervently, nobly, and often loved. In Margaret's sad story he carefully measured the utter self-sacrifice of woman's love. Into her character he gathered the fragrance of many crushed flowers, which haunts every scene.

Dante's masterpiece shows what a noble woman may become, and suggests to man a growing consciousness of absolute independence, high thought, and purity of soul.

Both these portraits were drawn by men; but let such laurels as even these poets wear, dishearten no pleader for woman, for better, far better, is the saint than the image, the life than the book.

In one of his last lectures on Robert Burns, in the great City Hall of Edinburgh, Professor Wilson told the story of a proud and accomplished lady of noble birth who was wont to walk at noon in her garden, when the plowman-poet, leaving his team in the furrow, crept about the hedge to steal a glimpse of her beauteous face. They came upon each other unawares at a sudden angle. She turned away in scorn from the cowering intruder; but the poet saw only her beauty, and soon one of his noblest poems was written and sent to her with apologies. "And here," continued the speaker, leading forward upon the stage a bowed and wrinkled, but justly proud, old lady, "here is the woman who inspired Burns to write one of the rarest tributes that genius ever paid to beauty."

Is it not nobler to be the muse than the poet, the Madonna than the shrine?

Let men organize, administer, invent; an infinite and no less noble field of work remains for woman in revealing new beauties of character, in originating new "allurements to truth and new incentives to virtue," in adorning the domestic and social world with the art of new and simple refinements, and all the hallowed influences of a higher life.

# SATAN AND MEPHISTOPHELES.

By OLIN A. CURTIS, of Lawrence University.

### BIOGRAPHICAL.

Olin A. Curtis was born December 10, 1850, at Frankfort, Maine, and educated in a thorough manner at Lawrence University, Appleton, Wisconsin, and at the Boston Theological School. In 1880 he joined the Wisconsin Methodist Episcopal Conference, and was chosen pastor the same year of the Court Street Church, Janesville, Wisconsin, remaining three years. In 1883 he became pastor of the Summerfield Church, of Milwaukee, Wisconsin, where he labored for three years. While upon this charge he delivered the memorial oration of General Grant for the City of Milwaukee. In 1886 he went to Germany, and was a student in the University of Leipzig for two years. Upon his return from Germany he joined the Rock River Conference, and was engaged as pastor of the Englewood Church, Chicago. In February, 1889, he was elected to the chair of Systematic Theology in the Theological School of Boston University, which position he fills with distinguished ability. He is a doctor of divinity, and a man of much intellectual culture. His college oration here given was delivered at the fourth annual oratorical contest, upon which occasion he was the winning contestant.

## THE ORATION.

Delivered at the Inter-State Oratorical Contest, at Madison, Wisconsin, May, 1877, taking first prize. Judges: Messrs. LYMAN TRUMBULL, C. C. COLE, W. F. VILAS, Rev. C. H. RICHARDS.

Prominent among the devils of fiction are Milton's and Goethe's. Representing the same Evil Being, they are yet as unlike as Macbeth and Iago—each character being as unique as it is masterly, both becoming only the more clearly defined as we study the entire family of demons from Marlowe's to Byron's. Whatever may have been the poet's intentions, whatever may be the critic's final decision, Satan and Mephistopheles are certainly heroes—the central figures of the two poems holding our attention with a grasp at once fascinating and terrible. In spite of our worthy purpose to hate devils whether in the body or out of the body, to be interested only in those creatures and those conceptions which savor of the divine, these brain-born fiends, in the presence of angels the holiest and humanity the most inspiring, command our thought, enchain our will, and marshal our emotions as with the mystic charm of Ismeno's deadly spell.

The body of Satan, in comparison with which that of our classical Hercules is pigmean, would be a burden sufficient to crush any other character in fiction; but, touched by Milton's remarkable genius, rendered formless and indistinct as well as vast, and thus having, as Macaulay has said, "none of the fee-faw-fum of Tasso and Klopstock," it seems perfectly adapted to his mental features, and serves but to increase what George Eliot calls "the grandeur of the wild beast."

Indeed, what body can be too enormous for Satan? Is there one aspect in which he is not utterly bewildering? Can we, amazed at the valor of Rinaldo and the aspirations of Napoleon, comprehend this devil who "durst defy the Omnipotent to arms? Here is an ambition that seeks the throne of God, and reaches after the scepter of eternity; a courage that feels no pain, knows no fear, dreams of no disaster; a daring that sweeps through the battle as the fiery breath of a simoon; a pride as obdurate as fate; an egotism absolutely infinite, speaking and acting as though conscious of strength to annihilate the Almighty and splinter his dominion; a grit so admirable that our thoughts at times all but leap the holy barriers, and cry out for the overthrow of the chariots of God!

Witness the manifestation of these various characteristics. Though wounded by the resistless sword of Michael, though defeated, his troops scattered in wild confusion, yet Satan had no thought of yielding, but cheers his comrades with more than the art of a Xenophon, then invents his "devilish enginery," and once more meets with fearless march the "rattling storm of arrows barbed with fire." Now his complete punishment has come. His flaming volley has been answered. His squadrons have been buried under the mountains, plucked from their foundations, and flung as pebbles speeding from the slingers brawny arm. The Son of God, with thunders "winged with red lightning and impetuous rage," has driven the rebellious multitude over the crystal wall. But Satan is not subdued. His arm has failed. His might has proved of no avail. His followers are "overwhelmed with floods and whirlwinds of tempestuous fire." His fairest hopes, like brightest skies, have vanished, but his heart is still invincible. Regrets are banished. Despondency and sorrow are spurned. Despising compromise; unwilling to repent, though the premiership of glory would come thereby; madly reckless as to results; bound to pay back the Almighty; meaning to shadow all heaven with sorrow, to agonize the Infinite Heart, to hush the hallelujahs before the throne—this Arch-Fiend determines to build up a rival kingdom out of the very chaos of hell, and, forcing his entire being into this one desperate purpose, he takes the black crown with that sad, malignant, terrible coronation speech, "Hail, horrors! Hail, infernal world!"

In striking contrast with the character of Satan is that of Mephistopheles, whom Carlyle has called "the only genuine devil of these latter times." Satan is the culmination of ambition; Mephistopheles, the quintessence of skepticism. In Goethe's metaphysical devil there is condensed every form of doubt, from that of the deist to that of the libertine. He is not only literally "the spirit that constantly denies," but, as Madame de Stael has said, "He expresses doubt itself with a tone of decision, which, mixing arrogance of character with uncertainty of reasoning, leaves no consistency in anything but evil inclinations." With what infernal irony he sneers at philosophy, declaring that an entire system may be built up with words, yet advising the anxious student to write away as zealously as though the Holy Ghost were dictating to him! With what bitter pleasantry, what diabolical coolness, what pitiless sarcasm he insinuates that love is a mere passion— spark from the animal; that virtue can always be bent like a reed under the tread of the storm! Mephistopheles would shatter every blessed hope and every cherished opinion; would blast whatever of zeal, whatever of trust, whatever of affection ennobles our toil and hallows our homes. Acting upon his tersely-worded theory, that "everything which has originated deserves to be annihilated," he would become the supreme destroyer of mankind. With words that sting like scorpions, with glances and motions as full of poison as were Armida's fountains, with a malicious grin more consummately hellish than is the atheism and blasphemy of Byron's Lucifer, this philosophical demon would undermine the foundation of the sciences, affirming that deduction is folly because there may be no mind, and induction absurd because there may be no facts; would overthrow religion, not with the argument of Hume, but by denying the reality of reason and testimony both; would call life a gigantic myth, and immortality a stupendous lie; would put an interrogation point after all existence, and utter the name of God with a rising inflection.

In his work of doubt and demolition, Mephistopheles exhibits an intellect vastly superior to that of Satan. The deceit that led the parents of the race to ruin was Japanese jugglery in comparison with the marvelous transformations by which Faust and Margaret were ensnared. Mephistopheles can adapt every power of his mind to any situation. Now he is as jolly as King Lear's jester; now as kind and attentive as a lover; now as metaphysical as Aristotle. Perfectly understanding the human heart, knowing all its points of weakness, just how it will meet every influence, he so transforms himself, body and mind, as to touch the one successful spring and accomplish the desired end.

Yet more wonderful than this adaptation is the utilization of forces. Satan is grand in his prodigality; Mephistopheles in his economy of power. Satan would have killed Valentine with a great expenditure of rage and strength; Mephistopheles does it quietly with an unseen turn of his forearm. The one never does by skill what he can do by might; the other never does by might what he can do by skill. Next to the Omniscient, Mephistopheles is the greatest economist in the universe. He gauges the breath of his anger, and wastes not even a sneer. Like Von Moltke, he plans everything, and never strikes without a map. He ruins men by the nicest mathematical calculations, and damns women from the swift conclusions of a syllogism. Where Satan would work through the mind, Mephis topheles works through the heart, seeing this to be the shorter route to death. He draws Faust from philosophy to pleasure, from thought to feeling, sending through his veins blood aflame with lust, realizing that once in the fiery furnace of passion, only those having with them "the form of one like unto the Son of God" can possibly escape without "the smell of fire having passed on them." He overcomes Margaret through her affections, clearly foreseeing that to these, and to these alone, she will make any sacrifice, casting even her precious garland from her; yielding to the tempter till her peace is gone, which she finds on earth never and never more; becoming enslaved till her heart is rich only in sad memories—till her loveliness has fled as a Magdalen's dream of heaven—till those pure

"Feelings that could once such noble life inspire,
Are quenched and trampled out in passion's mire."

This is Mephistopheles. Satan—revengeful, willful, haughty, intrepid, ambitious Satan—an archangel fallen, yet still resplendent with a lingering ray of his original glory—like the Coliseum, magnificent even as a ruin—seems worthy of the crown of sainthood in contrast with this mean, jeering, sarcastic doubter; this confident sophist; this cool, artful, cautious strategist; this malignant destroyer, grinning calmly at the damnation of souls; this "abortion of dirt and fire;" this counterpart of the real devil who has already crowded our lives with anguish, and filled this beautiful world with the bitter pangs of hell.

# FAITH AND DOUBT AS MOTORS OF ACTION.

By S. FRANK PROUTY, of Central College.

### BIOGRAPHICAL.

The subject of this sketch, Hon. S. F. **Prouty**, was born near Delaware, Ohio, January 17, 1854. His parents started with him to Iowa in the fall of 1855, and while journeying his mother died, and was buried at Mt. Pleasant, Iowa. His father, with the five boys and one girl, continued the journey to Knoxville, Iowa, where the motherless children found temporary homes with friends. "Little Frank" was placed in the keeping of a family where he succeeded in causing a generous amount of domestic infelicity. The "man of the house" fell in love with the two-year-old, white-haired boy, and wanted to adopt him; but "the lady of the house" took a decided dislike to "the brat," and resolved that the same abode would not accommodate both. It was finally resolved, in the interest of peace, that Frank should move again, and he was taken to his father, where he lived until he was eight years old. At this time misfortune overtook the Prouty home, and the boys were told that they would have to "hoe their own row." Although the youngest, Frank felt as much a man as any of them, and insisted on the right to fight the battles of life with his brothers. The right was freely given, and since that time he has depended on himself. He spent his boyhood in farming, and served as apprentice under most of the enterprising "grangers" within a radius of ten miles of Pella, Iowa. He attended school in winter, and prosecuted his studies at night and during vacation. At sixteen years of age he presented himself to the superintendent of public instruction of Mahaska County for a teacher's certificate, which he procured, after passing the examination, but he was too timid to ask a school board for a position. In 1871 he entered Central University, Pella, Iowa; then spent

two years at Simpson College, Indianola, Iowa, but returned and finished the classical course at Central University, in 1877, representing Iowa the same year at the inter-State oratorical contest, held at Madison, Wisconsin, and receiving the second prize. Upon his graduation he was tendered and accepted the chair of Latin and natural sciences in Central University, which he occupied four years. Later he was made vice president, thus has filled all offices from janitor to vice president in this university. While a student and teacher he began the study of law, and was admitted to the bar in 1881, and deservedly enjoys the reputation of being one of the ablest lawyers in Central Iowa. In 1879 he was nominated and elected, by the Republican party, the representative of Marion County, Iowa. Mr. Prouty is a member of the firm of Lesh, Prouty & Abbott, the largest manufacturers and exporters of walnut lumber in the United States. It is hoped his remarkable success will be continued.

## THE ORATION.

Delivered at the Inter-State Oratorical Contest, at Madison, Wisconsin, May 1877, taking second prize. Judges: Messrs. LYMAN TRUMBULL, C. C. COLE, W. F. VILAS, Rev. C. H. RICHARDS.

This is truly an age of doubt. The blind credulity of a few centuries ago has been followed by a natural reaction. Children no longer passively accept the creeds and traditions of their ancestors. The people have ceased to receive, without question, the utterances of clergy, bishops, priests or Popes, or to bow reverently to the declarations of the most lordly dignitaries. Scientists receive with mistrust the theories and even the data of their predecessors.

Everything, before it can be accepted, must not only be submitted to the focus of reason, but also be tested through the microscopic agency of distrust. First doubt, and believe only when forced by evidence, is the maxim of the age!

The present spirit of investigation seeks not so much to establish truth as to detect errors; not so much to confirm existing creeds, theories, and institutions as to overthrow them.

The spirit of doubt has been bold and aggressive. It has questioned the wisdom and perfection of nature, the genuineness of revelation, the existence of a God, the existence of matter or spirit, and even the existence of the doubter himself. There is scarcely a fact in history that has not been questioned. Not even those institutions, hoary with antiquity, and made almost inviolable by the universal acceptance of past ages, have been able to escape the searching blast of modern skepticism.

The fact that this age of prevailing doubt should also be distinguished as an age of unequaled progress, has led a certain class of writers who are wont to connect two contemporaneous events as cause and effect, to infer and freely assert that it is doubt "that is moving forward the wheels of progress." One writer has gone so far as to assert that "doubt has done more for the world than faith." If this be true, it is the greater motor of action; for it is action that blesses and renovates the world. Motion is nature's great purifier. Without it the crystal stream would become the stagnant pool, the vitalizing air a fetid and ruinous gas, and the universe one vast ocean of turbid stagnation. Perfect cessation in the social, no less than in the material, world generates impurity; it breeds vice and corrodes virtue.

All human action flows from principles of the soul. We recognize from the operations of the mind that it is apparently composed of certain principles and their opposite conditions—positives and negatives. Thus hope is a principle of which despondency is merely the absence or perversion. So with faith and doubt. One is the positive, the other the negative. One is the principal, the other the opposite condition. One is the natural, the other the acquired state of the mind.

But the fact that the child believes without evidence, and the aged person scarcely with it; the fact that faith finds its maximum in the mind of the confiding infant, and its minimum in the incredulous old man, proves that faith is the innate principle, and that doubt is only the result of frequent betrayals and flagrant abuses of natural confidence; that faith is the positive, and doubt the negative. It is a misconception when we attribute to nonentities moving agency. Heat expands, but cold does not contract.

Again, instead of a man's believing nothing without evidence, he naturally believes everything until evidence and the results of experience cause him to doubt. It takes a preponderance of adverse evidence of it to create doubt, but faith is the gift of the Creator. Skepticism is a disease of the intellect, for which the subject is responsible to the same extent that he is for a disease of the body.

Believing is the normal, doubting the abnormal condition of the mind. That which is abnormal may hinder, but cannot promote, action. It may retard, but, on the whole, cannot facilitate progress. It may tend to rest, but never to motion. Here theory and fact coincide. Our tendency to act in any direction is diminished just in proportion to our doubt in that direction. Though skepticism in one field, as regards effects or results, may turn our attention toward another, yet there must be faith in that other field before there can be action. It may stop from pursuing one course, but it cannot lead us along another. It may cause us to reject one thing, but it cannot induce us to lay hold upon another. It may restrain us in one direction, but it cannot, even by a reflex operation, propel us in the opposite. It may cause stagnation, but action *never*.

Its mission is to tear down, not to build up. Its power is wholly destructive, not constructive. It may, by the diversion of interest and the relaxation of energy, cause the monuments reared by ages to crumble, but it cannot erect others on their ruins. It may cause the scientist to reject a thousand theories, but it cannot stimulate him to form a single new one. Though he should doubt the soundness and validity of every known theory, and had no faith in any scientific investigation to develop other and better ones, there could be no action. Doubt may destroy, but cannot restore.

On the other hand, into whatever department of human enterprise we look, we find that faith is the power that moves every energy employed. Without it not one act could be performed, not one thought matured, not one plan executed. Without it every other faculty would become dormant, and every energy of the whole man paralyzed. Faith is the great motor of action. It is the wellspring of human energy.

But there is a higher form of faith than that which is centered upon an object of pursuit, to which this class of writers may refer. If they mean that such a faith has done less for the world than its corresponding doubt, that irreligion has done more than religion, it is but necessary to appeal to history and fact. In this appeal it matters not whether the faith was pure and enlightened or mingled with superstition; whether it rested upon a false or true Deity; upon Jehovah or an idol of benighted Africa — faith in its motive power is a unit. And when it is centered even upon a mythical deity, it excels, in the benefaction of mankind, its corresponding doubt, as motion transcends stagnation. The firm believer in any religion is endowed with an enthusiasm that lifts his mind above the whole visible world, above the power of perishable things, and above the fear of death itself. Hence the believing world has ever represented the highest activity. Religious faith has ever furnished the highest stimulus for the highest energy. It nerves the soul with Herculean strength in time of danger, and enables men to perform the most heroic deeds. It arms them with that Cyclopean power that enables them to accomplish the most stupendous works, to overcome the most insuperable difficulties, and move resistlessly forward on the highest plane of human activity.

Again, if you will turn to the smoky pages of the past, or the fresher pages of the present, though you will there find it recorded that religion has sacrificed thousands of human victims, both upon the altar and upon the field of battle; that its bigoted devotees have frequently waged war against the rights of others, and, perhaps, against the rights of humanity; that priestly influences have frequently stifled investigation and curbed free thought — yet you will there find the record of few real blessings that have come to the human race that have not been borne upon the wings of some religious faith. In every nation and every age it has formed the anchor of society, the basis of morality, the foundation of government. If at present you should dig deep beneath courts, laws, and offices, you would still find it underlying and forming the basis of the grandest governmental structures. Remove this, and they must fall. Blot from China faith in the doctrines of Confucius, and that old empire — that empire which has stood there immutable through centuries, that empire which has been preserved by an unchanging faith while every other government in the world has fallen or undergone a revolution — would crumble to pieces in a fortnight. Religion is the rock upon which governments must rest.  It is the only cement that can unite into a whole the diversified interests, or bind together the factions of a widely differing people.  When one of those ancient forms of religion fell, it carried with it not simply government, but letters, laws, and all the splendor of its civilization; all was anarchy and ruin, confusion and dissolution, until another religion gained supremacy, formed another government, and thus secured peace and harmony.

No government can long survive the egress of religious faith from the hearts and minds of her people.  Infidelity removes all restraint, lets loose all the fierce pent-up passions of man's depravity, subverts the very foundations of morality, and soon sweeps away the virtues of society and the institutions of good government.  Relaxing the higher energy, it calls into activity the lower and more debasing; removing the nobler stimulus, it increases the power of the ignoble.

Again, it is to this faith that the world owes its marks of the higher civilization.  It has established the colleges for the enlightenment, and the philanthropic institutions for the amelioration of mankind.  It has promoted science and *true progress*.  Instead of stifling investigation and curbing free thought, as is sometimes charged, it simply moderates wild and fanciful speculation.  At present, at least, it is moving forward the wheels of *true progress*, while infidelity is "throwing on the brake."

It has also made the world blossom with beauty and teem with grandeur.  It was this that inspired Milton, Dante, Virgil, Homer, Horace, and all the Hebrew seers to utter their noblest strains of poetry.  Examine the libraries of the world for proof of the assertion that the master productions in literature, in every nation and tongue, have been developed under the influence of the same power.

Sculpture and painting arose with heathen worship, and reached their culmination when Raphael and Angelo, with brush and chisel, wrought out their grand conceptions of a perfect yet incarnate Jehovah.

Here, too, architecture finds its origin and perfection.  If you were to wander far back amid the ruins of ancient architecture, and pause before the crowning perfection of "the glory of kingdoms and the beauty of the Chaldee's excellency"—

the temple of the old Babylon, rising tower above tower and column above column to the height of six hundred feet — and ask what power could have reared that marvel of colossal grandeur, the huge golden statute of Jupiter, resting upon the summit of the topmost tower, would tell you, in language that could not be mistaken, that it was faith in a divinity. If you were to wander over into Northern Africa, there the pyramids, Cheops and Chefrenes, the mighty monuments of antiquity, with their hoary heads still towering o'er the wrecks of time, would tell you that it was faith in a divinity that reared them. If you were to pass back to classic Greece and Rome, there the temples of Delphi, of Juno, of Olympian Jove, and of Diana, the grandest specimens of architectural grandeur, would tell you that it was faith in a divinity that reared them. If you were to stand by the pagodas of China, the cromlechs of Wales, the obelisks of Egypt, the mosques of India, or the ruins of those magnificent temples of ancient Mexico, they would all tell you that it was faith in a divinity that reared them. If you were to interrogate the finest specimens of modern architecture in the world, the cathedrals of London, Milan, and Rome, with all their richness of proportion and grandeur of effect, their lofty spires piercing the heavens, would tell you that it was faith in a divinity that reared them. Were you to repeat the interrogation to the thousands of spires and colossal domes that tower heavenward from Germany, France, England, and America, they would tell you that it was faith in the divinity of the Galilean Carpenter that reared them. This faith to-day is the mighty engine that is moving the world. It is the mightiest of the mighty powers that are shaping, moulding, and controlling the destiny of the human race. It is the heart of the great giant of progress and civilization. With every pulsation it sends life, energy, and humanity through every vein.

On the other hand, every dominant religion in every nation and time has had its legion of unbelievers. But what monuments of their achievements have they left us? To what really noble strain of poetry have they given utterance? What fine specimen of sculpture or painting have they given the world? What grand or magnificent edifice have they erected? What great and noble work have they accomplished for humanity? What colleges or benevolent institutions have they established for the enlightenment or amelioration of mankind? None! We seek for them in vain among the ruins of the past or the realities of the present.

Skepticism is a land of perpetual snows, where flowers never bloom and the plant of humanity never grows. Doubt, wherever found, paralyzes energy and congeals the well-spring of human activity. Faith gives life and energy. It is faith that moves the mind; "it is mind that moved the world."

# THE LONELINESS OF GENIUS.

By E. A. BANCROFT, of Knox College.

BIOGRAPHICAL.

E. A. Bancroft was born November 20, 1857, at Galesburg, Illinois. He prepared for college at Knox Academy, and entered Knox College, Galesburg, Illinois, in 1874. He took second prize in declamation in both freshmen and sophomore years, and took first prize in oratory in his junior year. At the convention of the Illinois Inter-Collegiate Association, held at Evanston, October, 1876, he was elected president. He received the first prize at the Illinois contest, held at Monmouth, October 18, 1877, on oration "The Need of the Hour," and nine colleges were represented in this contest. At the inter-State contest, in May, 1878, St. Louis, Missouri, he received the first prize among six State representatives, on "The Loneliness of Genius." In 1878 he was graduated bachelor of arts from Knox College, and in the fall of the same year entered the Columbia College Law School, New York, and was graduated from it bachelor of law. In May, 1880, he was admitted to the bar of Illinois, and began the practice of law at Galesburg, and is now a member of the prosperous firm of Williams, Lawrence & Bancroft. In January, 1881, he argued the contested election case of Nicholas E. Worthington vs. Philip S. Post, on behalf of General Post, (Republican,) before the committee on elections of the 50th Congress, for the seat in the House as representative of the Tenth Congressional District of Illinois; the committee, though Democratic, reported unanimously in favor of General Post. In 1880 Mr. Bancroft was elected presidential elector for the Tenth Congressional District of Illinois, on the Republican ticket The following pages contain his oration, which is worthy of particular note.

## THE ORATION.

Delivered at the Inter-State Oratorical Contest, at St. Louis, Missouri, May, 1878, taking first prize. Judges: Hon. A. TAFT, Bishop THOS. BOWMAN, Hon. BENJAMIN HARRISON, Hon. WM. HYDE.

Insects swarm; the lion forages alone. Swallows consort in myriads; the condor dwells companionless in the awful solitudes of the Cordilleras. Weakness wars with thousands; might battles a Goliath. Littleness is gregarious; greatness is solitary. The grandest realization of civilized society is the man of genius. His individuality is of the most distinctive type, and by its very intensity necessitates his insulation. But what is genius? What is life? Call it transcendent mental power; intensity of the intuitive and inventive faculties; say that it is of the heart, innate, soul-born, incommunicable. But is that all?

The mind perceives, the heart feels, and the whole being vibrates with the pulsations of the great truth or strong passion, struggling mightily to the birth. Then genius, by a common instinct of nature in travail, withdraws from the multitude, and in silence and in solitude, inswathes the bright children of its soul. Not in courts nor palaces nor classic halls nor coteries of the learned are deepest emotions felt or embodied, grandest truths discovered, or sublimest conceptions begotten or born; but from Sinai's slopes and the shores of Gennesaret, from the chamber of blindness in London and the felon's cell at Bedford, have come the revelations that bless mankind.

Emerson says, "Veracity derives from instinct and marks superiority in organization." So we may say, lonelines derives from nature and marks superiority in endowment and delicacy in organism. These we conceive to be the main factors in the loneliness of genius, and shall so consider them.

Superiority of endowment—the first and chief cause of loneliness in men of genius.

An almost necessary concomitant, the peculiar charm of lofty intellects, as of mountain-peaks, is solitariness. Were the hundred Alpine summits equally elevated, Mont Blanc would little engage the poet's pen or the tourist's eye. But peerless and cloud-wrapt, he towers in cold sublimity to companionship with the stars. So genius, upborne by a faith that gazes upon the ineffable, holds lofty communion with the universal Soul above and around it.

Think of the Prophet at Horeb; the royal Buddha in the caves of India; the divine Dante wandering like the shade of an unburied Greek; Gibbon weaving his chaplet of immortelles by the lonely waters of Leman, and Byron gathering on the deserted shores of the Ægean the jewels which to-day glitter in the diadem of his fame. Oh, the solitude of great minds! How they shun the crowd and seek peace and inspiration amid the solemn beauties and lone sublimities of nature! They wander through "the pathless woods;" they linger on the wave-washed beach, awed and thrilled by the deep anthems of the sea; they stand alone upon the mountain-tops and hear unterrified the voice of storms. 'T is a voice of nature—they know it well. Like the eagle, the *Oioros*—the "lone-flyer"—of the Greeks, they gaze with undimmed eyes upon the sun of truth. This is the loneliness of genius; or rather it is the expression, the outward symbol, of an inherent isolation, which often is hidden, yet is part as well as characteristic of all genius. Like Burns, the man of genius may mingle in the busiest scenes of life—at the plow with simple peasants, at the board of Edinburgh's nobility—yet his soul is ever "like a star, and dwells apart." He stands

> "Among them, but not of them: in a shroud
> Of thoughts which are not their thoughts."

Neither craving their applause nor fearing their displeasure, he is self-contained without arrogance, elevated without haughtiness, learned without pedantry, superior yet without vanity. Beings of a nobler faith, they seem ambassadors or visitors from the courts of a higher sphere, and are estranged from the world by the peculiarity of their nature and their mission. The laureate of loneliness was the youthful Shelley. His eye caught the light of a coming dawn, and his soul the freedom of a looked-for age. His life was wed to the interpretation of the soul within, and the grander soul around him. He worshiped nature, ofttimes heard "the still, sad music of humanity." Beside him place the unpoetic, tender-hearted Lincoln. His deep, sad eyes and pensive hours gave many a token of a loneliness, hidden from the popular eye, yet real and pathetic beyond expression. His was a character grandly simple. Unconscious and spontaneous, yet vigorous and brave, it is the most unique, solitary, beautiful in our history.

The peculiarly delicate mental constitution of genius, especially if environed by unpropitious influences, is another and a frequent cause of intense lonesomeness.

Lord Byron's misanthropy and alienation illustrates this. His life was made up of the widest and wildest extremes and antagonisms. His nature warred with its environments, and his environments mocked his nature. The springs of his life were early embittered, and he felt alone in a hostile world. Born amid enemies, he died amid strangers. A lyre so finely strung could not be so roughly swept and no string be broken. Think of our wandering Pleiad of poesy, the Byron of America. With the temperament of a delicate girl he struggled with the coarse natures of a great city. He was a frail and beautiful exotic amid the sharp thistles, stunted pines, and gnarled oaks of a northern clime—a trembling fawn among the uncouth denizens of the farm-yard. Early and sadly Poe died as he had lived—alone; and the brightest star in American literature went out in darkness.

But these men of genius are insulated more by their fineness of mental mechanism and their superlative sensitiveness than by the rough treatment of the world. And this utter absence of sympathy is often their heaviest and keenest grief. Gray's epitaph says, "He gained from heaven—'t was all he wished—a friend." Ah! that is it! Admirers, patrons, flatterers—they all have these; but how few have friends! And without intelligent sympathy genius is as much alone in the thoroughfares or parlors of a metropolis, as by the sullen crater of Ætna or the voiceless shores of the Arctic sea.

But isolation not only results from the nature but also enhances the power of genius. It concentrates and matures intellect and imagination; it deepens and intensates every motion; it makes the soul self-centered and self-directed, and it counteracts the enervating and dispersive influence of society. The one law of society is "Conform," and against it the unconscious spontaneity of genius must rebel.

Society discusses grave topics flippantly, or considers trivial subjects seriously. Only to itself does the soul tell its inmost thoughts, convictions, and emotions. Moore and Coleridge, and Dickens, by joining too often in the dissipations of society, undoubtedly diminished the strength and vigor of their genius, and brought their grand careers to an untimely close.

Although the influence of mental isolation is highly favorable to intellectual development, it is often detrimental to disposition and character. Melancholy is the form it commonly assumes. To the youthful genius the tendencies to doubt and despondency are almost irresistible. His mind at first forceful, buoyant, and original, soon feels the conservatisms of the world pressing upon and confining it like the fabled iron shroud. He fancies himself a young Enceladus beneath an Ætna of outgrown forms. If he submit as to the inevitable he sinks into a gloomy pessimism in whose firmament there shines no star. If he resist, his misfortune begets a bitter defiance of mankind and a scornful indifference to their affairs. He is the cynic or the misanthrope, the Diogenes or the Timon.

But it is when men of genius escape these phases of solitariness, and reach the sphere of a grander, nobler, purer loneliness, that they attain to the ideal. When, forgetting the enmities of the present, they calmly await the glory of the future; when they exchange the mantle of selfish loneliness for the garb of philanthropy; when, from the misery, the exile, the dungeon, or the scaffold, to which an ungrateful people has consigned them, there comes a voice of prayer, "Forgive them, for they know not what they do," ah then their genius transcends humanity — becomes divine. How sublime their silence before their accusers! What can they say to the ignorant and the superstitious? Stand by Socrates and Bruno and feel the utter folly of speech: "And when He was accused of the priests and elders he answered nothing, insomuch that the governor marveled greatly."

One closing thought seems voiced from the subject we have discussed: it is the ministry of genius to the children of men. Not useless are these God-made men on whom abides "the light that never was on sea or land." Though dwelling companionless and high, yet are they apostles of good to the millions who tread the lowliest vales of earth. The else too somber web of life they brighten with threads of purple and gold. Into dull souls they breathe a quickening spirit. To the groveling and earth-bound they are angels of a nobler and

better life. Interpreters of deeper mysteries, they hold ajar
for us the doors of the ineffable. Heralding all grander truths,
they are the pioneers of civilization, the exponents and prophets
of that Golden Age for which humanity waits.

# DANTE.

### By J. GERRY EBERHART, of Cornell College.

## BIOGRAPHICAL.

J. Gerry Eberhart was born July 27, 1856, at Shrewsbury, Pennsylvania, and is of Scotch-Irish and German parentage. When nine years old he was converted and joined the Methodist Episcopal Church. He attended academy three years at Shrewsbury, and then his father placed him in Lebanon Valley College, Annville, Pennsylvania, when but thirteen years old. At fifteen years of age he attended Cornell College, Mt. Vernon, Iowa, one year, and at seventeen years re-entered and continued five years, graduating in 1878; *in cursu* he received the degree master of arts. While in college he was president of the oratorical association, and manifested notable interest in the literary society, and received one of the gold medals at the inter-State oratorical contest, when President Harrison was one of judges. Mr. Eberhart's early ambition was in the law business, but feeling toward the close of his college course especially called to the ministry, he entered Drew Theological Seminary, Madison, New Jersey, to prepare himself for the Master's work. His began his labor in Central Pennsylvania Conference under the presiding elder, and afterward joined the Rock River Conference, of Illinois. At the expiration of three years he moved to Flagstaff, Arizona, the only missionary point on the Altantic & Pacific Railroad from Albuquerque, New Mexico, to Barstow, California. One year later he located at Prescott, and was chaplain of the council of the 16th legislative assembly. He was sent to Central City, Colorado, by special appointment of Bishop Bowman; he was also located at Ouray, Colorado. He eventually returned to the Rock River Conference, and is at present located in Kent, Illinois, devoting his time to preaching and lecturing.

## THE ORATION.

Delivered at the Inter-State Oratorical Contest, at St. Louis, Missouri, May, 1878, taking second prize. Judges: Hon. A. TAFT, Bishop THOS. BOWMAN, Hon. BENJAMIN HARRISON, Hon. WM. HYDE.

The history of a nation is the history of her great men. Dante was the prophetic exponent of the heart of the Middle Ages, the embodiment of the character, and the realization of the science of his day. A character original, pathetic, and angelic, whose inspired soul led the intellect in its train. Tasso, Spenser, Goethe, Byron, and Milton bathed themselves in the light of his resplendent genius.

His writings are as subtle as logic and as sublime as nature's laws. The "Divina Commedia" is his masterpiece. He incorporated into his immortal work the learning, philosophy, religion, and popular traditions of the mystic age. The universe was his field of labor; eternity the goal of his endeavor, and the solitude of thought his studio.

A pioneer in literature, he cast upon the waters bread which is feeding the starving millions to-day. Having entered the "Holy of Holies" he has wandered through the labyrinths of the human heart. The triple-headed dog Cerberus ceased his barking, and competition fled from Dante as "from the glance of destiny." To him was given the keys of the bottomless pit. Devils trembled at his approach.

He lived as if seeing Him who is invisible. An angel incarnate, he recognized simply mind and spirit, and was not polluted by the touch of *earth*.

Who shall breathe a word against him, or say he was not conversant with the sentiments and principles which are the living springs of beauty? With one stroke of his forearm having shattered the kingdom of papacy he fled from the terrors of torch and dagger, and wandered an exile in all lands. His persecutors coveted his fleshless palms and lifeless form for their city, ready to place them in "the damp vault that weeps o'er royal bones."

Dante's poetry differs from Milton's as the picture-painting of Mexico from the hieroglyphics of Egypt. The images of Dante are concise and level with the common mind, while those of Milton are elaborated for the chosen few.

"If you examine Italian art," said Cornelius, "its decline begins when painters ceased to carry Dante in their minds." He was the connecting link between medieval and modern literature. In him the latter had its birth. It mattered not whether chasing the butterflies of youth, or all aglow with life's meridian glory, the chief magistrate of Florence, the immortal dreamer, or a banished hero, he was the same man of destiny. Mounted on thought's fantastic pinion, he sailed from mountain-top to mountain-top and from glory to glory. The populace acknowledged him as prophet, priest, and king, and with trembling hand, as if in the presence of the supernatural, exclaimed, "See there, the man who has been in hell!" Like Luther, he had heard the cry of others, "If there is a hell, Rome is built over it!"

He cringed before no foe, and, filled with that holy enthusiasm, the sure premonitor of success, his fame widened, and stars came out to adorn his crown. When he went out in death no night followed. He lives in the bright light of his example, enshrined in the hearts of a worthy posterity, and he shall be forgotten only when men cease to revere genius and virtue, and trample upon their cherished memorials.

America—thanks to her own honored poet, Longfellow—begins to appreciate the transcendent intellect and pure soul of Dante. Who has not experienced the soul-subduing awe of his solemnity, or been raised to the lofty heights of his sublimity? Who has not felt the gloomy pathos and keen sarcasm and personality of his verse? He converted heathen antiquity into Christian mythology, and built up a new heaven and a new earth. No muse called by fancy from the fabled heights, no ambition to spread a sounding name abroad, gave the world the grander efforts of Dante; but we owe all to the inspiration of a young and beautiful woman.

Dante once stood, as the shadow of a devil, in the background; but, under the glowing light of modern criticism and truth, he is transformed into an archangel wearing the victorious sword of a Michael, ready to smite the red dragon of the seven-hilled city, though standing upon the Prince of Darkness at the very mouth of hell.

As the simple light is seen on the mountain before the monster Vesuvius belches destruction upon listless Pompeii, so, silently, under a propitious star of the Italian constellation, Dante began his state. He came—a mental and moral light, a savior and not a destroyer, in the fiery times—to free the bondsmen and point out the higher path of a Christian civilization.

His age, like ancient Pompeii, now lies buried, and only by digging beneath the surface of his literature is it truthfully revealed. His literature unveils not only the history of his times, but also the foundation of his creative energy, upon which he reared the fabric of his fame.

He exemplified futurity to the material eye by the personified presence of living actors. Thus, with rich hues of reality, he made his scenes more impressive. He even clothed the myths which shock and amuse, while they flee from our grasp as "a shadow or a mocking spirit."

Dante shines by no reflected light. A star of the first magnitude, the center of all attraction, he shines in the firmament of creative mind.

The images of Dante are not rude forms struggling into notice, striving in vain to maintain their equilibrium. They burst upon us as the first view of the sea, holding the eye by their infinity, and filling us with a longing to examine them with a closer gaze.

Dante loved solitude, not the solitude of slavish fear which shrinks from sight, but grand and peculiar he rose like a pyramid above the gloomy desert of the fourteenth century. With eyes upon the subjective phenomena, inward, yet an accurate observer of the objective, he recognized the material as typical only of the ideal and the divine. He stood alone, because head and shoulders above his fellows. He weighed the nations in the even balance of his justice.

His land is one of enchantment and wild despair. Everything wears the garb of vivid personality. The mystic chain of friendship is unbroken. The trees are so many tongues. The rended rocks tell their history. The myrtle into which Polydorus had been metamorphosed, when struck by the rude hand of desire, bleeds, and utters sorest plaints from its wounded side. The animals shake pestilence from their shaggy manes. The air moans in agony. The rivers run red to the sea. And only by worshiping at the shrine of changeless

Providence are we led out to the "ever-green mountains of life."

Dante's devils are to be hated. They are monsters of hideous mien and immense proportions. His Lucifer does not appear as an archangel ruined, but as *"a seraph willfully fallen."* He bears no marks that would solicit sympathy, but maintaining his obdurate pride is willing to wear the crown at the bottomless pit, an Arch-Fiend, rather than bow to the Lord Almighty.

Dante is led through the realm of Paradise by the celestial smile of Beatrice, who is the embodiment of divine science. Her smile deepens until high on the wings of rising faith he sees "grace culminate in the ever-blessed Trinity in unity, where unto is taken forevermore the glorified humanity of God Incarnate."

And now the wanderer returns and seeks repose in Florence, the fairest home in Italy. Ah! thou too, Florence, dost thou spurn him from thy bosom? Has the common mother forgotten her offspring? Is this rejection the fruit of his abundant sweat and toil in thy behalf? Dante becomes the adopted child of Ravenna.

"On thy hoary shores, fortress of fallen empire!
Honored sleeps the immortal exile."

Hear, fairest Italy! Arise! Shake off the dust from thy garments, and take thy place in the front rank of nations! "The spirits of thy sons are standing on every step of the temple of genius since the twelfth century." The children call thee blessed, for Dante, the immortal Dante, greatest of them all, sleeps in thy bosom. Ye streams that go dancing into the sea, sound his praise! Ye torrents, thunder it in your awful plunge! Ye soft skies, wreath yourselves in smiles and weep tears of joy! Ye silent voices of nature, whisper it to the winds! Ye winds, carry it upon your wings the world over! Ye purple hills, tell it to the stars! Ye fiery battalions that tread the celestial way, sing it to the music of the spheres! Dante's ministers on trembling pinions wait to catch their master's least commands. Time, the tomb-effacer, covers up all things human. Empires rise and sink as waves of the sea. The proudest works of man are short-lived, and "dust to dust" concludes the noblest song. The lofty marble and bronze will crumble and fall. The iron bands will burst asunder. The everlasting hills will sink into nothingness. The earth will vanish as a scroll. The burning orbs that gem the radiant brow of night will wander "rayless and pathless;" and midnight, universal midnight, will reign.

But Dante ever lives, and his spirit grows brighter by time. He sung, impelled by the power that rules in Heaven, and then gave his golden harp into angels' keeping, and it awaits his master touch to answer in sweeter strains in the morning of the resurrection.

# IAGO.

By R. M. La Follette, of Wisconsin State University.

### BIOGRAPHICAL.

It is that great disparity between the humble log-cabin and the honored chair of State which truly shows the great possibilities of an American life. Mr. La Follette's life has been one of this true American type. The rapidity of his political and social growth has been as marvelous as that of any American statesman. Robert Marion La Follette was born in a log-cabin in the town of Primrose, Dane County, Wisconsin, June 14, 1855. When six years of age his parents moved to Argyle, in a neighboring county, where his time was divided between working on a farm and attending a district school. In 1873 the family moved to Madison, and here he attended a private academy preparatory to entering the State University, where he was admitted to the freshman class in September, 1875. His early college work was characterized by his activity in the debating societies, and in literary work as editor and joint-owner of the university press. In his junior year he was elected by the Athenean Society as its orator in junior exhibition. In his senior year he represented the university in the inter-State contest, at Iowa City, Iowa, winning the prize on his oration "Iago." This literary masterpiece, combined with its faultless elocution and delivery, established his reputation as a writer and orator. He took his diploma with the class of '79, and entered the law school in the fall of the same year, which he attended only one term, completing his law studies in an office. He was admitted to the bar in 1880, and in the fall of the same year was nominated and elected by the Republicans district attorney of Dane County. This office he filled with such conspicuous ability that at the following election, in 1882, he was re-chosen by his county, notwithstanding formidable opposition and the fact that the average plurality against his

ticket was over a thousand. The severest strain upon the powers of a member of the legal profession comes in the trial of cases. Tested thus as a master of the points of his cause, in quick perception, and close discrimination in examination of witnesses, and the gift of exposition to court and jury of the law and facts involved, Mr. La Follette is pre-eminent. The reputation earned by him as a lawyer, together with the popularity and friendships attaching to a winning and genial personality, brought him before the people of the capital district as their most desirable candidate for Congress, and in 1884 he was nominated and elected congressman of the third district. He was the youngest man in the 49th Congress, being but twenty-nine years of age when his term commenced. He was re-elected to his seat in Congress and again in 1888, and was unanimously renominated by the Republicans of his district in 1890, but in the political revolution ensuing upon the introduction into Wisconsin State politics of compulsory education issues, made one of the numerous candidates defeated, his district thereupon losing not only a faithful and tireless representative, but one of unimpeachable private and public character. Among his speeches in Congress, winning him wide commendation, are more particularly his discussion of the River and Harbor Bill of 1885; his reply to Speaker Carlisle's speech on the Mills Bill; his defense of the Lodge Election Bill; his advocacy of the constitutional power of Congress to tax manufactured compounds deleterious to health; and his speech in endorsement of the Tariff Bill of 1890. Outside of his public work he has been called upon to do much public speaking. During his first term in Congress he was chosen to make the annual address to the Howard Law School, at Washington, to pronounce the oration at the Grant memorial exercises held at the Monona Chautauqua Assembly, and to deliver a political address in Chickering Hall of New York. As a campaign orator he is greatly in demand; his style is simple and direct, his vocabulary copious and Anglo-Saxon, his argument inductive, and thought clear; backing this is the gift of oratory, a voice musical and magnetic, and the taste and discrimination of a trained literary mind. In 1880 Mr. La Follette married Miss Belle Case, of Baraboo, Wisconsin, who had been his classmate in the university, and to whom upon graduation in

1879 was awarded the Lewis Prize for the best commencement oration. In addition to her university training Mrs. La Follette also took a full course in the Wisconsin University Law School, and was the first lady to receive a diploma from that institution. She has proven herself a most worthy and inspiring sharer of the honors, trials, and responsibilities of her husband's professional and political life. At the expiration of the present Congress he will return to his home, at Madison, and resume the practice of law. We predict for him a future which will realize the promises and expand the reputation gained in ten years of public service as lawyer, orator, and statesman.

## THE ORATION.

Delivered at the Inter-State Oratorical Contest, at Iowa City, Iowa, taking first prize. Judges: Prof. W. H. Harris, General Gibon, and others.

### ABSTRACT OF ARGUMENT.

1. Mental analysis of Iago.
   Has but two of the three constituents of the mind.
   Loss of emotional nature has cost him his moral parts.
   What he lacks in feeling, he has gained in knowing — he knows everything, feels nothing.
2. Originality of his methods of meanness, as shown in his relations to the other characters of the tragedy.
   Display of his intellectual acuteness — his power of dissimulation, his manner and his means.
3. He is a being without conscience, but his acute mind redeems him to us as a subject.
   His questioning his "reasons," the result of his mental mechanism, not the protest of conscience.
4. Contrasted with Richard III. Iago is more perfect as a devil, Richard more perfect as a villain. Richard's conscience finally asserts itself; Iago has none, hence, is his superior in pure hellish consistency.
5. Iago, Shakespeare's conception of the "Evil Principle;" hence, the vagueness of his fate, which can be explained in no other way. It is consistent with a devil — not with the villain of a tragedy.

Shakespeare's Iago personifies two constitutents of mind — intellect and will. These alone are the springs of his action, the source of his power. What he lacks in emotion he has gained in intellectual acuteness, but the result is deformity. The character is not *un*-natural; it is fiendishly natural. His reasoning power is abnormally developed; but he has no feeling, no sympathy, no affection, no fear. His is the cold passion of intellect, whose icy touch chills the warm life in all it reaches. He is an intellectual athlete, and is unceasing in his mental gymnastics. His contempt for all good is supreme; his greatest crime is his greatest pleasure, and his own hypocrisy gladdens and intoxicates him. Whatever is most mean, whatever is most hard, whatever is vilely atrocious and dangerously difficult, he seizes with greedy glee. Skeptical of all virtue, to him love is lechery, truth-telling stupid goodness, and lying a daring to be ingenious.

The emotions are the native soil of moral life. From the feelings are grown great ethical truths one by one, forming at last the grand body of moral law. But Iago is emotionally a cipher, and his poverty of sentiment and wealth of intellect render him doubly dangerous. Here we have the key to his character—he is possessed of an inflexible will, of an intellect pungent, subtle, super-sensual. He not only knows more than he feels, he knows everything, feels nothing.

The other characters of the tragedy of Othello—a tragedy which Macaulay pronounced Shakespeare's greatest—are but puppets, moving at the will of this master. He reads them at a glance, by a flash of instinct. He wastes no words on Roderigo other than to make the "fool his purse." But upon Othello he plays with most subtlety, and infinitely greater zest. Upon him he exercises his crafty ingenuity; and the "double knavery," the "how? how?" whets him keen. Now flashes forth the invisible lightning of his malignant mind, and woe to all virtue within its reach. Now we see his character in all its artful cunning, all its devilish cruelty. With what marvelous skill he makes his first attack! He does nothing in the common way. His methods have the merit of originality. He does not assail Desdemona's virtue with a well-conned story, but is seemingly surprised into an exclamation, appearing to utter his suspicions by the merest accident. And when he has engaged Othello's ear, note his matchless cunning; he comes and goes, and comes and goes again, with his ingenious inuendoes; changing like the chameleon, quick to take his cue from the Moor, yet craftily giving direction to the other's thoughts; cursing Cassio with his protestations of love, and damning Desdemona while joining in a benediction to her honesty. The "constant, loving, noble nature" of the Moor changes quickly under the "almost superhuman art" of Iago; but too well he knows the human mind to gorge it with suspicion; and with every dose of poison gives just a little antidote. With pious self-accusation, he says, "'Tis my nature's plague to spy into abuses," and oft my jealousy shapes faults that are not;" but carefully adds, "It were not for your quiet nor your good to let you know my thoughts;" and is equally careful to tell them; smothering with one hand all suspicion of his perfidy, and kindling with the other the consuming fires of the Moor's jealousy.

Iago's manner of practicing on Othello is only matched by the means he employs. Like the genuine devil, he destroys the entire household — not through some unguarded vice, but through its very virtues. He sets all goodness by the ears. The strength of the Moor's affection is made a fatal weakness; and, more than this, the very medium of all their misery is she

"Of spirit so still and gentle that her motion
Blushed at herself."

Iago and Desdemona! Strange, unspeakable union of opposites! Weird harmony of discords! Somber mingling of a smile and a sneer! O the poet whose genius could compound these elements without an explosion! O this "unequal contrast between the powers of grossness and purity!" That Desdemona, whose child-like nature is a divine fusion of innocence and chastity, should be played off against a moral outlaw — a being whose livery is "heavenly shows," and whose logic is the "divinity of hell" — is a juxtaposition appalling, fascinating! 'T is Dina in the talons of a Harpy. That virtue should be 'turned into pitch,' that "out of goodness" should be made the 'net to enmesh them all,' that innocence should become the instrument of the infernal, is a "moral antithesis" that preludes the oncoming of chaos. And it comes like the quick night, and consummates the tragedy; while over all, in sullen silence, gloats the imp of darkness.

Somewhere Thomas Carlyle has said, "There are depths in man that go to the length of the lowest hell, as there are heights that reach highest heaven;" but Iago is a magnet with only one pole, which ever points toward the infernal. Why is it, then, that this character does not disgust us? Why do we follow his intricate windings with such intense interest?

Why do we tolerate him? We find the answer in his great intellect. This is the core of his character—abstract intellectuality united to volitional force, devoid of all morality, divorced from all feeling. He is hardly human, yet he sounds humanity like a philosopher. He is wanting in ethical parts, yet he makes the nicest moral distinctions. He is a fraction, yet greater than a unit; a part, yet more than the whole. He is a paradox. In his deep schemes we nearly forget the villain. His triumph over all obstacles pins the attention to his intellectual powers. He is "instinct with thought." This redeems him to us as a subject, and yields another explanation for what has been termed his "little trace of conscience." His self-questionings, his subtle sophisms, his cataclysm of reasons, are not the weak protest of a moral part, but the logical outcome of a sleepless intellect. He is emphatically a being of reasons. He will do nothing except he furnish to himself the "why." It is not that he requires these reasons as a "whetstone for his revenge," it is not that his "resolution is too much for his conscience," but rather that he revels in reasons, that his hungry mind will have its food. He "suspects the lusty Moor," and fears "Cassio with his night-cap, too," on occasion; not that he dreads to destroy either without some motive, but because his mental constitution demands a reason for all things. Schlegel defines wickedness as "nothing but selfishness designedly unconscientious;" but Iago makes no effort to deceive himself, for he says:

"When devils will their blackest sins put on,
They do suggest at first with heavenly shows,
As I do now."

He does not care to justify himself, except as an intellectual satisfaction. He desires no moral vindication. In fact he commits crime merely for crime's sake, and there is no sin that he will not claim as his own. Think of it! a being who clutches at wickedness with all the greed of a miser. Thoroughly passionless, coldly intellectual, he is forced into the self-confession that he is no libertine; yet fearful lest the admission has cost him one hellish trait, he quickly adds that he stands "accountant for as great a sin." This is a moral defiance sublimely hideous, but hardly reconcilable in a being with even a "little trace of conscience." Were there a single golden thread of

moral sense to knit him to the good of humanity it would shine
forth when Desdemona, whose only offense against him is that
she is pure, sinks under his cursed cunning. But it is a quality
he feel not, knows not, and what Coleridge calls *"the motive-
huntino of a motiveless malignity;"* this constant combing of his
wits for reasons is simply a service performed at the mandate
of his craving intellect.

These are the premises from which, as a conclusion, we deduce Iago—a character without a conscience.

Mark the "steep inequality" between him and Richard III.:
The Duke of Gloster, born with teeth, a twisted body, and a
majestic mind, cut his way through those of his own flesh to a
throne. Malignant and artful, hypocritical and heartless, he
"seems a saint when most he plays the devil." Monster, he
stands apart from men; he is "like himself alone," and he
stalks along his bloody course a solitary creation. Brave, he
has the audacity to defy destiny, the impudent confidence to
enter the lists against the Unknown. But hidden away somewhere in his black soul is a germ of conscience, disguised as
superstitious fear—a germ of conscience which starts forth
when that towering will is off guard; coming in the thin substance of a dream, yet so terrible that the remorseful "drops
hang on his trembling flesh." Here is his humanity, his mortal
weakness, and through this the "all-powerful and ever-watchful Nemesis" hurls her lance, barbed to the shaft with retribution. Pursued by croaking phantoms, scourged by the invisible
lash of violated conscience, he flings himself into the conflict,
and with a royal flourish, in perfect keeping with his character,
closes the tragedy. His death satisfies the equation of right.

Richard and Iago possess some qualities in common: both
have mighty intellects; both are wily, cunning, crafty; both
dissimulers; both actors. But farther than this they are
profoundly unlike. Richard III. is more humanly terrible;
Iago more devilishly perfect. Richard loves nothing human;
Iago hates everything good. Richard is arrogant, passionate,
powerful, violent; Iago egotistical, cold, cynical, sly. Richard
is fire; Iago, ice. Richard III. is more objective; Iago, more
subjective. Richard would pulverize the universe; Iago would
like to reverse the order of things. In point of satanical finish
Iago is Richard, and more. Richard III. murders many and

sweats with horror; Iago few, and forgets remorse. Richard III. mounts the throne of England on a score of dead bodies; Iago wins the throne of hell in three strides. The conscience of Richard wakes from its throne; Iago has no conscience. Richard III. is a monstrosity; Iago, a psychological contradiction.

We offer Iago, then, as Shakespeare's conception of the "Evil Principle." And how perfect the creation! In the whole course of his crime he betrays never a weakness, never a check of conscience — nothing to mar the elegant symmetry of his fiendishness. From the time he lays down the postulate that "I am not what I am" till he attains his infernal majority, he is the same refined, pitiless, sarcastic devil. He is often surprised, but he is never disconcerted. He plans, but it is because he likes the mental exercise. It has been said that "deep rogues take all their villainy *a priori*; that they do not construct plans in anticipation." Iago's carefully perfected schemes would seem to rebuke this philosophy were it not that they appear, rather, meat for his mind than directions for his diabolisms. Indeed it is in those unpremised scenes where the occasion fails to fit his plans, where all the odds are arrayed against him, that he achieves the greatest triumph. This is nothing short of Stygian skill, and it is just here that he attains the dignity of a devil. That dignity would have been sacrificed in his death. By all the principles of dramatic tragedy Othello is his fit executioner. Significant fact! we are only promised that his "punishment shall torment him much and hold him long." This is to appease the moral demand, and in its vagueness the poet seeks to avoid a decline in tragic intensity. This we offer as the ethical and æsthetical reason for the indefiniteness thrown about Iago's fate by the dramatist. He had pushed his creation to the verge of the finite: punishment was demanded, none could be devised which would requite him.

The full course of tragedy, the mighty evolution of its events, must yield an apt sequence, a sublime completeness, else it fails in its aim. Schiller says, "Life is great only as a means of accomplishing the moral law; and nothing is sublimer than a criminal yielding his life because of the morality he has violated." With the single exception of Iago, Shakespeare has availed himself of this principle. The Thane of Cawdor tops all his murderers with his own head; Lady Macbeth bleaches in death the "damned spot" from her unclean hand; Richard III. seals with his own blood on Bosworth field the sublime in his career; but Iago is just beyond the reach of death, and we can fancy him disappearing in the darkness of which he is a part.

There are two fitnesses in a villain's death—the moral fitness and the tragic fitness. The one, the ethical satisfaction at the inevitable recoil of the broken moral law; the other, the grandeur of a *finale*. To condense into one moment the whole of life, to put a fiat on existence, to engulf a soul in the awful immensity of its own acts—this is sublime; but to have conceived and brought forth a being so super-physical, so positively devilish, so intensely infernal, that his death would be pathos—this is genius.

And this Iago. The polished, affable, attendant; the boon companion; the supple sophist, the nimble logician; the philosopher, the moralist, the scoffing demon; the goblin whose smile is a stab, and whose laugh is an infernal sneer; who has sworn eternal vengeance on virtue everywhere; who would turn cosmos into chaos. This compound of wickedness and reason, this incarnation of intellect, this tartarean basilisk, is the logical conclusion in a syllogism whose premises are "Hell and Night." He is a criminal climax; endow him with a single supernatural quality, and he stands among the devils of fiction supreme.

# MAHOMETANISM AND ITS ENEMIES.

By J. A. BARBER, of Oberlin College.

## BIOGRAPHICAL.

J. A. Barber was born at Iona, Michigan, in 1855. It was at the age of twenty-two he graduated from Oberlin College, Oberlin, Ohio. The following year he served as superintendent of the schools at St. Marys, and then located in Toledo, and became principal of the high school, resigning at the end of the year to engage in the study of law. He was admitted to the bar October 3, 1882, and has since been actively engaged in the practice of this profession with great success. He is now prosecuting attorney of Lucas County. The oration, on following pages, delivered by him while a student of Oberlin College, secured to him the second prize for oratorical excellence.

## THE ORATION.

Delivered at the Inter-State Oratorical Contest, at Iowa City, Iowa, taking second prize. Judges: Prof. W. H. HARRIS, General GIBON, and others.

The progress of the human race has been slow but sure. In the revolutions of human activity, principles, institutions, and religions have sprung up, fulfilled their mission, and fallen into the grave of buried epochs.

When we judge of a factor of civilization, reason demands that we lay aside all prejudice. Neither can we judge by the standard of our own age; but the tribunal before which every institution must be tried is the condition of the human race at the time of that institution. We wish to examine the religion of Mahomet as a factor of human progress, and it is our purpose to show that Mahometanism has had a beneficial influence upon mankind. It has been but a short time that the world has been fair in judging the true character of Mahomet. For eleven centuries men looked upon him as a cheat and imposter and an enemy of mankind. Now all the greatest and most candid writers agree that Mahomet stands forth as a sincere, earnest, God-loving man. His soul longed to lead his people to a nobler life. In like manner, the writers of the past, blinded by hate or prejudice, have denounced Mahomet's religion as a curse to human happiness and a barrier to human progress. They have forgotten the good in his religion, and the good it has accomplished. They have looked only at its evils, and then told us that it has checked the progress of mankind. We think that a fair examination of his religion, and its influence, will lead us to agree with many of the ablest minds of to-day that such a view of Mahometanism is wrong. The religion of Mahomet changed the destinies of the world forever. One-fifth of the human souls that have lived and died upon this earth for the last twelve centuries, have drawn their inspiration, their happiness, and that highest and most divine of all earthly joys — the hope of an immortal life with an eternal God — from the teachings of Mecca's humble prophet. One hundred and eighty millions of men live upon the earth to-day whose eternal destiny is shaped by the doctrines of the camel-driver of Arabia. This, then, is the problem: in the divine order and harmony of the world, in the mysterious laws of human progress, has the birth of Mahomet, upon which rests such a burden of human destiny, been a curse? I know what the truthful believers in a kind and loving Providence will say. Impossible that one man could determine the eternal fortunes of one-fifth of the men who have lived for twelve centuries, were it not to work for the highest good of God's creatures! They will tell you that when Mahomet, hunted by his enemies, stood a hated and helpless prisoner in the hands of the officers of Medina, "when the lance of an Arab might have changed the history of the world," they will tell you that something more than human power stayed that lance.

But I wish to demonstrate, by the laws and facts of progress, that Mahometanism has had a beneficial influence upon the world. The first argument that the enemies of Mahomet bring against his religion is that it is full of fundamental errors, and from this they conclude that it has checked human progress. No one ever held that the religion of Mahomet was perfect. But we have it on the authority of all great minds that his religion, in its conception and grandeur, stands next to Christianity. A kind of Christianity, says Carlyle. There are great and grand truths in the religion—truths which appealed to the noblest impulses of those wild Arabian souls. We admit that there are great errors in his system, that he gave his sanction to many evils; but let us remember that Mahomet found these indulgences practiced unquestioned from the time his race issued from the caves of barbarism. Have men denounced Solon's laws? They were not perfect, yet they were the best the Athenians could receive. Have men hurled their philippics against Moses? He allowed polygamy. He allowed slavery. He permitted the institutions of primitive society. He did not abolish one of them; he could not. He mitigated their evils. Mahomet did the same. He could not unmake the manners of his people. He found Arabia steeped in spiritual torpor. From time beyond memory the night of sin had settled around them. His morality is not perfect; yet what a wonder that so grand a system could be reared in twenty-five years upon the ruins of one of the basest idol-worships that ever stained the annals of men. So far as the logical consequence of this objection is concerned we might admit it, and it would not prove that Mahomet's religion had checked human progress. If it can be shown that his religion was suited to the condition of the times, and to that part of the race which received it, it has been demonstrated that it has a beneficial influence upon the world. In the most glorious epochs of ancient civilization, when the human mind had reached as high a development as had ever been equaled, when the youth flocked to the schools of philosophy and oratory, when the muse of poetry sang her loftiest strains, and the theaters echoed with the beautiful conception of creative minds, at that very time the streets of all the cities were adorned with the marble and the temples of heathen gods. Above the azure vault of heaven, Jupiter, Bacchus, and the other gods, were believed to be reveling and taking part in human passion and human crime. Yet no one ever said that the worship of Jupiter was detrimental to ancient civilization. It formed a bond of union, without which, Max Mueller says, society cannot exist. It formed a stepping-stone of human progress. It was the only religion, which, in that condition and part of the world, could stir the highest impulses of men. Thus, when we judge of the influence of Mahometanism, we must discuss not the creed of Mahomet, but whether it suited the times and people that received it.

The second argument that the enemies of Mahometanism bring to show that it hindered human progress is, that it entered Christian ground and hindered Christianity. I know that the Christian religion had to give up the cradle of its infancy; and when it became known, "a nerve was touched," as Gibbon says, "which vibrated to the heart of Europe." Let us go back to our tribunal to weigh this argument— the condition of the times. Palestine was bounded by the fire-worshipers and the star-worshipers. Christianity had failed to weaken the idolatry of those savage millions. The Christian religion itself, in the East, had become paganized. In the dark night of superstition and sin, it had fallen into a state of corruption and idolatry. For six centuries Christianity held its sway in the East. What is the uniform testimony concerning its results? It had ceased its rapid conquest. It had fallen into superstition and sin. Star-worship and fire-worship were unchanged. Hallam, the least enthusiastic of writers, testifies that society had sunk into the depths of ignorance; that, "in the shadows of this universal ignorance, a thousand superstitions, like foul animals of night, were propagated and nourished." If, in the light of such facts, it is said that Mahomet's religion entered Christian ground, we reply in the language of Milman, a great and candid writer, that Islam was better, far better than the idolatrous forms of Christianity which it supplanted. It is said that his religion hindered Eastern progress; we answer in the words of Hallam, that "Mahometanism is the only form of religion that has proved itself suited to the nations of the East." How in the light of history can we fling upon Mahomet the charge of hindering Eastern progress? Are all other nations of the world progressive save those under his religion? Can a religion which teaches the unity of God, which teaches temperance and chastity, which teaches the divine principles of benevolence and prayer, check the progress of society? The worship of Jupiter and Bacchus did not hinder ancient civilization, yet how wrong was that worship compared with the teachings of Mahomet. Historians tell us that Eastern society is what it was in the time of Solomon, what it was in the time of Abraham.

Oriental society has been non-progressive. The Chinese, the most advanced, are as stationary as the pyramids of Egypt. We can see but one answer to the non-progressiveness of the East—it is the nature, nature, nature of the race.

We will now support the affirmative of this line of argument —that the human race has been made happier, because Mahomet, by something more than human power, issued from the caravans of the desert to shape the fortunes of Ishmael's sons. We argue that Mahometanism has been beneficial, first, because it was a mighty reform. Generations and ages rolled into oblivion, and the wild Bedouins of the desert had remained unnoticed. For ages, of which the pen of the historian can never write, the sun had risen upon the wandering, warring, robbing tribes of the Arabian wastes. They had never dreamed of that sublimest of truths—there is but one God. They had never enjoyed that most divine of all earthly joys—the hope of an immortal life with an immortal God. They had never drawn a breath save under the basest idol-worship. Poor, savage, half-human, half-brutish creatures! But they were not always to be so. In the words of Voltaire, the turn of Arabia came. Mahomet in his boyhood days had learned of God. He longed to raise his people from the night of sin, and to lead them to a nobler life. He could not reveal to them such a religion as the voice of Judea proclaimed six hundred years before. But such a religion as could come from his rude, untutored, fervent, God-loving soul, he gave them. "Destroy your idols. Cast off your blasphemous idolatry. Ye are mocking God. God is great. He made us all. He guards us and cares for us. Serve him. He alone is good. He only has power to save." This inspired their wild souls with enthusiasm. They began a career of progress, and there was inaugurated one of the greatest reforms that ever shook the affairs of men. If you prefer to hear on this point the greatest prose writer that now lives, he will tell you that "to the Arab nation it was a birth of darkness into light. Arabia first became alive by means of it; glancing in splendor and the light of genius, Arabia shines through long ages over a great section of our world."

Again, we argue that Mahometanism has been a beneficial factor of civilization, because its mission seemed to be demanded by the condition of the times. We have seen how

Christianity has fallen from its state of primitive purity. It had become paganized. Heathen rites had been introduced. In the East were seen men bowing to images, as heathens do to their heathen-gods. The whole Eastern world was immersed in ignorance and superstition. The Church was torn with discords and dissensions. Yes, long before the "Sermon on the Mount" had ceased its rapid conquest, such was the state of the Christian nations. All the rest of the world was in idolatry. Where was there hope? Mahomet comes. He offers them a sublime monotheism. He offers them a religion which teaches temperance and charity, a religion of prayer, "a really spiritual religion." The Saracen sword demonstrated the majesty of God, and one-fifth of the race was saved from the worship of gods of wood and stone. Thus it was suited to the condition of the times. I would like to give the opinion of Milman on this point: "Islam is entitled to disdain the vulgar polytheism of the East, the fire-worship of Persia, or either the depraved forms of Judaism and Christianity."

We argue, lastly, that Mahomet's religion has made the world happier, because it gave a powerful impetus to the growth of the human mind. One writer charges Mahomet with making progress a crime; yet for five hundred years the excessive brilliancy of Arabian learning dimmed the radiance of all the rest. Throughout the most inglorious period of the world's history they held up the torch of learning to humanity. If we can only get before our minds that "inconceivable cloud of ignorance" which overspread the whole face of the world; if we can only see how strong a connecting link between the old civilization and the new, Arabian learning was, we shall know how much this argument weighs. They roused the world of its sleep of ages, unshackled the human soul, and gave a new impulse to progress. It was the Arabs who, during the darkest ages of Europe's history, summoned the muses of poetry and history. It was the Arabs who turned the philosophy of Plato and Aristotle and the great minds of ancient civilization into new channels of progress. In the science of astronomy they excelled every nation that had ever inhabited the earth. They invented the sciences of chemistry and algebra. All candid minds agree that Arabian learning gave a wonderful impetus to the human intellect. Throughout the

Saracen Empire the streets of all the cities were adorned with colleges and school-houses. Schools of philosophy and science dotted portions of all continents then known.

In the light of all this, in the light of history, in the light of human reason, can we conclude with the enemies of Mahomet, that, in that final tribunal before the bar of God, one-fifth of the men who have lived since the year 600 will rise up to curse Mahomet as an eternal barrier to human happiness? Although we may not understand why the Saracen sword glittered in the once fairest portion of our earth; although we may not understand why the blazoned banners of the Moslems waved over the birthplace of the Christian religion, why the columns of Mahometan mosques now cast their shadows over so large a section of the world; although we may long to see the spires of the Christian church towering among those nations of the East; although we may long to see the time when the posterity of the wise men of the East shall again be guided by the Star of Bethlehem, when the religion of Jesus shall be proclaimed from the altars of Mahometan mosques — yet, after all, would it not be better to conclude with Richelieu, the old white-haired cardinal of France —

"Come, let us own it: there is One above
Who sways the harmonious mysteries of the world?"

# POE.

### By L. C. HARRIS, of Iowa College.

## BIOGRAPHICAL.

L. C. Harris was born June 17, 1857, at Grinnell, Iowa. His early education was obtained in the Grinnell high school, and later he entered Iowa College, which is also located at Grinnell. While in college he entered the contest for oratorical honors, and with his oration on "Poe" he was triumphant. After leaving college he entered the law department of the Iowa State University, completing the course in 1882. In the fall of the same year he went to Dakota to engage in the law and real estate business, and settled in La Moure County. He resided here one year when he was elected register of deeds and county clerk, which position he held until the 1st of January, 1889. Mr. Harris is now practicing law, and is county attorney for La Moure County. He is an efficient officer, as an evidence of which he has been engaged in public work for several years, and is a man of many admirable qualities.

## THE ORATION.

*Delivered at the Inter-State Oratorical Contest, at Oberlin, Ohio, May, 1880, taking first prize. Judges: Hon. THOMAS A. HENDRICKS, Messrs. OWEN, BRAND, and others.*

There have appeared at different stages of the world's history minds so anomalous in their nature, so totally at variance with those surrounding them, so unnatural and equivocal in their construction, that they have seemed more like errant spirits from the world beyond than those possessing the attributes and propensities of common mortals.

Prominent among the names in this strange order of beings occurs that of Edgar Allan Poe. He combines in a remarkable

degree two elements of mind seldom found united—analysis and imagination. These form the ground-work of his genius; they are the source of his wonderful power. No two faculties could be more opposite in their effects. Their union in him gives to many of his subjects the effect of what can only be expressed by the contradictory phrase of the *spiritually material*. He treats the most ideal themes in the most realistic manner. He is both poet and mathematician. He conceives with all the vividness of the former, but he reasons with all the coldness and precision of the latter. He is living fire hedged in with ice. He reduces the wildest play of passion to the most exact order. He unites the severest logic to the most exuberant fancy; the heat of passion to the coldness of reason.

A too close observance of the poetical and ideal part of his nature has gained for him the appellation of *dreamer*. He *has* his moods of abstraction, but he is not the typical dreamer. His piercing acuteness, his minuteness of detail, his subtle distinctions, his refined reasonings, all separate him from the purely meditative mind. The dreamer is passive; Poe is active. The dreamer diffuses his faculties; Poe concentrates them. The dreamer revels in the mysterious; Poe will have nothing to do with it, only as he can explain it. The dreamer surrenders himself to contemplation and reverie, till his own individuality is lost in that of the objects around him; Poe never loses himself in his abstraction—he is most keenly alive when most absorbed.

Mark the contrast between the strength, clearness, and precision of his intellectual, and the wild disorder and disease of his moral and æsthetic, faculties. He naturally possessed delicate perceptions and refined sensibilities. But what do we find in his tales? A nature attuned to the harmonious and the beautiful, reveling in all that is discordant and hideous; a mind intoxicated by the fiendishness of its own creations, indulging all that is self-destructive; all the natural, genuine emotions of the heart blighted and turned awry; hope driven into the icy caves of despair; joy banished into rayless caverns of gloom; poetic fervor turned into maniacal fury; feeling frozen into frenzy; smiles withered into sneers. In fine, the impression produced by these weird compositions is that of a demon mounting to a throne of evil eminence on the wreck of all that is pure and beautiful; and, having attained it, gazing down with fiendish glee upon the ruins below. The diseased condition of his mind we see manifested in the unnatural delight he seems to take in dwelling on the subjects of death and decay. In one of his tales he says: "I have imbibed the shadows of the falling columns of Tadmor, Balbec, and Persepolis, till my very soul has become a ruin." That is it. It is always beauty and grace dethroned; shattered columns, crumbling walls, and tottering arches; the lingering smile on the lips of death; the false and treacherous bloom on the features of disease; "the gilded halo hovering round decay"—it is all these that his morbid fancy seizes upon with such greedy avidity.

He cares nothing for mere external objects only as they excite his emotions. Therefore he always chooses such subjects as are suggestive of melancholy and sadness. He ever represents love as in the icy clutches of death—not that he may show his affection for the dead, but rather as a means of gratifying his abstract love of grief. He has a morbid craving for unnatural sensations. He feeds on mockeries. He taunts himself with the hopelessness of his despair, and takes a strange delight in this process of self-torture. His most intolerable anguish is his keenest joy; the more painful his emotion, the more pungent his pleasure; the greater his grief, the more delicious his sorrow.

But how shall we account for this perversion of his nature? That a mind should indulge in all that is self-destructive, that the very order and nature of things should be reversed, that out of cosmos should come chaos, and out of beauty hideousness, seems a moral antithesis—inexplicable. The explanation of this apparent contradiction is to be found in a peculiar tendency of his nature—his morbid habit of introspection.

Hawthorne, the profoundest moral philosopher that America has ever produced, has said, that of all the practices in which a mind may indulge this one of introspection is the most pernicious. Poe is a slave to it. His eyes are ever turned inward to a "heart gnawed with anguish." Here within this spiritual laboratory he dissects, analyzes, watches. He notes each passing breath of emotion. He catches each fluctuating shade of feeling. He studies with painful minuteness the creeping sensations of crime, guilt, sin, and remorse. He pursues with nervous intensity the darkest thoughts as they steal stealthily through the chambers of the heart. He loves to see the delicate tendrils of the soul quiver with agony or pulsate with joy. And it was this process of critical self-analysis, this peering into the inmost recesses of the soul, this cold, analytic dissecting of an emotion as the anatomist would a nerve, this lying in wait for the play of passion, this trailing a thought through all its tortuous windings—it was this that shattered Poe's sensibilities and dulled his perceptions. His characters are but the logical sequence of this intense subjective tendency of his mind. In none of them can there be found a complete and harmonious blending of all the elements of mind and soul. They are simply the incarnations of a thought; mere abstractions of crime and guilt, frenzy and despair, clothed with flesh and blood. All their sympathy, love, and fear is absorbed by a single animating principle. They have but little to link them to humanity, and possess more in common with the denizens of hell than with the inhabitants of earth.

The many conflicting tendencies found in Poe would seem to almost justify a belief in the duality of mind. He was a strange compound of opposites, a curious blending of harmonies and discords. In him "fire and frost embrace." At times he was mild, gentle, and affable; again, fierce, passionate, and moody. Now he would be charming or electrifying a circle of friends by his wonderful eloquence; and now, sitting apart in some secluded retreat, muttering to himself in dismal monologues. One moment holding you enraptured by his visions of wondrous beauty; the next, chaining you, petrified with terror, among his dismal phantasms, built up in forms of "gloomiest and ghastliest grandeur." To-day soaring away into the far-off realms of imagination; to-morrow wandering in the gloomy labyrinths of his own soul. "At night the hero of a drunken debauch; in the morning a wizard of song, whose weird and fitful music was like that of the sirens."

Poe has often been called the Byron of America. In many respects they are similar. Both are egotistical, passionate, arrogant; both have a morbid love of melancholy, gloom, and death; both are the victims of passion and diseased self-contemplation. Poe resembles Byron in his ethical, but not in his mental, qualities. Byron is powerful, vigorous, synthetic; Poe is subtle, acute, analytic. Byron has broader comprehension; Poe has keener perception. Byron treats of individuals; Poe only of principles. Byron is more objective; Poe, more subjective. Byron broods over his wrongs; Poe analyzes his emotions. Byron dwells upon his sorrows with morbid self-pity; Poe dissects his with frenzied pleasure. Byron was driven into his own consciousness by forces from without; Poe entered his more from innate necessity. Byron is not only conscious of self, he feels the gaze of the whole world; Poe forgets the outward in his intense concentration on the inward.

In other points they stand in closer relations, but still remain apart. Byron is cynical, sullen, morose; Poe is gloomy, sorrowful, despondent. Byron is a misanthrope; Poe is a hypochondriac. Byron wages war with all mankind; Poe is ever contending with the elements of his own nature. Byron has but little of idealism; Poe has nothing of sensualism. Byron has more of human sympathy; yet Poe has less of scorn and sarcasm. Byron's passions come hot and seething from the heart; Poe's are as cold as intellect itself. Byron crushes all sentiment and feeling; Poe reverses them. Byron seems like a "mocking devil, laughing at the world in rhyme;" Poe like a scoffing demon, exulting in his own fiendishness.

This, then, is Poe—the saddest, loneliest figure in all literature; who gave the cypress to love, and the myrtle to death; who sounded the lowest depths of wretchedness and laughed at his own misery; who made of life a living death, and chanted the requiems of despair over the dead hopes of his own soul. The melancholy and gloom in which he enshrouded himself has tinged with sadness all that he has written or said. No Ode to the Nightingale or Skylark from Poe—his was to the sable-winged Raven, the type of his sorrow. He was ever pursued across life's stage by the passions of his nature, like Orestes fleeing the Furies; and he will ever hold a place in the memory of men rather for what he might have been, than for what he was. Goethe has been called the poet of the universe; Byron, the poet of the individual; but Poe is the poet of the soul.

# THE EVOLUTION OF GOVERNMENT.

By RICHARD YATES, of Illinois College.

BIOGRAPHICAL.

Richard Yates was born at Jacksonville, Illinois, December 12, 1860. In 1873, at the age of thirteen, he entered Whipple Academy, the preparatory school for Illinois College, and three years later entered the college. The first year in college he received the prize at the annual declamation contest; second year he was chosen delegate to the Illinois inter-collegiate contest, held at Lebanon, and was there elected president *pro tem.* of the association. He ever manifested particular attention to these contests, and on various occasions took prizes, the most auspicious being the inter-State contest, at Oberlin, Ohio, May, 1880, when he was awarded a gold medal as second prize on his oration, "The Evolution of Government." He graduated in 1880 with the degree of bachelor of arts, and three years later received the degree of master of arts. The first summer after leaving college he was engaged as city editor of the Jacksonville *Journal.* In the fall he entered the law department of the University of Michigan, at Ann Arbor, joining the *Phi Delta Phi,* and becoming vice president of the national council of the fraternity. At the expiration of the first year he discontinued his law studies and resumed the newspaper work. In 1883 he returned to the law school, completed his studies, and was admitted to the Michgan bar in April, 1884; two months later he was licensed by the Supreme Court to practice in Illinois, establishing an office at Jacksonville. In 1885 he was appointed city attorney by the mayor and city council, re-appointed in April, 1886, and at the close of his second term, a change in the law having made the office elective, he was unanimously nominated and elected by the Republicans, and re-elected in 1889. He has filled every office in the Young

Men's Republican Club of Morgan County; was one of the nine delegates from Illinois to the first national convention, at New York; was chosen delegate to the State convention in 1881; and in 1890 was delegate to the legislative, congressional, and State conventions. He has been twice urged to become a candidate for the legislature and once for county judge, but each time refused. It may be said Mr. Yates is a born politician. His father was a member of the Legislature of Illinois from 1842 to 1850, a member of the United States House of Representatives from 1850 to 1854, was Governor of Illinois from 1860 to 1865, and United States Senator from 1865 to 1871; he died at St. Louis, Missouri, November 27, 1873. His mother, who still survives, remains his pride as when a boy. Mr. Yates is a member of the Round-Table Literary Society, a Knight of Pythias, a Mason, a Knight Templar, and an Odd Fellow; he was a member of the Morgan Cadets, Company I, Fifth Regiment, Illinois National Guard, remaining a private throughout his term of enlistment, from 1885 to 1891. He is a consistent member of the Young Men's Christian Association, and the Grace Methodist Episcopal Church. In 1888 Mr. Yates married Miss Helen Wadsworth, a very estimable young lady.

## THE ORATION.

Delivered at the Inter-State Oratorical Contest, at Oberlin, Ohio, May, 1880, taking second prize. Judges: Hon. THOMAS A. HENDRICKS, Messrs. OWEN, BRAND, and others.

Throughout all Christendom to-day scientists are zealously discussing the laws and principles of evolution. It is considered an established proposition, that from everlasting to everlasting, in the heavens, upon the earth, and throughout the entire universe, there is constant change, growth, and improvement. The same great principle has unerringly held good in the history of the nations. From the time when mankind first realized the necessity of association for mutual benefit, a steady growth and improvement have constantly been taking place in the science of human government. First barbarism held sway both in the East and West. Ancient India, China, Arabia, Gaul, and Britain, were simply races of the rudest barbarians. Then, after the lapse of centuries, the second form of governmental association was achieved. As men began to be more attracted together, and commenced to build immense cities and dwell fraternally in large communities, some restraining, governing power became necessary, able or ambitious leaders began to exercise their talents, and to assert their privileges, and the issue was despotism—the system under which Persia, Egypt, and the far-famed empire of the Montezumas reached their climax of civilization. Next, the transitory republics of Greece and Italy, with their more advanced systems of politics and their more liberal institutions, for a time redeemed the world from the gloom that had been spread over it, only to fall from their high estate and to plunge into deeper despair the well-wishers of mankind. But although the failure of Grecian and Roman Republicanism recalled to some extent the old order of things, men were not so tractable as before; and unable longer to endure the oppressive exactions of a system so unjust as despotism, they effected the formation of the more limited monarchies of the Middle Ages. As time passed on the condition of politics was still more favorably changed, and the way was prepared for the monarchies of modern times, such as Germany, Austria, Italy, and Russia, all of which are great in many elements of national stability. And finally, rising from the foundation laid when the Magna Charta of 1215 was wrested from King John, the British Empire is seen pursuing its career of glory—the home on every continent of freedom-loving men, the arbitrator of the world's affairs, the greatest and grandest of European nations—the model monarchy of history.

Meanwhile the lovers of perfect liberty had not been idle, and all over Europe republican forms of government had sprung into being. But these republics, established by men unaccustomed to the taste of the sweets of liberty, inhabited by peoples to whom political freedom seemed a dream and not a reality, permeated with time-honored respect, and even reverence for rank and title—these republics, in which aristocracy and love of fame and pride of name still held a firm footing, were far from that perfection to which the science of government must in the end attain. However, in the fullness of time the grand result of this evolution was to be reached. Barbarism had accomplished its mission. Despots and kings had satisfied their ambition upon the thrones of the world, and the world itself was ripe for a new and more advanced form of government for the people. But nowhere in Europe or in Asia could a land be found whereon to erect the fabric of this new and mighty empire; and nowhere was a people to be found over which to build it, and into whose keeping to commit it. The Power that dwells above, seeing His creatures' need, prepared a land for this new nation, and sent out over the waters to discover it one greater than Noah. The land was found — a continent of imperial grandeur, destined to become the home of an imperial confederation of States. A people to inhabit this realm was providentially prepared. Fleeing from persecution, they gladly sought and settled its shore, and in due time the new nation came forth revealed to the world — an actual fact. It was indeed a prophetic coincidence, that, at that very moment when, as Carlyle says, "The French kingship was perishing in the death of Louis XV., the most Christian King," the dying monarch's closing ears were saluted by muffled sounds borne across the Atlantic — sound new in our centuries. For behold, a Pennsylvanian Congress gathers, and ere long, on Bunker Hill, Democracy announces, in death-winged rifle-volleys, that she is born, and whirlwind-like will envelop the world!

Granting that there is an evolution in government, and that it has been sufficiently demonstrated in its progress in history, we cannot escape the conviction that our republic is the grand culmination of this evolution. True, some declare that every nation and form of government has its period of existence, and that just as Greece, Rome, and Judea fell from their mighty power and lofty position; just as republicanism has again and again proved a failure in France; just as Germany, that gave to the church Martin Luther, and to literature John Gutenberg, is wasting away by the oppressions of a haughty nobility and a tyrannical ministry; while Italy, the land of Dante and of Michael Angelo, is also decaying; just as every civilization known to humanity has gone down at the end of an existence of about five centuries. The day will some time come when the United States, and with them the republicanism in which we glory, shall fall a prey to the diseases of political senility, and finally be stricken from the face of earth. This assertion we may confidently attempt to refute. Greece, unrivaled in the beauty of her poetry, the profundity of her logic, the grandeur of her philosophy, and in all the excellence of her literature, fell because she had exhausted the idea, that philosophy alone was essential to man's well-being. Rome, unequaled in jurisprudence as she was in martial prowess, fell only when she had exhausted the two-fold theory of Law and War as being necessary to the full attainment of true manhood. Judaism was founded upon the idea of religious symbolism, and owed its fall to the fact that it had exhausted that idea. So also republicanism in France was indebted for its many failures to the fact that *republican* France always speedily became *infidel* France, and that the Goddesses of Liberty and Reason always held sway there together whenever the inspiring strains of the Marseillaise had roused the French patriots to another effort for freedom.

With the American nation it has always been different. Our fathers began, as it were, just where other nations left off. It was divinely ordained, that the founders of this republic should be men of transcendent intellect, of finished education, of cultured conscience, of refined sentiments — true noblemen. Never in history did a nation start with so much intelligence, so much culture, so much conscience, as inspired the American colonies to battle for their independence. Other struggles for liberty have taken place. Leonidas had withstood the hosts of Persia at Thermopylæ; but he fought for local freedom. Tell had opposed Gesler; but it was for the sake of his native canton. Cromwell had resisted his king; but the revolution led by Cromwell in the seventeenth century was a war against a dynasty, and was inspired by selfish motives unworthy an Englishman. But the American revolution was not for limited or local freedom — it was for all men. And all that preceded that struggle was but tributary to that event. The exhaustion of the various theories of Grecian, Roman, and Jewish politics; the demonstration of the insufficiency of imperial individualism for the moral culture and elevation of humanity; the plain proof that the union of Church and State has been a failure in the past — all these facts tend but to show that a government wholly of, for and by the people; a body politic which should secure to the greatest number the greatest good; a nation whose fundamental maxim should be the golden rule of Christian ethics: "Do unto others as you would have them do unto you"—that such a nation, the heir of all ages, should be the result of the grand evolution of government.

Such a nation now exists, the noblest of republics; and there can be no doubt, that if there is to be still further advancement in governmental science, the issue will be a model republic upon American soil, and that model republic—the grand culmination of centuries of struggling for civil, political, and religious liberty—will be the United States of America; the nation whose attributes are illustrious lineage, vast territorial domain, royal power, rare intelligence, perfect liberty, religious toleration, pure morality, and the glory of distinguished deeds. May we not hope, that as age after age rolls into the abyss of the past, and generation after generation takes its stand and acts its part in the stupendous drama of history, each shall, in characters of living light, write its name higher and higher upon the temple of fame, and urge on the final triumphs of universal liberty and universal truth!

# THE PHILOSOPHY OF SCEPTICISM.

### By Charles F. Coffin, of DePauw University.

Delivered at the Inter-State Oratorical Contest, at Jacksonville, Illinois, May, 1881, taking first prize. Judges: Mr. Dyer, Hon. Edward P. Kirby, H. F. Carriel, M. D.

It has been justly said, that the shadow of riches is poverty, the shadow of power is slavery, the shadow of virtue is vice; and with equal justice it may be said that the shadow of belief is scepticism.

England had her Jeremy Taylor and her David Hume; France had her Pascal and her Voltaire; America has her Joseph Cook and her Robert Ingersoll.

How does it occur, and what does it mean, that these two great intellectual forces are so often found together? Does it mean that they are related as cause and effect? Does it mean that faith can be purchased only by paying the fearful price of scepticism? With such vital questions as these confronting us, it is of the highest importance that we examine candidly the relation of Scepticism to Theology.

As a common ground "from which to reason and to which refer," it will perhaps be admitted that law prevails in the realm of mind no less than in the realm of matter, and that mental phenomena no less than physical, should be interpreted in the light of rational principles.

For no general phase of human thought, whether it relate to government, to philosophy, or to religion, ever sprang spontaneously into being; but every current theory of state, every doctrine of modern philosophy, every tenet of modern theology, is the outcome of the slow and toilsome growth of ages. And each in turn represent centuries of human thought, centuries of human experience, centuries of human suffering. If over the soil of fair America to-day a proud republic waves her flag, it is because out of the terrible conflict of the past, out of the tyrannies of despots and the rebellions of the oppressed, out of the decay of states and the disasters of revolutions, there was born and flourished in human consciousness the idea of self-government. If the philosophy of to-day is broad and deep and rational, it is because it is the quintessence of the yearnings and the strugglings which, since the dawn of history, have impelled the human mind to search for the unknown. And just so, I take it, is scepticism the outgrowth of certain antecedent mental forces which may be ascertained and classified, just as the forces which produced the Protestant Reformation, the French Revolution or the American Rebellion may be ascertained and classified. The demonstration of this involves a consideration of the law of human growth, the method of human progress. In this man differs widely from nature. In Nature there are no epochs; no conflicts between the conservative and the radical. She has no revolution, no reformation. The shuttle of her mighty loom moves incessantly to and fro, and now she weaves a rose, and now a lion, and now a man; but all is quiet, gradual, uniform.

With man, progress has been a ceaseless conflict between the radical tendencies of thought and the conservative tendencies of institutions; between the gradual unfolding of human consciousness and the stubborn fixedness of the organic forms of civilization. Indeed, human progress is not unlike a volcanic eruption. For a long while the open-mouthed mountain stands out against the sky a dead, harmless mass of rock and earth. Yet down in the subterranean caverns, at its base, the volcanic fires roll and hiss and sputter, till at last, no longer able to be confined, they rush forth in ungovernable fury. The sky is first reddened with flame, then darkened with clouds of ashes, rivers of molten lava pour over the country, devastating fields and destroying cities. So human thought, smothered by oppression, goes on, dimly defined and unexpressed in the great brain of humanity, till by a coincident development of like thoughts and tendencies, like passions and feelings, it breaks out and defiantly laughs conservatism and tyranny to scorn. Old institutions are suddenly swept away; old modes of thought are discredited. The wheels of the human chariot, deep in the rut, are lifted out and placed on a new highway. New relations are formed, new institutions are created; and these in turn become the conservators of past development and the barriers to future progress, till another crisis comes and another revolution solves the problem.

The human mind is so constituted, that, when compelled by external or arbitrary power to bide any extreme of thought, sooner or later it will escape from the bonds of authority, and on the principle of the equality of action and reaction, rush to the opposite extreme. What was Voltaire? He was a reaction. What was David Hume? He was a reaction. What is Robert Ingersoll? He is a reaction. These men, sceptics though they are, and censure them as we may, are nevertheless martyrs to the inexorable law of their own being, and the irresistible laws of human progress. They are to a great extent created and destroyed by their own environment. And so long as progress shall be by revolutions, it will have its victims, its brutalities, its social and intellectual ostracisms, its smoking stakes, its clanking chains, and its times of fire and blood.

It is in the light of human history, and in the light of the psychological law of reaction, that scepticism is largely traceable to the antagonism between man's religious consciousness and his religious institutions—I may say, between the progressive tendency of the religious spirit which is in man and the conservative tendency of his theology. For, while most of the great sciences have been studied with almost perfect freedom, and have been open to perpetual revision, theology has, to a great extent, been studied in fetters. The students of the other sciences have sought facts, their use, their meaning, their law; they have acknowledged no pre-established standards; they have been bound by no traditions; they have employed no Procrustean beds on which to torture ideas. Reluctant as we may be to admit it, so much can scarcely be claimed for theology as a science. It has frequently resisted all growth and development of its creeds. The aim of theologians has too often been not so much to express the highest, the freshest, and the purest religious thought of a particular age, as to formulate a system of theology which should be final, to establish some external standard by which theories of ethics and forms of doctrine could be tested as by some mechanical process. The result is inevitable. Sooner or later a conflict arises between thought and dogma. Doctrines are still avowed and defended that are so unsatisfactory to right reason, and so far behind the development of man's religious nature, that thinking men are repelled from the church, and are led to doubt, to criticise, to deny. Therefore it is in this conflict between the conservative spirit of theology and the progressive tendency of religious thought, and also in the fear of the church to allow the human mind full sweep in its investigations and inquiries, that we find the genesis, the philosophy indeed, of scepticism.

Having diagnosed the disease, do we pronounce it fatal, or is there yet hope? Must scepticism continue to be the skulking shadow of belief? continue to darken the lives and future anticipations of so large a part of humanity? Is it, and must it ever be, as the great essayist has said, the very "Nemesis of faith?" Or may not we expect to see this grim monster vanish before the enduring light of truth?

Listen to the answer borne on the winds from all parts of the earth: Yes, there is hope. In the name of sturdy Germany, there is hope. In the name of brilliant France, there is hope. In the name of modern India, Africa, and Japan, there is hope. In the name of the God of Nations, there is hope.

But the remedy for scepticism must be based on the nature of its cause. Theologians must abandon the cherished idea of a final system of theology. So long as there is an undiscovered fact in the universe, so long as human nature is subject to growth, so long as there are imperfections in the human mind, there can be no government of man wholly by rule, there can be no law which does not admit of a doubt in its application; and concerning the Beyond, there can be no creed which precludes the possibility of change. In the march of the finite towards the infinite, there can be no halting-place till humanity, "Above the low-hanging clouds, like mountain-peaks that look forever into the face of the clear blue heavens, and gaze on the unsetting stars, shall look up into the face of the Divine and dwell among principles that are unchangeable and eternal."

Furthemore, the church must throw wide open the doors of free inquiry. Nothing is more fatal to error, and more serviceable to truth, than investigation. And nothing so protects error and so hinders truth as the fear and suppression of investigation. The brave men who are willing to bear the pain of honest thought, must often sacrifice their prejudices and have great havoc made with their fondly cherished illusions. But there can be no permanent value in a false position. Though a temple be builded as broad as the earth and as high as the heavens, and though its vaulted dome glitter with all the wealth of Ormus and of Ind, yet if its foundations be in the sand, the "eternal movements of the Divine floods will sometime undermine it and sweep it away."

The fatal mistake made by the Roman church was the suppression of individual thought. It granted no liberty. It encouraged no freedom. It shut the Bible. It imprisoned the mind. It scowled upon invention and discovery with a baleful and malignant eye. And although the reformation broke the power of this absolute intellectual tyranny, and started the swell of a revolutionary wave which broke only when its agitated waters kissed the peaceful shores of liberty-loving America, yet so thoroughly was the very atmosphere permeated with the spirit of intolerance, that to the present day there is more or less of a conflict between the men of science and the men of religion.

Until this discordant element is cast out; until the free reading of the book of nature is accompanied by the free reading of the Book of God, the voice of the scoffer and of the sceptic will not be hushed. America stands in the front rank to-day, guarding the very outposts of religious freedom, and with anxious vision she gazes toward the citadels of Europe, and with bated breath she asks: Watchman, what of the night? She cannot mistake the answer: Lo! the morn appeareth. Christian men are occupying the posts of the enemy. Christian men sweep the star-sown fields of space with their telescopes, and know of a truth that "The heavens declare the glory of God." Christian men, with hammer and microscope, study the mysteries of the rocks and the wonders of the deep. The church is beginning to "prove all things." With an army of trained thinkers in her service—with her Lotzes, her Presenses, her Cooks, and her Hopkinses—she is pushing her investigations in every direction and into every province of thought. She is rapidly pushing her way up through the clouds of prejudice and superstition, through the mists of error and ignorance, to the lofty heights of Christian scholarship, from which, with purified vision, she can sweep across the whole realm of thought, and view things in their right positions and true relations. As Savage says, she is beginning to understand, that, "just as all life, whether it reveals itself in the viscous globule that palpitates in primeval seas, in the lichen that creeps over the rocks, up through all the ascending forms of plant and animal, till you reach the infinitely involved brain of a Newton, solving a problem in calculus"—has its source in the one creative God of the universe; and so all truth, whether it be the Vedas of Brahmin, the Koran of Mohammed, or the Bible of the Christian; whether it be on the banks of the Ganges or the Jordan, in the valley of the Tigris or the Nile, it, too, is from God. When these grand conceptions shall be realized in human consciousness—and they will be—when faith and reason shall join hands, and call upon the Author of All Truth to sanctify the union- and they will do so- then may we expect the progress of man to become like the growth of nature. Revolutions will no longer call for the sacrifice of human blood. If a dogma shall become obsolete, or a constitution cease to express the will of the people, change will no longer mean the marshaling of armies on the field of battle; it will no longer mean the carnage of Austerlitz and Waterloo, of Bunker Hill and Yorktown. It will no longer mean the beheading of Charles I., or the assassination of Alexander II., but the old will be merged into the new as quietly as an Arctic summer night breaks into dawn; as peacefully as "the summer blooming of the flowers, or the sudden softening of the air." Religious institutions will grow with the growth and expand with the expansion of man's moral and religious nature. Scepticism, robbed of the very soil in which to sow its seed, specter-like, shall vanish away; and by the side of tyranny, oppression, and intolerance, it shall lie down to its eternal doom—

"Unwept, unhonored, and unsung."

# PROGRESS, ITS SOURCES AND ITS LAWS.

By OWEN MORRIS, of Carleton College.

### BIOGRAPHICAL.

Hon. Owen Morris, of St. Paul, Minnesota, was born on the 12th day of August, 1858, in Anglesey, Wales. He attended the national school in his native land. When ten years of age he came with his parents to America, and settled near Mankato, Minnesota. Here he attended the common schools. While very young he took several prizes, at Welsh Eisteddfods, for compositions and recitations. In 1874 he entered the preparatory department of Carleton College, Northfield, Minnesota, and in 1881 graduated from that institution with the degree of bachelor of arts. In 1884 he received the degree of master of arts. While at college he mainly supported himself by working for his board. In 1881 Carleton College first entered the oratorical association. The entry was, as it were, at the last hour, necessarily limiting the time for preparation. On the night of April 28th Mr. Morris was awarded first prize at the home contest; on the very next night, the first prize at the inter-collegiate contest; and on May 4, at Jacksonville, Illinois, at the inter-State contest, the second prize, but receiving the vote of one out of the three judges for first place. Up to this time Carleton College through him enjoys the distinction of being the only institution in the State which has taken a prize at an inter-State contest. In 1882 he was elected to represent Blue Earth County in the Minnesota Legislature for the years 1883 and 1884. In 1882 he also entered the office of the late Hon. Gordon E. Cole, Faribault, Minnesota, as a law student; was admitted to the bar on an examination in the Supreme Court in 1885, and on January 1, 1886, became partner of General Cole, at St. Paul, and continued in that relation until Mr. Cole's death. He is unmarried, lives with his widowed mother, and enjoys a fair and increasing practice.

## THE ORATION.

Delivered at the Inter State Oratorical Contest, at Jacksonville, Illinois, May, 1881, taking second prize. Judges: Mr. DYER, Hon. EDWARD P. KIRBY, H. F. CARRIEL, M. D.

From the very beginning of human society two of its most important forces, Radicalism and Conservatism, have waged a bitter warfare. Social and moral advancement only furnishes them different questions for debate, and new battlefields on which to fight. Time, so far from assuaging the conflict, seems rather to aggravate it. Like the ceaseless heaving of the ocean, it is now subdued and scarcely discernible, and anon vehement and irrepressible, agitating the social mass to the very core.

Conservatism is peculiarly sensitive to the influence of antiquity, clings tenderly to the past, and sighs for the purity of the fathers. Dust-covered volumes, recording the valiant deeds of ancestors, compose its library. The chambers of its imagination are adorned with quaint pictures of tournament. Rusty casques and swords decorate its halls. By its endeavor to control religion it has made the church a storehouse of abuses and a citadel of tyranny. Occasionally it may have checked the muddy stream of Error. Far oftener it has damned the crystalline river of Truth, and doomed the world for ages to the drouth of gloomy superstition. It chills enthusiasm, dreads the future, and appeals to custom and selfishness, rather than to righteousness and truth. Without self-sacrifice, it yet sacrifices self.

Radicalism, on the other hand, is opposed to everything that is tainted with antiquity, and is impetuous and extravagant in all its actions. It fights against authority, despises custom, and makes the end to sanction the means. To-day a peace-maker, it condemns carnage and war; to-morrow a demon, it may overshadow Bartholomew's Day, or deluge another Palestine with the blood of rash fanatics. It is a madness that would go through oceans of blood merely to satisfy its caprice concerning ideal right. It hurls contempt on principles which have been vindicated before Cæsar's judgment-seat and avowed at the stake. The fanatical votary of Quixotic change, it violates shrines by its polluting touch. Disregarding the warnings of experience, it plunges headlong into the terrible whirlpool whose flood but hastens it to certain ruin. Here are the two conflicting forces—the one as the mountain torrent, rushing into the fruitful valley, scattering destruction on every side; the other, as the stagnant pool, emitting noisome malaria and destroying every form of life. Both, under the control of an all-wise Providence, mysteriously unite to form the majestic and ever-flowing river of Progress.

Philosophers have theorized much concerning progress, but their theories have only enveloped it in greater obscurity. Prejudiced antiquaries, viewing the subject in an unfavorable light, hold that there is no such thing as progress. In support of their views they cite evidences from exhumed cities, seats of culture and refinement rivaling those which are the pride and glory of modern civilization, and affirm that they have searched the earth in vain for a living Homer or Plato, a modern Daniel or Paul. They see the present plainly with all its ruggedness and deformity, its harshness and discord; but they have forgotten that time has erased the blots from the face of antiquity, giving it a brilliant color, and subdued its harshest tones into a mellow murmur. Let them use for a season proud Romes' farm implements, as described in the Georgics, and they will return with renewed relish to their patent plows, seeders, and threshing machines. Let them take a pleasure voyage in one of Homer's crooked-beaked galleys which crept timidly along the sea coast, and they will be proud to embark on the modern soul-inspired steamship. We may not be able to boast of a prophet like Daniel, or an apostle like Paul, yet we can boast that we have outgrown the civilization which tolerated the casting of the one into the lion's den, and the staining of the axe with the other's blood.

Champions of lost arts are behind the times. Their ideas are ghosts which have passed the termination of natural life, and yet, like the mythological Grecian heroes, wander on this side of the impassable river, only because they have been denied the due rites of burial. In the darkest periods of history, amidst disappointment and opposition, turmoil and anarchy, society has never suffered a retrogression. When Truth and Virtue seemed asleep, when Science had laid down her telescope and Philosophy her torch, it was only to arouse from their slumbers refreshed, ready to pursue with renewed vigor their accustomed path, not in a circle toward a lost excellence, but directly onward toward a millennial perfection.

Healthy progress is not the result of accident, but it is governed by immutable law, and moves with steady, even revolution, like the steam engine controlled by its governor. The growth of the short-lived mushroom is rapid and sickly, while that of the giant-limbed oak, which endures for centuries, is by slow degrees. It was not the few hours of struggle at Marathon, at Waterloo, or at Gettysburg, that determined the fate of nations. The real arbiter was a public sentiment produced by diligent and long-continued preparation, and reaching its culmination in these sharp and decisive contests. "The first furrow drawn by an English plow in the thin soil of Plymouth was truly the first line in our Declaration of Independence."

During the infancy of the race physical strength was the greatest power. The highest ambition of the ancient Greek was to be victor at the Olympic games. His great ideal was a Hercules or a mighty Zeuss. The human body, in those early days, was as it were a new garment, and was worn for a long time, sometimes even for many centuries apparently undamaged. Now it is an old vesture, easily torn, and scarcely lasts "three score years and ten." Yet, through the rents in this mantle of flesh, the great soul within sends forth its light upon the path of invention and discovery, and asserts itself as still the lord of creation, great enough for nature to obey. Instead of the ancient throwing of javelins and wrestling matches we now have intellectual contests. Mind triumphs over matter. Mind duels with mind on the field of investigation. Mind compresses the whole universe into a circle commensurate with man's stature, and there, where all things are within the focus of its power, transmutes them almost to its own spiritual nature. At the present day physical weakness is not severely censured, nor is physical strength especially praised. Men do not cautiously shun the one nor passionately seek the other, while the reproach of mental debility is the object of universal dread. Formerly might be seen armed Achilles in his golden chariot, while Socrates, bareheaded and barefoot, plodded his way in the mud. To-day behold the prize-fighter in the gutter, while the Websters and Carlyles are enshrined in the hearts of the people. The roll of honor of the present day contains only the names of those who have worked out the grandest problems of human progress, and given the greatest impulses for good to the race, and of those noted for physical strength only so far as they have exerted it in vindicating the great principles of justice and right.

Progress is nowhere more apparent than in the domains of science, philosophy, and religion. Many centuries ago, when man was but a school-boy in the realm of science, the Creator asked him the question, "Canst thou send lightnings that they may go and say unto thee, Here we are?" and his puerile reply was, "Behold I am vile, what shall I answer thee? I will lay my hand upon my mouth." But now, since man by rapid strides has left the alphabet far behind, an answer to that question entirely different would be given. The great Jehovah thrust the lightnings in his hands, and he sends them forth as ministering servants.

Philosophy may be as old as Plato in form, yet its methodical application dates only from Bacon. Induction and deduction till then separated joined hands. Fact superseded fancy, and reason was hailed as supreme.

Religion, though breathing in the sacrifice of martyred Abel, was never so untrammeled as since the thunder tones of the sixteenth century shattered the bulwarks of papal power and proclaimed to the world intellectual and moral liberty.

As the graduated columns along the banks of the Nile indicated the elevation of the waters, so, at wide intervals, along the river of progress, there are such names as Archimedes and Newton, Plato and Bacon, Huss and Tholuck, indicating the tidal rise in its three tributaries — science, religion, and philosophy.

Now, man revels in a wider theatre of art and invention than ever before. Fearless of Pluto, we descend into his dark regions, and rob the earth of its secrets. Defying the forked lightnings of ancient Jove, we scale the heavens and solve their mysteries. The crude philosophy of our fathers has been developed, purified, and made practical. Freed from the shackles of ancient thought and superstition, it is handed down to posterity an improved heritage. The Bible has become our charter of freedom. Those whom armies have made free in name are now taught to be free indeed. Liberty, sought for in Egypt and wept for in Babylon; honored at Marathon and disgraced at Pharsalia; liberty, for which Demosthenes pleaded, Luther prayed, and Madame Roland died, is now and forever triumphant. Universal equality moves on to bloodless victories. Instead of the mire of selfishness we have the clear waters of philanthropy and Christian benevolence. Such are the present results in the fields of science, philosophy, and religion; politics and ethics of two forces, either of which alone would have ruined all advancement. The future will be still brighter. **The morning star of a millennial dawn is already above the horizon.** The glorious day will soon appear, when all shall enjoy the prerogatives of liberty, virtue, and truth, and equality of **rights** shall be the first of rights.

# THE OLD AND THE NEW CIVILIZATIONS.

By FRANK G. HANCHETT, of Chicago University.

### BIOGRAPHICAL.

Frank G. Hanchett was born at Kaneville, Illinois, October 2, 1856. He attended a country district school until ten years old, after which time until sixteen years old he helped his father on the farm, and attended school three months each winter. He then attended the village school at Kaneville two terms. At seventeen years of age he entered the West Aurora High School, graduating June, 1875, in which year he entered the Chicago University, and graduated in the classical course in 1882. During the time from entering the preparatory school until graduating he taught school four terms, which delayed him considerably from completing the university course earlier. His first success is dated at the sophomore contest, in 1880, when he delivered an oration entitled "Horatius at the Bridge," and was awarded first prize; at the junior contest, in 1881, he delivered an oration entitled "The Jews," and was awarded first prize. In the fall of the same year he represented Chicago University, at Bloomington, Illinois, in the inter-collegiate contest, delivering an oration entitled "The Old and New Civilizations," and was awarded first prize. In May, 1882, at the inter-State contest he delivered the same oration, and was again awarded first prize. In 1883 he gratuated from the law department of Iowa State University, and opened a law office at Aurora, Illinois, where he has since resided. The same year he married Miss Lizzie L. Scott, of Kaneville, Illinois. He is still an active member of the Delta Kappa Epsilon faternity, a member of the board of education of the West Aurora public schools. In 1888 Mr. Hanchett was elected State's attorney of Kane County, which position he fills with great credit. He is a prominent lawyer, and an honored citizen.

## THE ORATION.

Delivered at the Inter-State Oratorical Contest, at Indianapolis, Indiana, May, 1882, taking first prize. Judges: Hon. NOBLE C. BUTLER, Judge J. S. FRAZER, Rev. OSCAR C. MCCULLOCH.

There is a tendency in man to swing, pendulum-like, from extreme to extreme. We can trace it from the individual with his hobbies and eccentricities, to the masses with their ever-varying and unreliable public opinion. We can mark it in the more slow and steady sweep of thought from century to century, and from age to age; in the alternate succession of days and nights of civilization — dark ages and golden ages of light.

It is this tendency in man that accounts for the two opposite extremes of what we term the old and the new civilizations — the civilization that dazzled the world with the Golden Age of Greece; and the civilization of which the nineteenth century is but the morning light; the civilization which recognized the *spiritual* Plato as the supreme monarch of thought; and the civilization which crowns the *practical* Bacon as the greatest philosopher of the world. Eras which may be distinguished as the Age of the Beautiful and the Age of the Useful.

This old civilization was a magnificent garden, in which the Beautiful, the Spiritual, and the Ideal, were cultivated with the choicest care, and in which the Useful, the Material, and the Practical were rooted out as rank and unsightly weeds. From this well-tilled soil grew and blossomed poetry, from whose fragrance the poets of all ages have drawn their sweetness; eloquence, whose unrivaled periods still ring in our ears; architecture, which has ever been the model and marvel of the world; sculpture, to whose divine beauty our boasted age still bows in admiring worship.

But with however much of admiration we may look back upon the glorious achievements of these old Greeks, we must still admit that they went to the extreme in the cultivation of the beautiful and the neglect of the useful. Their philosophers scorned the idea of debasing their knowledge for the advancement of the useful arts. They had famous sculptors, but bungling mechanics; splendid rhetoricians, but stupid doctors; dreams of delightful repose in the Elysian fields, but no vulgar vision of spring mattresses on this side of the Acheron! Steam might have lifted the lids of tea-kettles before the eyes of these old dreamers for endless centuries, but railroads would still be unknown. To their imaginative minds the thunder-bolt told no tale of the telegraph, but was the rattling of Jove's chariot-wheels over the golden pavements of heaven.

In the fullness of time there came into the fields of thought a practical husbandman, Francis Bacon, who was not satisfied with mere *flowers*, which however beautiful could but please and adorn, but desired "*fruit*," which could supply the more necessary wants of man. He therefore left this old garden of beauty, and in far broader fields scattered the seeds of a philosophy which was destined to bring forth rich harvests of usefulness. The fruits of this great philosophy have ripened into what we call the practical age—an age which with equal propriety might be termed the age of miracles—an age in which thought busies itself with the great problem of benefiting the condition of man—an age in which the hidden secrets of God have been found out and man's powers invested with the powers of omnipotence, until his feeble voice has been made to echo across continents and his thoughts to pass beneath the billows of the deep—an age in which the petty quibbles of metaphysicians are accounted secondary to the great inventions that lessen the burdens and perplexities of life— an age in which the poet who is contented with picturing the outer manifestations of things has been displaced by the scientist, who delights in searching out the inner secrets of the universe. But nowhere have the glorious triumphs of this age taken more practical form than in the modern home, which, crowded with the countless comforts and conveniences of life, is a veritable heaven in comparison with the palatial but empty abodes of the Golden Age of Greece, or the turreted but desolate castles of the senseless age of chivalry. In fact, the nineteenth century is one sublime and bewildering panorama of practical achievements.

In keeping with that tendency in man which carries him to the extreme, we observe that the same causes which have produced such great practical achievements have also produced a practical and material spirit in the age, which tends to dwarf and deaden the very noblest sentiments in man's nature. In the fields of modern thought the coarser plants of material prosperity have so overshadowed the more delicate flowers of poetry that they have made but a feeble and spindling growth. This spirit of the age would prize electricity more than immortality, and look with more pleasure upon a man-made machine than upon a God-inspired sentiment. It is a significant fact that all of the greatest poets lived before the age of material prosperity; that the genius of this age is drifting into the channels of trade, and instead of a Shakespeare, a Milton, or a Raphael, we have an Astor, a Jay Gould, or a Vanderbilt; that our scientists return from their search for the useful in the world of matter with their eyes spiritually blinded. These things point to the fact that our practical age, with all its boasted blessings, by absorbing the mind with the baser truths of matter is disqualifying it for the higher truths of the spiritual. This modern materialism has swung to its maddest extreme, and taken its most definite form in its attack upon religion. Puffed up with his meagre knowledge of one small world, little man attempts to prove there is no God in the great universe. We are told that man has no soul, that immortality is but an empty dream, and religion but the sickly child of ignorance and superstition. Thus would our age, with its material clutch, strangle the very divinity in man and leave him but the monarch animal of the world.

Physical science is the idol of the age, and the man who has perchance found a few bird tracks in some antediluvian rock is an illustrious hero. With what profound wisdom we have discovered that the first horse had five toes! How wise we are for having learned that there are 90,000 species of beetles, and possibly more! But is there no mental science? Was he right who asserted that "as the liver secretes bile, so the brain secretes thought?" "Can the scientist lay open our moral structure with his dissecting knives?"

We do not forget that our age "which draws its water from wells that are sixty centuries deep," by the natural laws of progress, is in the advance of every preceding age; but we criticise the extremely practical and material tendency of our age, which has produced a large class of narrowly practical men — men who see utility only in that which ministers to their immediate and physical wants; who are devoted soul and body to business, for the transaction of which they have become mere machines; who consider poetry and religion as fit only for women and children; men, who are forever crying in the language of Dickens's Gradgrind, "In this life we want nothing but facts, sir, nothing but facts;" men, whose imaginations, the wings of the soul, have become so heavy with the mud of the material things in which they grovel, that they can never soar into the lofty regions of thought where man asserts his kinship with heaven, and suggests that he has an immortal soul. Better be a philosopher and live in a garret, better be a poet and an heir to poverty, than one of these narrowly practical men surrounded with every comfort and luxury that the nineteenth century can offer.

Thus we see that what we term the old and the new civilizations have been the extreme developments of opposite ideas.

Happy will be that age, if it may ever dawn upon the world, when the central ideas of these two civilizations shall be wedded in harmonious equality, when the love of the beautiful and the love of the useful shall each have its designed place in the symmetrical development of man; then shall he have the poet's eye to see all the varied beauty in nature and in sentiment, and the keen perception of the scientist to search out all that is useful to man in the hidden secrets of God.

# THE CAUSE OF THE GRACCHI.

By Arthur J. Craven, of Iowa State University.

## BIOGRAPHICAL.

Arthur J. Craven was born at College Hill (now Lancaster), Indiana, on the 12th day of December, 1857. His parents removed to Minnesota when he was three years of age. They lived in Minnesota six years and then moved to Iowa, where he grew to manhood. He commenced teaching when quite young to obtain money for a college course, and at nineteen years of age entered Iowa State University, Iowa City, graduating therefrom in the regular collegiate course June, 1882. In his junior year he took first prize for oratory in a contest composed of members of his class; in the following year he represented the university and the State at the inter-State contest, taking second prize on the oration given on the following pages. In this latter contest he had not been on his feet a minute before the glare of the foot-lights so annoyed him that every preconceived idea with reference to his subject vanished, and he was compelled to extemporize as best he could for a few moments before again getting on the beaten track of thought and language. After graduating he taught school one year in order to pay up his indebtedness at college. He then read law with Judge Winslow, at Newton, Iowa; was admitted to the bar February, 1884. Mr. Craven was married to Miss Emma Kerr, of Newton, Iowa, removing the same year to Helena, Montana. He was a member of the constitutional convention which framed the present constitution of Montana. The firm of Leslie & Craven is one of the most enterprising law firms of the State, and their business is rapidly increasing, which success they well merit.

## THE ORATION.

Delivered at the Inter-State Oratorical Contest, at Indianapolis, Indiana, May, 1882, taking second prize. Judges: Hon. NOBLE C. BUTLER, Judge J. S. FRAZER, Rev. OSCAR C. MCCULLOCH.

Ideas, not swords, have filled the past with ruins. Rome was not destroyed by barbarians. True, they captured and pillaged and destroyed a city whose name was Rome, but the fair mistress of the world, the pride of her children, had long been dead; and when the lands of the North stretched out their strong arms to seize a bride, they embraced a corpse.

Ideas, not swords! And among the ideas that scourge mankind none is more potent than that of man's inequality — asserting that men are *not* of the same blood, that we are *not* free and equal, that I shall be king and you shall be slave. It sounds the tocsin of war on the world's battle-fields. It is the great Goliath of history, striding through the centuries, overturning kingdoms, obliterating empires, challenging republics; but no youthful David with sling and stone has yet stepped out from the ranks of the people who can slay and behead this giant of tyranny. As Americans we boast that the Declaration of Independence was his death-warrant, and that our political fabric towers high above his grave. But whence comes this cry of monopoly and the warnings against centralization? Is it merely the wail of human discontent? Are not the rich becoming richer and the poor poorer? Does not monopoly dip its hands into every bushel of wheat — yea, even into the standing grain? The tattered children of poverty, nursed and swaddled in the deadly shade of corporation, tugging at the skirts of their mothers for bread — are they really hungry? In the dreary past, you say, cloud-crowned pyramids and mouldering ruins of lofty cities whisper of slavery. In the battle-fields of yesterday we see the victory of human rights. Yes; but this bloody monster of inequality rises from its very grave. Formerly it was serfdom, now it is monopoly; yesterday it was slavery, to-day it is centralization. Take away its part from the long drama of history, and the play has lost its meaning. Exterminate this principle from the politics of to-day, and you relieve our statesmen of half their cares.

Agrarian reformation derives its importance not merely from its tragical interest in history, but from the fact that it is strangely applicable to present politics. History, with all its ceaseless repetitions, has resurrected from the buried past no problem of such continual importance as the use, rent, and ownership of land. The past resounds with the tread of soldiery, the cries of slavery and despotism; but exclusiveness of land possessions is the basis of conquest, the foundation of slavery and revolution, the very corner-stone of despotism. Wide-stretching acres made the lords of feudalism; serfdom is the product of tenantry. Ireland to-day, with her rags and her stripes, is the sad epitome of agrarian abuse.

Land, indeed, is *real* estate. It endures though government and race be swept away. It fosters conservatism. It checks revolution. It gives courage to patriotism. Mercenary troops have won few victories. From the firesides in peril stretch the mystic chords of sympathy along which flit messages that spur trembling armies to victory.

It was this importance of land ownership as a factor of patriotism which filled the mind of Tiberius Gracchus. On his journey to Spain as an emissary of the Roman government, he clearly saw the dark cloud of imperialism drifting over the desolated fields of Italy. The small land-owners had been driven out. Their homes and mortgaged farms had been seized by the centralizing hand of the rich. With their homeless families they had sailed across the seas to the colonies, or had fled to Rome to join the ranks of an idle army, or swell the hungry multitude which fawned at the feet of ambitious demagogues, and sold their votes for bread. Honest toil had lost its incentives. Free labor could not compete with the drudgery of slaves. Slave gangs of stammering barbarians looked sadly from the fields upon the crowds of free laborers flocking to the city. Homes were dear, but what were all the pleasures of domestic life compared with the terrors of serfdom? One way, and one way only, led to distinction and glory; and that lay over the bloody corpses of battle-fields, or through the passions of the forum. Rome was the center of the world. Her returning armies came back with standards of victory. Long processions of triumph, glittering with the spoils of conquest, were marching beneath her arches. Philosophers and teachers endowed her with knowledge. The forum was hushed by the spell of eloquence. Her streets were thronged with strangers But the surrounding fields yielded scanty harvests to the labor of slaves, and over the proud hills and lofty domes of the city hung a cloud of famine which neither sunshine nor breeze could ever dispel.

The very causes which contributed so largely to the renown and outward strength of the republic were hurrying it forward to a speedy decline. Increase of conquest made an increase of captives. The slavery of the captive destroyed the liberty of the freeman. And as farther and farther the tread of the Roman legions advanced through surrounding nations, when far in the East the boundaries were marked by the line of Roman spears, when their standards were raised beyond the Alps, and Roman sails fluttered in every harbor, the broad Mediterranean was freighted with living cargoes, and Rome became the slave-market of the world. Her great men boast no more the love of country. They count their money, measure their domains, dress forth their banquets, awake the lyres and timbrels, and with floods of ripe Falernian drown the little left of virtue. The laws, the laws of common right, the guard, the wealth, the honor, the safety of the nation—who has sold them, defaced, and corrupted them? Why do they guard the rich man's cloak, and tear the poor man's garment from his back? Why are they in the grasp of wealth a sword, and in the hands of poverty a broken reed?

On a heart warm with patriotism, this political condition could not fail to make an impression. On this journey to Spain Tiberius resolved upon the agrarian reform, which determined his career. On the summits of the mountains fringing the northern border he paused and looked back upon Italy. Below were the plains which lately bloomed with the happy homes of peasantry. Away in the distance rose the outlines of Rome. There was his home of royalty—his father the consul; his mother, Cornelia, the daughter of Hannibal's conqueror. There he was the petted favorite in the most distinguished circles of aristocracy. There he was taught and trained by Rome's greatest teachers and orators. There he had married the daughter of Appius. There, indeed, lay the path of glory; but it was paved with the oppression of the weak, and wet with the tears of the poor. In the valleys wandered the step-son of Italy. On the breeze was borne the clamor of the rabble in the distant city. And there on the mountains, looking down on a land rendered sacred by the memory of his fathers, he closed his eyes upon visions of wealth, and formed his plan for the relief of his country — a plan as stainless and pure as the snow which crowned the mountain-peaks above him.

In the crowded forum behold the sad tragedy of republics. On the one side iron-fingered monopoly with its deeds and its bonds; on the other, a nation of beggars pleading for bread. Tiberius rises from the side of the aristocrats, and demands that a law already passed should be enforced; that the land of conquest, which Rome had provided for her beggared children, should be wrested from the hands of wealthy usurpers and distributed to those for whom they were designed; that a commonwealth of small land-owners would prove a balm for pauperism and make a bulwark as strong as adamant against centralization. He is scourged and mangled by that maddened aristocracy, and finds his grave in the sands of the Tiber. A brother grows to manhood, and rising in that same forum pleads for poverty, and his lifeless head is held before the gaze of the multitude and rolled at the feet of his mother.

Go seek for the sorrow which bears the dregs of grief, where tears are relief and breaking hearts are voiceless, and you find it not with the warrior counting the loss of the battle, not with Napoleon standing lone and pensive at St. Helena, gazing above the raging billows toward sunny France; but go rather where Rachel is weeping, where Cornelia, and Niobe of Rome, asks no greater comfort than that the world, that history, should only call her the "Mother of the Gracchi."

Volumes have been filled with the results of the failure of her martyred sons. True, it is only the wind that plays with the idle leaves, but it heralds the tempest which will rend every fiber of the forest. The sculptor carves his marble and the poet weaves his verse; but the deadly virus courses through the veins of the state. The vulture of destruction broods over the imperial city and perches upon her lofty pinnacles. Murder strides through senate halls and creeps with drawn daggers to the bedside of sovereignty. Virtue gathers her spotless robes, and flees. The palace of marble overshadows the lowly hovel. The tread of armies wakes the echoes of civil discord. The rivers are stained with the blood of those who lately toiled along their banks. On the peak of the mountain frowns the fortress of the noble; on the plain below, in all the pains of serfdom, toil the subjects of the empire.

Almost two thousand years have rolled on. Time has wrought his mighty changes. The kind face of old Mother Earth has grown scarred and worn by the care of her quarreling, restless children. Civilization has fled from her cradle in the East. She has plowed the continents and sailed the seas. Here under western skies she has built her cities and raised her monuments. To-day we wander back and search for the footprints of her youth. Every mound is sad with its story, every ruin speaks; but none more plainly and solemnly to this republic of the West than the columns and temples crumbled and decayed because **the cause of the Gracchi was lost.**

# THE POLITICAL MISSION OF PURITANISM.

By JOHN M. ROSS, of Monmouth College.

## BIOGRAPHICAL.

John M. Ross was born at Monmouth, Illinois, and is the son of Rev. Robert Ross, one of the founders of Monmouth College. He received his education in the Monmouth schools and college. He was the successful orator of the tenth inter-State contest, which occurred in 1883, at Minneapolis, Minnesota. Here it was declared he is an orator by natural talent, and by thorough study acquired the perfections of an orator. Upon graduating he accepted the professorship of mathematics in Tarkio College, Missouri. Two years later he began the study of theology, in the United Presbyterian Theological Seminaries of Xenia, Ohio, and Allegheny, Pennsylvania, graduating from the latter institution March, 1888, and began his ministration as pastor of the Oakland United Presbyterian Church, of Pittsburg, where he still remains their favorite pastor.

## THE ORATION.

Delivered at the Inter-State Oratorical Contest, at Minneapolis, Minnesota, May, 1883, taking first prize. Judges: Hon. ANGUS CAMERON, J. W. STEARNS, Hon, S. M. CLARK, Rev. Dr. LITTLE, Gen. A. B. NETTLETON.

The essence of Puritanism was belief in God and liberty. The Puritan believed in God; but so did the Cavalier. The Puritan believed in liberty; so did his Teutonic ancestor. But men had learned at last to grasp the dual truth of man's freedom and God's sovereignty. Belief in God and belief in liberty were welded into one. The Cavalier believed in God and the divine right of kings. The Puritan believed in God and the inalienable rights of the people. This belief was not a mere abstract conception; it was a soul-stirring energy, and

was potent for good. It produced earnestness, fearlessness, devotion to duty, rugged strength, moral sublimity. 'T was this belief that nerved Hampden to resist his king; animated Cromwell's Ironsides; taught Vane how to die; wrung majestic music from the harp of Milton; thrilled a whole nation with lofty enthusiasm; opened up to the world broad vistas of progress.

The separation of the English Church from Papal Rome was an act of kingly self-aggrandizement. The sovereign became supreme in both spiritual and temporal affairs. Civil liberty was little advanced. Rather were the coils of arbitrary rule drawn more tightly. Ecclesiastical tyranny re-enforced that of the crown. This double-headed despotism of church and state made its lair behind the throne. When attacked it slunk into its den and securely defied pursuit. Before the monster could be throttled, the throne itself must be battered down. Thus Puritanism in resisting the encroachments of the spiritual order antagonized the crown. Organizing opposition to arbitrary rule, it carried reform into governmental affairs and became the champion of popular rights. Earnestly, heroically, resistlessly, the Puritan threw himself into the struggle. He protested against superstition and tyranny. He plead for knowledge, truth, righteousness, liberty. The grandeur of his idea impressed itself upon his work. While the Cavalier was dazzled by the glitter of royalty and rewarded by the smile of his king, the Puritan was devoted to the uplifting of his race and sought a reward which fadeth not away. The former represents the tinsel age of chivalry; the latter, the golden age of humanity. The Cavalier struck his lyre and sang of war, knighthood, gallantry, the splendors of regal power; and the siren song died away. The Puritan tuned his harp and sang of liberty, justice, mercy, the glories of a heavenly home; and that melody re-echoes evermore.

Conflict was inevitable. Liberty was the issue. The two principles—the popular and the arbitrary—marshaled their forces for the contest. If the Cavalier deserves respect for his loyalty in rallying under the banner of his king, the Puritan commands admiration and gratitude for defending the cause of popular liberty. If the Cavalier feared innovation with its accompanying evils, the Puritan dreaded despotism with its baneful blight. The Cavalier loved pomp and power; the Puritan hated shams and oppression. If there was somewhat of fanaticism in the acts of the Puritan, there was much of servility in the character of the Cavalier. The fanaticism sprang from excess of earnestness; the servility, from lack of high motives. The Cavalier fought for royalty and personal triumph; the Puritan, for constitutional liberty and popular rights. The policy of one tended to centralization of wealth and power, to thralldom and national decadence; that of the other, to development and progress. The Puritan was not a Jacobin—not a Nihilist, finding a mad delight in the work of indiscriminate destruction. He was an ideal revolutionist, destroying the evil, preserving the good. Did he aim sledge-hammer blows at the formalities of the church? Yes; yet he cherished true religion. Did he with stubborn strength oppose his king? Yes; yet he loved law and order.

But why was the Commonwealth so speedily succeeded by the Restoration? Why did the people fail to maintain their ascendency? Because they were fallible. Conceptions of truth are at first vague and imperfect. The dawning of great ideas is like the dawning of the sun. In the first glimmerings of light men catch distorted and sometimes even grotesque views of things around them. It was so with the Puritan. As light increased and more rational views prevailed, propositions which had appeared reasonable became palpable absurdities. The dominant party was loaded down with odium. The people had been trained in the school of tyranny. They were not prepared for self-government. They could dethrone their king; they could not crown themselves. Anarchy impended. The Protectorate was a child of necessity. Given conditions as stated, and Carlyle's solution of the problem is the only adequate one—the strongest soul, the Hero, must rule. With the death of Cromwell coherence was lost. Disintegration followed. Hence the Restoration. The old despotism, however, could not be permanently reinstated. The Puritan idea survived the fall of the Commonwealth. It disseminated itself, molding the sentiments of the nation. The fantastic visions of the early dawn vanished before the on-coming light. In English society, through all its fluctuations, there was a durable element of progress. The shuttle of thought glided rapidly to and fro; but the fair fabric of truth was woven at last from the contending opinions of men. The Revolution of '88 establishes a constitutional government, and "Freedom rears her beautiful, bold brows."

But the Englishman could not fully appreciate Puritanism. His prejudices were too strong. Then as now he prized liberty, yet his affections were centered in himself; his sympathies were bounded by his native island. He made the same mistake that men have ever made. He forgot that a principle once accepted must be accepted in its entirety, and must produce its own legitimate results. And just here is the reason that "God's first temples" have so often echoed with the harsh notes of war; just here is the reason for the convulsions which have upheaved society; just here is the reason that humanity has advanced along a road macadamized with the bones of martyrs. Puritanism was not for a nation alone; 't was for humanity. It had formulated a creed too broad for England. Only in a new land could it fully realize its lofty ideals. Its best elements sought in America a home. Here Puritanism itself became more pure. Here it outgrew the deformities which disfigured it in England; but its essential truth endured, for that was imperishable. That the two principles, love of liberty and reverence for law, are not antagonistic but are complements of each other; that they are the bulwarks which defend society from tyranny on one hand and from anarchy on the other; that together they form the Gordian knot which despots cannot cut nor communists untie — this was the sublime affirmation of New World Puritanism; and this affirmation is the rock upon which our Republic rests. Love of liberty inspired the sturdy yeomanry of New England in the contest for independence; reverence for law unified society and saved it from the awful doom which a few years later settled down on France like night. In the New World, as in the Old, the progress of Puritanism has been in the face of opposition; but its development through successive generations is that which has given unity and dignity to American history. In our own century it has waged its mightiest conflict and achieved its crowning triumph. In the campaigns of the civil war those principles which had been vindicated at Marston Moor and Naseby were again at stake. In the maintenance of national sovereignty, in the destruction of the slave power, in the enfranchisement of the negro, these principles were again triumphant. The broad-minded statesmen who framed the Constitution had preferred to employ a circumlocution rather than admit, even by implication, the atrocious proposition that there can be property in man. They had appealed to coming generations to vindicate their wisdom, and their appeal was not in vain. At Gettysburg and on other battle-fields it was decided — finally, we trust — that the Puritan idea is not local but universal in its application; that it is true for all races and for all time. Admirable indeed were the results of Puritanism in England; but the extent and potency of its influence must be viewed in the Republic of the West. In England it was revolutionary; in America, constructive and creative. In England its mission was to remodel an ancient building, but the old frame-work marred the symmetry; in America it erected a new edifice founded upon faith in God and devotion to the rights of man. Unhampered by old institutions it here found room for development, and developed. It cast off localisms. It represented enlightened, liberal views. It molded character. It built up institutions. It became both the germ-principle and the conservator of a nation's life. In England it secured liberty for Englishmen; in America, spurning with broad generalizations the narrow confines of time and place, it proclaimed liberty as the birthright of all men. Here Freedom reared her holiest temple and opened wide its portals to the world. Here shall this temple stand, let us hope, until the grateful nations worship at its shrine.

The Puritan was human, and therefore fallible. In rude, ungraceful strength, mountain-like, he stands out on the landscape of history. The angular outlines of his character offend some in this fastidious age. It is well we can laugh at the eccentricities and crudities of his thought. It is not well if we fail to appreciate his moral grandeur and the debt we owe him. It is not well if we seek to hear only the minor discords and are deaf to the noble music of his life. Let it not be forgotten that to the Puritan, as Hume testifies, England owes the whole liberty to her constitution. Let is not be forgotten that when in America "stern Democracy hymned its world-thrilling birth and battle song," the spirit of English Puritanism was present and inspired that strain. Let it not be forgotten that upon the continued activity of this Puritan idea depend the advance of Anglo-Saxon civilization, the stability of American institutions and the maintenance of the dearest rights of humanity.

By the Puritan were originated or promulgated those ideas which are the political master-principles of to-day; principles upon which rest the governments of modern England and America; principles upon which depends the prosperity—aye, the political salvation of the world. Representative government, universal equality, education, and freedom in its highest, grandest sense—freedom of conscience, which brings freedom of thought, freedom of action—all bear testimony to the influence of Puritanism. Though as a political organization it perished when its work was done, as a spiritual force it *lived*, purifying and directing public sentiment, changing the arid wastes of history into gardens of wealth and beauty. "Time has softened its asperities," but strengthened its devotion to truth. The old Ironside sleeps his dreamless sleep, but the soul of Puritanism "is marching on." As once it wrested Liberty from the tyrant's grasp, so to-day in the face of maddened mobs it asserts the majesty of Law. Nor will its works be complete till universal right prevails, and men are freed from every chain, save those by which "this whole round earth is bound about the feet of God."

# THE SAXON ELEMENT IN CIVILIZATION.

By DANIEL M. KELLOGG, of Beloit College.

BIOGRAPHICAL.

Daniel M. Kellogg was born November 8, 1859, at Whitewater, Wisconsin. His father, who was a brilliant lawyer, died when the subject of this sketch was eight years of age. His mother was a lady of culture and great piety, and her son attributes his success to her Christian training. Mr. Kellogg received his elementary education in the schools of his native place. He entered the preparatory school of Beloit College at the age of twenty, continuing until graduated. In college he was especially fond of literary and oratorical work, never failing to take the prize at a public debate or contest. At the inter-State contest he was awarded second prize on his oration, "The Saxon Element in Civilization," which appears on the following pages. Upon completing his education he taught school in Kansas three years, after which he returned to his native place and engaged in the study of law. For several years Mr. Kellogg has been prominently identified with the temperance cause, holding positions of responsibility and trust. When in college he espoused the cause of the Prohibition party, but later became convinced that better results could be obtained by non-partisan effort and renewed his allegiance to the Republican party. In September, 1888, he was chosen by this party at Whitewater, Wisconsin, as the champion of the Republicans, in a joint debate with Hon. Walter Mills, "the little giant of Ohio," who represented the Prohibition party. So well did Mr. Kellogg acquit himself on this occasion that, on the following evening, his fellow citizens serenaded him and presented him with a handsome purse as an appreciation of his effort. He was afterward employed by the Republican State Central Committee, and made over forty speeches during the last

campaign. In August, 1889, Mr. Kellogg was married to Mrs. Carrie Hayes, a lady of high attainments. About this time he received a government position in the office of the secretary of the interior, and now resides in his pleasant home on H Street, Washington, D. C.

## THE ORATION.

Delivered at the Inter-State Oratorical Contest, Minneapolis, Minnesota, May, 1883, taking second prize. Judges: Hon. ANGUS CAMERON, J. W. STEARNS, Hon. S. M. CLARK, Rev. Dr. LITTLE, Gen. A. B. NETTLETON.

Prominent among the races of men stands the Saxon. Nursed in the forests of Germany, rocked in the cradle of the ocean, in childhood transplanted to his island home, his early surroundings tended to develop a vigorous manhood. It is said that the giant trees of the West rear themselves in one massive trunk far above the surrounding forest and then stretch out their lofty branches to the unhindered light of the sun. So through the centuries the Saxon has attained his development, and to-day the branches of this mammoth tree, penetrating the extremities of the world, receive nourishment from the parent trunk.

Stability has ever marked the course of the Saxon. With steadiness of purpose, with persistent action, he has stamped his impress upon the world's civilization. When the tide of Germanic tribes swept over western Europe, the Frank, the Goth, the Lombard, in a few generations were entirely absorbed by the vanquished races, but the Saxon not only conquered the Briton, he so transformed him that the Celtic element formed but a small part of the English race. Wherever it has come in contact with a foreign people, either as conqueror or conquered, the Saxon element has prevailed. The savage Dane became a part of the English nation, and in a short time in customs, manners, and language, was essentially Saxon. The Norman was the conqueror in battle, and vainly attempted to guide and curb the destinies of the Saxon race, but on that broader battle-field, in the conflict of the ages, where nature's unerring law secures the survival of the fittest, there the victor's wreath rests upon the brow of the Saxon. In the colonization of the New World other races, partially adopting native customs, have produced a mongrel and semi-barbarous civilization; but the Saxon, rigidly maintaining his identity, scorning external compromise, infuses into all races his national life. The proud Spaniard sinks into the indolent Mexican, but the Englishman is ever true to his race. The Saxon, moreover, is a radical, but a conservative radical; not overturning society to right a wrong, but beginning at the root of things, starting with a firm foundation, after careful consideration, he uproots noxious evils, and engrafts new principles upon the old stock, choosing the golden mean between rash radicalism and unalterable conservatism. Deeply imbedded in the foundation of modern enlightenment, intricately interwoven in the web of human progress, to eradicate the Saxon element would cause the whole structure to totter and fall, would rend into shreds the entire fabric. Exterminate it in one place and it will appear at another, and like the mountain-moss will take root and flourish upon the bare rock. Such is the stability of the Saxon element in civilization.

A natural fitness for government has ever characterized the Saxon. The equality of mankind was with him an innate principle. Self-government was an inherent right. The town-meeting and trial by jury, ancient Saxon institutions, are the foundation of all modern civil liberty. Representative government, the stumbling-stone of kings, was a Saxon principle. The Normans attempted to supplant Saxon freedom with the feudal system of the continent, but through centuries of conflict English liberty has continually been in the ascendant. The divine right of kings, taxation without representation, restraint of thought and action, have all been shattered by the principles of Saxon liberty; and to-day the "great commoner," who guides the destinies of that world-encircling empire, is a representative of the people, while the descendant of William the Conqueror sits a figure-head in Windsor Castle.

Saxon liberty comprises principles which were unknown to the ancient republics of Greece and Rome. Roman and Grecian law concentrated all within the State. The State was everything, man nothing. For the advantage of the State virtuous and worthy citizens were banished or even executed. Saxon freedom was based on the liberty of the individual. The earliest enactments of the British parliament were for the relief of personal grievances. Throughout English history the great struggle for liberty was a struggle for personal liberty. The principles of Saxon freedom triumphed, and that triumph has tolled the death-knell of tyranny everywhere, sundered the shackles which fettered genius, turned with lightning rapidity the wheel of human progress, and materially altered the history of mankind. From the crumbling castles of feudalism, royalty and aristocracy look forth upon the world which is fast eluding their grasp, hear with amazement the busy hum of modern industry, behold with wonder the lofty flights of low-born genius, perceive the *insignia* of empire vested in popular sovereignty, and the crown and scepter, emblems of medieval majesty, only retained as a matter of political convenience.

The moral element has had a controlling influence in English civilization. The Saxon was intimately related to those wild nations of the North, whose mythology, fierce and brutal as it was, yet in the grandeur of its conception stirred the human soul to its very depths, inculcated sublime sentiments of life, death, fate, and destiny, and stood in strong contrast to the loose voluptuousness of the Olympian deities. The gloomy regions of the North and the lives of its inhabitants, alternating between the extremes of energy and repose, had a strong tendency to nurse reverential sentiments. Among vast forests of perpetual twilight, among mountains rugged with ice and crested with storms, and amid the dismal vicissitudes of northern winters, the flitting shadows that traversed the wild scenery became spiritual visitants, while the mysterious sounds of hill and valley were regarded as their supernatural voices. Calm, cool, deliberate, self-reliant, with a stern sense of duty, the Saxon possessed those elements of character which preserved English civilization intact from the enervating tendencies of wealth and power. When Christianity shed its beams of light over Europe, its tenets were readily adopted by the Saxon race. The doctrines of the equality of man and individual responsibility to God, were aptly fitted to the Saxon mind. To the fickle Celt and spiritless Roman, Christianity was but a substitute for the old pagan religion. In niches dedicated to the shrines of the gods, were placed the images of the saints. The Virgin supplanted the voluptuous Venus, and the Bishop or Pope ruled in the stead of Pontifex Maximus. But the Saxon, penetrating the film of formalism which obscured the sublime truths of Christianity, and comprehending the divine doctrines of that gospel which brought salvation to man, has accomplished more than any other in spreading the teachings of the world's greatest benefactor. When the struggle of the reformation roused Europe from its fatal lethargy, the Saxon was foremost in the contest between protestantism and papacy. Beneath his powerful blows priestcraft fell. Absolutism was unbearable to his independent nature, either in church or state. Freedom of thought and action was first recognized upon English soil. On the rugged rocks of New England the Puritan fitly exemplified the truest type of Saxon character, and his stern individuality has permeated and controlled our entire national life. The moral strength of the Saxon holds him out in bold relief from the family of races, leading mankind to a higher and happier sphere of existence, as the snow-capped mountain peak rears its hoary head high above the floating clouds and gazes out from the finite to the infinite and eternal.

Firm, free, and true, the Saxon element is destined to penetrate civilization with enduring power. Widely differing from the barbaric splendor of the ancients, it is also strongly contrasted with the highest phases of modern enlightenment. How unlike the Celt, whose varying course of life, and sudden leaps from the depths of degradation to the heights of glory and renown, have kept the world in constant wonderment. Fickle, fiery, pliable, without organizing force, his grandest efforts result in chaotic confusion. Incapable of self-government he suffers for centuries the yoke of dire despotism, and then in one vast unorganized bulk, overturns government and establishes anarchy. Thus, like a pendulum, he swings backward and forward, from tyranny of the autocrat to the tyranny of the mob, ignorant of the true principles of government, until touched by the elements of that higher civilization which is gradually assimilating the world. The genius of the Celt is the child of circumstances; the genius of the Saxon, the inevitable result of continuous effort. The one, by chance, produces the unbalanced yet brilliant Gambetta, the other through the irresistible logic of events evolves the peerless Gladstone, a crowning gem in Saxon civilization.

English civilization has inoculated the world. The Czar in his snow-bound palace strives to imitate English methods. The African chieftain traverses oceans to ask of England's queen the secret of Saxon civilization. The exclusive Mongolian opens wide his gates and hastens to adopt English customs. Saturating all society with his subtile power, permeating all phases of humanity, infusing his spirit into the life of every nation, engrafting the product of past civilizations upon the parent stock and using them as his own, transforming the customs of the world, surpassing the Greek in beauty, the Roman in strength, the ancient in philosophy, the modern in science, the Saxon continues to complete his divine destiny, in absorbing, amalgamating and assimilating mankind.

# JUDAS ISCARIOT.

By CHARLES T. WYCKOFF, of Knox College.

## BIOGRAPHICAL.

Charles Truman Wyckoff was born in Farmington, Illinois, the 16th of October, 1861. The log school house of early childhood, and rude, pine desks, well whittled, gave place in later years to good grammar and high schools, where there is less of whittling and more of true education. In September of 1879 he entered Knox College and academy. He took a moderate though increasing interest in the exercises of composition and elocution. However he made great progress in these studies, and in '83 was one of the members of the senior and junior classes who received the appointment to the preliminary trial for a contest in oratory. The subject, "Judas Iscariot," was suggested to Mr. Wyckoff as one not worn threadbare. It was afterward jokingly said his success was due partly to his audacity in taking such a theme. But he passed the trial which made him the representative of his *alma mater*. On this same night he started for Dakota, there to live six months on a claim. October 5, 1883, Judas, though such a villain, was again privileged to be victorious at the Illinois inter-collegiate contest. And now for the final trial—inter-State contest. In May, 1884, the battle was on, and ended in "Judas Iscariot" winning first prize. After graduating from Knox College Mr. Wyckoff entered the Chicago Theological Seminary, finishing the course in 1887. On invitation from the faculty of Knox College he delivered the master's oration, "Judas Maccabaeus," an admirable production. Shorty afterward he went to Japan, and engaged in teaching music and kindred departments in the government school at Osaka, but has been transferred to the Doshisha School, at Kyoto. He is recognized as an able instructor, and is a gentleman who commands esteem.

## THE ORATION.

Delivered at the Inter-State Oratorical Contest, Iowa City, Iowa, May 1884, taking first prize. Judges: Hon. S. M. CLARK, Col. C. A. CLARK, Hon. E. H. CONGER, Prof. N. C. DOUGHERTY, Rev. R. NUTTING, D. D.

The hero-worship of the world has made few mistakes. Party spirit may blind for a moment; the passions of men may sway the judgment for a time; but the verdict of history seldom errs. In that tragedy of eighteen centuries ago the clear, white light of a character supremely divine, falling upon one of the actors, casts a heavy shadow across the field of history—a shadow which continues to lengthen and darken. Historical criticism and philosophical investigation fail to disperse the gloom which shrouds the character of the Iscariot; nor wipe the stain from his name. Each generation adds its seal to the verdict of condemnation. Nevertheless there are in these modern days, especially among the Germans, but with a following among us, apologists for the crime of Judas. These apologists say that the arguments to prove that he was actuated by the motives usually attributed to him, are insufficient; that the cause was inadequate to the result; that ambition or avarice never would have impelled him to a crime so enormous as the betrayal. What exaltation could ambition find in the death of Christ? Could avarice, that gloated enviously over the costly outpouring of the alabaster box of ointment, be induced to commit so dark a crime for the paltry sum of thirty pieces of silver? Judas was not a traitor *per se*, but upon examination his motives are bright with the light of patriotism, though the result be shadowed in unanticipated gloom.

To him as a patriot holding the popularity of the prophecies, the vision of Christ coming in earthly power and glory as King of the Jews was perfectly natural. He did not understand the spiritual attitude of Christ. He caught no glimpses of the divine plan; but he saw the iron heel of the Romans crushing the Jewish nation—a nation which had bowed its neck in bondage only twice in its long history—once in the early dawn of that history under the shadow of Egypt's gigantic temples and palaces, and again by Babylon's winding rivers and floating gardens. He saw the people worshiping Christ as they had worshiped no one before. Here was an opportunity to drive the Romans back to their homes on the Tiber; to make the Jewish people a ruling nation again with Christ as their king.

All this, they say, and more, Judas saw and felt with the burning, passionate fire of a Jewish patriot. And why did not Christ accept these opportunities when all seemed ready for such action? Once, twice, thrice, aye, many times had the cup of kingly power been pressed to his lips, and as many times refused. This nature, so divine, seemed nevertheless to lack something. To Judas alone it was clear. This inaction was the result of indecision of character. This fault must be remedied. He must supply the lack. He must precipitate Christ into such a crisis that he would be compelled to exercise in his own defense that mysterious power so often used for others. That crisis was the betrayal.

Thus the defenders of the Iscariot endeavor to show that Judas was not impelled to the betrayal by ambition or avarice; that neither of these was sufficient to account for the result; that the real motive was patriotism, and the betrayal the means by which he hoped to elevate Christ to the kingship, and the Jews to the leadership among the nations.

But are these arguments in defense of the Iscariot valid? Was he a patriot? Does his general character harmonize with such a supposition? A patriot is full of love and devotion. He sacrifices himself for his country and his people. He glows with enthusiasm. But Judas was not only selfish and corrupt, he was also morose and cynical. There was no feeling in his breast which could sympathize with the impulse that prompted Mary's noble gift. Suspicion of others was continually creeping into his mind, and the dark, flitting shadows of burning passion skulked in the recesses of his soul. What feeling was there here to knit a nation together for victory, to stir and thrill men to deeds worthy of heroes? The dark, scowling countenance of Leonardo da Vinci's Judas well expresses his sinister character.

Not only his character, but also his course of action precludes the supposition that he was a patriot. As a patriot he would have left incomplete no arrangements by which success might be insured to his understanding. But not even a hint was given; none to the impetuous, fiery Peter; none to the loving John; none to the people who but a few days before had shouted hosannas to the son of David. No one knew of the plan, if plan there were, to re-establish the Jewish kingdom with Christ at its head, save the dark, silent Man of Kerioth.

Then, again, the betrayal took place at the lonely hour of midnight, when all the people were sleeping after the busy day. The birds had ceased their singing in the olive groves of Gethsemane, and nothing was heard save the sounds proceeding from these two bands—Christ with his disciples, praying that prayer of agony; and the mob of soldiers and priests, with their lanterns and spears, with their curses and eager longings for the death of the Nazarene. The hour was unfavorable for patriotism, but favorable for perfidy. No patriot would have chosen such a course. In such circumstances no result could be expected from the betrayal but the death of the betrayed.

The words of Christ and his disciples concerning Judas, reveal his true character. Surely, after three years' intimate association with him, these chosen companions, better than any one else, understood his real motives. "Judas Iscariot, who also betrayed him," are the only words which the troubled, shuddering heart of the disciple could utter. How full of terrible import the words of Peter. "He went to his own place." Note especially the words of the beloved disciple: "Then Satan entered into him." As on a wild and fitful night the angry storm-fiends wail their mournful requiem through the air, so in the heart of Judas rioted and raged the dark fiends of passion. Think you there was patriotism here?

"Christ," says John, "needed not that any should testify of man; for He knew what was in man." But what says this divine reader of hearts; "Father, those that Thou gavest me I have kept, and none of them are lost but the son of perdition." "Have not I chosen you twelve, and one of you is a devil?" And if the Iscariot had been a patriot would Christ have said, "Judas, betrayest thou the Son of Man with a kiss?" Christ recognized no love in that kiss; no warm, patriotic spirit in that greeting; nothing but the signal for betrayal and death.

To account for the betrayal of such a Master, avarice is inadequate; but as an opening for a horde of more malignant passions, sufficient. It was but the small crevice in the dike, through which a sea shall yet rush.

And what were these more malignant passions? Examine

the last few days of the tragedy.  Go back to Bethany, to that quiet retreat which Christ was soon to leave forever, to the supper and to the royal anointing.  No word but of love and adoration had been spoken by that little company.  But upon our ears grate harshly the words of Judas condemning the waste of the precious perfume.  Out of harmony and out of sympathy with the spiritual elevation of the company, Judas feels more than ever his isolation.  The fires of anger and hate, of disappointment and revenge, filled his heart.  These passions now hold him fast, and as he leaves the feast and hurries along the dark road to the priests at Jerusalem, the mutterings of the coming storm are in his soul.

And do you know what revenge is in the human heart? How it pursues its victim, unrelenting, unpitying, through lapse of years and length of distance, till at last the fearful end is reached?  Then he who so lately pursued is hunted to the death by the dread furies of remorse.  Then Judas, blinded by rage and hate, with silent longing for revenge burning in his heart, followed his victim.  Then came the betrayal; then the suicide of despair.  Not till Christ has been condemned and the wild shouts of "Crucify Him" fall on his ears does Judas begin to realize the enormity of his crime.  Then, indeed, conscience shows him the dark path he has been treading, and the awful precipice of guilt to which he has brought himself.  He is overwhelmed with bitter heart-rending remorse, in which is no pulsation of sorrow or repentance, but only the dark, wild despair of evil beholding itself.  The thorn-crowned head turns upon him with a look of unutterable reproach and sorrow.  Now the divine face vanishes, and the air is "with dreadful faces thronged and fiery arms."  The satanic legions exult in fiendish glee over the fallen man.  They crowd around him; they mock at his remorse; they jeer at him; they seize him and drag him, shuddering to their own gloomy abode.

Thus fell the Iscariot into the dark depths of his own condemnation.  Thus the verdict of Judas himself, the verdict of Christ, the verdict of all the following ages, is our verdict — **Judas was a traitor.**

# THE UNITY OF SCIENCE AND RELIGION.

By GEORGE L. MACKINTOSH, of Wabash College.

## BIOGRAPHICAL.

George L. Mackintosh was born in Gugsboro County, Nova Scotia, January 1, 1859, and is of Scotch parentage. The first twelve years of his life were spent on his father's farm. He then attended the Academy at New Glasgow; later taught school. In the fall of 1878 he removed to the United States. Shortly after his arrival he entered Wabash College, Crawfordsville, Indiana. He was a faithful student, and graduated in 1884. After leaving college he studied law, but subsequently studied for the ministry. His first charge was as pastor of the Presbyterian Church at Winamac, Indiana, where he still faithfully serves. He delivered the second prize oration, printed on the following pages, when a student of Wabash College. It is an excellent oration, and the product of a only a week's labor.

## THE ORATION.

Delivered at the Inter-State Oratorical Contest, Iowa City, Iowa, May, 1884, taking second prize. Judges: Hon. S. M. CLARK, Col. C. A. CLARK, Hon. E. H. CONGER, Prof. N. C. DOUGHERTY, Rev. R. NUTTING, D. D.

Men seldom seek truth for its own sake. The personal and professional element enters largely into all their investigations. Theologians are more eager to uphold their theology, and scientists to defend their theories, than is either to strive for truth in its broad and comprehensive unity. This tendency in man's nature, while it has imperative uses, has led to nearly all the conflicts and disputes of the world of thought. Most of all has it caused the seeming discord between some of the truths of religion and science. Through the whole course of human thought this antagonism has prevailed. Two principles seems to run parallel in every age and civilization, and, indeed, in each individual mind. The one is embodied in empirical science; the other, in religious faith. Intellect is the controlling force of the first; reverence, of the second. The former is iconoclastic and aggressive; the latter, conservative and restraining. Developed in harmony, they are the counter-balancing forces on whose nice adjustment must ever depend the symmetrical advancement of the human race. But if either is advanced at the sacrifice of the other, harmony of movement is destroyed, and beneficent progress is impossible. Religious faith without intellectual enlightenment is superstition. Intellect without the restraining influences of religion inevitably drifts into atheism and despair. Pendulum-like the world has swung from one to the other of these extremes. On the one hand we have the unquestioning faith and reasoning superstition of the Middle Ages; on the other, the impious audacity and coarse materialism of the French philosophers. The former reduced a beautiful and lofty faith almost to fetishism; the latter raised reason and shame to the throne of Divinity. Each in turn had overstepped its proper boundaries, and assumed to itself the whole province of thought. Each had scornfully rejected the claims of the other in order to secure absolute power to itself.

Even in the nineteenth century the conflict for supremacy goes on with unabated vigor. Once more to-day we are told, in no modest terms, that this is the age of science; that science is the light of the world, before which the penny rush-lights of religion must inevitably pale into insignificance. What, then, is this mighty science? Science is what man knows of sensible things and their relations, and its utmost bounds are man's capacity to know. With indomitable courage science has gone forth to meet the mystery that confronts it. From star to atom it has left no field untried. Measuring illimitable spaces or gauging a molecule, calculating the age of a planet or an insect, it is ever patient, persistent, and daring. No nook of visible creation has escaped its penetrating eye. Its ambition knows no bounds. To build a pyramid from whose lofty summit the whole domain of knowledge might be surveyed has ever been its cheering and inspiring hope. In pursuance of this design individual facts are classified; classes are systematized and united in the idea of unvarying law. Here science ends. And what is law? Is this a word to conjure with and climb the empyrean of divinity? "Law," says Montesquieu, "is the necessary relations that arise from the nature of things." Has science, then, in reaching a law established an ultimate principle? Does the law of gravitation keep the planets in their orbits and maintain the harmony of the spheres? Does the law of evolution generate genus and species? Law is but the method of force. Law is a pure abstraction. Beyond law must be the real impelling force, and of this science gives no explanation. All science falls short of the final explanation of things. Astronomy ends with the nebular hypothesis; chemistry, with the atomic theory; and geology fades into the illimitable ages of the past. Physical science reaches out in every direction, and is met at all points by a blind, impenetrable infinity. It is indeed a torch in the night, but as it grows brighter it only renders more palpable the darkness beyond. As it is multiplied it only widens the circle of the unknown.

If science is unable to solve the problems of the physical universe, how shall it answer the questions of a higher existence? Astronomy may calculate the almost infinite path of a comet, but what science the dying emperor's question, "Whither goest thou, oh my soul?" Chemistry may resolve the physical universe into its elements, but what magic art has analyzed a single human emotion? Biology may trace the descent of species and reveal a plausible evolution, but who has found the germ of being? In the depths of every human soul, in the dreams of sleep, in every flower that lifts its head to heaven, in every senseless, useless clod is lodged a mystery far transcending scientific skill to comprehend.

Must we then agree with Compte that in "positive science" the range of thought is exhausted? Must we reject all we can not comprehend, reduce all our views and beliefs to the five senses, make human nature but the refined brutish instinct, and this short pittance of time our only immortality? From such dismal conclusions of the intellect, the soul instinctively recoils and finds within itself a protest against such petty limits. From other than scientific sources comes positive knowledge. From the depths of consciousness comes certain proof that beyond all this array of phenomena and from there reigns supernal power. The institutions of the soul are real phenomena, and they connect man with an infinite invisible to which mere science can never attain. This is evinced in the common consciousness of mankind. It is seen in the sculpture of the Greeks and the painting of the great masters. It is found in the Vedas, the Koran, and the Bible. It is typified in the Valhalla of the wild Norsemen, and the Nirvana of the stolid Burmese. It is sung in every line of genuine poetry, from Homer to Tennyson. It is proved by the temples of the past and the living faiths of the present. Through every age and civilization this idea has run like a thread of gold, and modern science from its very inability to destroy it only adds another proof to the accumulated evidence of the ages.

It matters not that astronomy has demonstrated the infinities of heavenly motion; beyond all is the Omnipotent Power that sways the whole. It matters not that geology has shown the earth to be a child of law; law is an index of divinity. It matters not that biology has shown an evolution in the organic world; at the ultimate term of the series, though that term be infinity itself, stands the first great cause. Beyond the reach of human sense is found the larger arc of the great circle of truth. Here, where science can never go with hammer, or scalpel, or telescope, lies the distinctive region of faith. Here, where science ends, religious faith takes up the argument and carries it to its logical conclusions, far into the domain of the infinite.

Some have speculated on the religion of the future, and predict a time when all religion shall dwindle to the proportions of a classic myth. They have ill studied the soul in its higher relations who indulge in such speculations. Religion of some kind is a necessity to human existence. It is the aggregate of those forces which most clearly distinguish man from the brute. It is the law of the soul as much as gravitation is the law of matter. Whatever forms it may assume, under whatever aspect it may appear, so long as man is man religious sentiment must endure. It contains elements of truth that are eternal. They were true when the stars sang together at the birth of creation. They will be true when the last man stands on "this bank and shoal of time."

Truth often presents to man a fragmentary and uncertain aspect. But a keener vision and a steadier gaze reveal a harmonious unity. This is the eternal truth of which science and religion are but the infinitesimal fragments. From this standpoint all petty conflicts and disputes fade into mere nothingness; the spectre of human prejudice is removed and the pure white light of God is revealed. In this faith we hope and believe that those forces, which at times seem antagonistic, are in reality the beautifully adjusted parts of a great whole, and that all human wisdom, science, and philosophy, will yet be grouped in a harmonious, beneficent unity. Somewhere there must be a border-land, as yet dim and uncertain, where science is religion and religion science; and where both unite to form a colossal eminence from which man may, with some philosophy, survey the highway of existence stretching from the present to the limitless future. Here is the pyramid which neither faith nor science can build unaided, but which both may raise to form the highest excellence of human wisdom. Here, at last, the unity of truth will in some degree unfold itself to mortal sight.

When not science or philosophy or anything else but truth shall be the pole-star of thoughtful men; when science, philosophy, and revelation, shall move in converging lines; when scientists shall be theologians and theologians scientists; when all sects may pitch their tents in harmony on the broad field of a generous philosophy, then will the destiny of the human race be fulfilled and the grand epic of civilization completed.

# THE CONFLICT OF LABOR AND CAPITAL.

By ALBERT J. BEVERIDGE, of DePauw University.

## BIOGRAPHICAL.

Albert J. Beveridge was born in Highland County, Ohio, October 6, 1862. While yet a child his parents removed to Moultrie County, Illinois, where he worked on the farm, and in the logging camps cutting and hauling logs, until he entered DePauw University, Greencastle, Indiana. He graduated from this institution in 1885, and paid his way with money earned during vacations and prize money won during his college terms, having won every contest in which he took part during his entire course. His masterly effort, "The Conflict of Labor and Capital," he delivered at the inter-State contest of 1885, and won first prize. In 1884 he stumped the State of Indiana, under the direction of the Republican State Central Committee. He has spoken during every State and national campaign since then, under the direction of the State Central Committee. In December, 1885, he began the study of law with McDonald, Butler & Mason, at Indianapolis, and upon the dissolution of this firm, in 1887, was made chief law clerk of the firm of McDonald & Butler, until he opened his own office in January, 1889. He has enjoyed a profitable practice, with steady and rapid growth; his specialities being corporation and commercial law. He was married November 24, 1887, to Miss Kate Maud Langsdale, of Greencastle, and they now reside in their happy home on Christian Avenue, Indianapolis, Indiana. Mr. Beveridge has attracted much attention through his legal efficiency, especially in the cases of State of Indiana *ex rel.* Yancey *v.* Hyde, 22 Northeastern Reporter, 644; and the State of Indiana *ex rel.* Worrel *v.* Peelle, 22 Northeastern Reporter, 654, and 24 Northeastern Reporter, 440. Mr. Beveridge represented Messrs. Yancey and Worrel, which cases arose because of the conflict between Governor and Legislature.

## THE ORATION.

Delivered at the Inter-State Oratorical Contest, Columbus, Ohio, May, 1885, taking first prize. Judges: Rev. H. W. BAYLISS, Hon. S. M. CLARK, Hon. J. W. HALLSDAY, Gov. H ADLEY. Dr. E. K. YOUNG, Dr. J. HECKMAN.

### GENERAL ANALYSIS.

INTRODUCTION.
    I. Principle originating most conflicts.
    II. Principle solving such conflicts.
    III. Application of above to conflict of labor and capital.
DISCUSSION.
    I. Importance of the labor problem.
    II. Social extremists already moving.
    III. Positions of these social extremists.
    IV. Positions of social extremists refuted.
    V. Our present society equal to the problem.
    VI. True causes of the conflict.
    VII. True remedy the removal of these causes.
    VIII. Forces preventing removal of these causes.
    IX. These forces must therefore be overcome.
    X. Methods of overcoming them.
CLOSE.
    I. Summary.

Most conflicts result from reactions. The French Revolution was a reaction against the oppression of caste, with Rousseau to lead it. Skepticism is a reaction against conservative creed, an Ingersoll leading it. Socialism is the reaction of labor against capital, Henry George leading it.

Such extremes can never solve a problem. Upon the passionless heights between, whence unprejudiced reason may sweep the whole field of thought, is ever found the comprehensive truth. The French Revolution resulted in the rejection of extremes—the union of individual liberty and social restraint. Eventually science and dogma must reject extremes; faith and reason must unite. The solution of the labor problem must be the abandonment of extremes—the union of labor and capital.

This conflict is filling the universal mind, dictating political platforms, anon bursting into riots and strikes, like the complaining murmurs of a coming storm. But eight years since, it kindled the flames at Pittsburg, and sent terror to every city in our land; it inspired the late riots in Hocking Valley and South Bend, and waxing fiercer and fiercer, running bullets unseen, mustering forces invisible, it will, if unchecked, one day rouse us with drum-beat and bugle-call.

Increasing population brings it each day nearer. Already we have 1,000,000 unemployed men; already 2,000,000 laborers secretly organized; already fifty newspapers spreading sedition and excess; and our population is doubling every twenty-five years!

Great cities cradle this conflict. With a Chicago, a New York, a San Francisco, a score of cities like Paris, what must we expect? With a hundred equal to Marseilles, what? When the fortunes of Vanderbilts, ill-gotten, ill-kept, are filling the masses with bitterness, what? Ah! was Macaulay dreaming when he told of our coming Huns and Vandals? Was Wendell Phillips a madman when he said that the problem of the rich and poor would yet try our souls as slavery never tried them? A problem, this, to which we must address ourselves now, ere extremists throw labor and capital into armed conflict.

Already these extremists are moving. Already in behalf of toiling poverty have such intellects as Rousseau, La Salle, and George, proclaimed war against our social system. They represent ideas, and they must be heard; for an idea, glowing with the immortality of some man's convictions, can not be silenced but by convincing argument.

These extremists demand the overthrow of our social system. They ask: "Why this vice and wretchedness among the poor? Why have they not equal happiness with the rich? Because society is unjust; conditions unequal. Because one man owns a thousand acres while his neighbor is famishing." Their remedy is, "Right the injustice; make property common, as air is common, and sunlight and starlight; make conditions equal, as nature made them equal. With poverty swept away the cause of the theft and murder and misery will be gone."

But their argument rests on false premises. Vice, sloth and attendant wretchedness prevail, not because of poverty; poverty prevails because of them. It is the old, old problem of human nature and its frailty, and human nature they disregard.

Is their remedy just? What gives property its value? Some man's toil; some man's thought. Yonder marsh is worthless; drain it and it teems with richness. Is it right, when one man gave it value, for all to enjoy it equally? Manifestly not.

Equality of condition is neither right nor natural. Great capacity deserves more than mean capacity. An Edison deserves more than his engineer. The parable of the talents flashes back the vision of justice, and upon justice is society founded; and though the rains descend and the floods come and the winds blow and beat upon it, it shall not fall, for it is founded upon a rock.

Their remedy is as impossible as it is unjust. Could you make property common, condition equal? Who should dwell upon the shores of the Hudson? Who amid Arizona's sage-bush? Who should choose? Who decide? Would there be no favoritism, no fraud, no dissatisfaction? Ah, look just beyond this frost-work of socialism, and there flashes the bayonets and the swords, rough-ground of anarchy, aye — grim and blackened warriors stand to their smoking guns! Equality of condition is impossible until sunlit mountain and laughing valley are level plains, climate uniform, and all men equals in body and in brain. Indeed, men are like nature; here a crag, and yonder a dell; there a Jungfrau with beetling cliffs and crown of snow, yonder a generous plain; anon a dismal swamp where pestilence broods.

Equalize conditions and every motive to effort dies. No sweat of brow, no sweat of brain, never a glorious deed nor work of genius if improved condition does not reward it. Better the whirlwind of enterprise than the dreamless sleep of such equality. Voiceless yet would be the golden harp of Shakespeare, silent the song of Milton, still the fairy fingers of Mozart, unfilled with westward winds Columbus's sails, unreared our temples of learning, and wrapped in the shadows of a dream undreamt this mighty civilization, but for the magic touch of private enterprise.

No, not equality of condition, equality of privilege is the principle of justice. Equal privileges to build fortunes if one can; to lead armies, if one can; to be an Humboldt, if one can. This principle it was that gave us liberty; that handed the instant lightnings down to Lincoln; that stormed those heights at Lookout — equality of privilege — and the tattered battle-flags, torn by the shells at Yorktown, at Shiloh, at Gettysburg; the monuments of those who fell upon the furrowed fields where our heroes fought for the rights of men, calls upon us to preserve that principle forever! God grant that the day may never dawn when socialism attempts to execute its theory, for the sun of that day will set red amid the roar of cannon, and upon the ruins of our Republic some Cæsar may build his throne!

Is our society, then, sufficient to solve this problem? Yes. In the name of popular education, in the name of temperance reform, in the name of Him of Nazareth, it is indeed sufficient.

But if society is equal to the question, why the conflict? The solution means the removal of the cause. What, then, is the cause of the conflict? Not society's injustice? No. It results because right relations are distorted; because demagogues have cut the cords of confidence binding labor and capital together. Mutual distrust is the moving spirit. Labor and capital forget what each owes the other. Capital forgets that labor creates its wealth; that labor is human, with sacred rights; forgets that "rank is but the guinea's stamp, the man's the gold for a' that;" forgets this, and fixes wages, not where they should be, but as low as labor can live upon. Labor forgets that capital alone can give it employment; that capital, like all force, must be massed to accomplish great ends, and that scattered it would be powerless as the shorn Sampson; forgets that labor receives 95 per cent. and capital but 5 per cent. of all the value industry creates, and that capital is the directing force which renders this industry possible; forgets that the true nobility of labor is "brave struggling, not repining;" that every force today is lifting labor up. Let the toiler pause and think. For his sake thrones are falling and the world is yielding to the royalty of thought and toil. For his sake science searches the mystery of force and life, and, at the portals of the tomb, almost grasps the mystery of death. Every influence — college or church, statesman's thought or law of matter — whatever today is a living force is shaping in this century the golden age of the workingman; yet, under all, is the hand of capital guiding, moulding, building. Labor and capital must remember these things; labor must remember that capitalists deserve more than workingmen for the foresight and responsibility that create enterprise; capital must give labor the wages of justice — wages that rise and fall when profits rise and fall; confidence must be restored, and this problem will vanish like frost in a flood of sunshine.

But confidence is impossible while three classes remain — the ignorant, the criminal, and the poor; and if the school can not overcome the ignorant, the church the criminal, and both united to temperance the indigent, then alas for the future of society!

Thus universal education becomes a social necessity. Ignorant labor can not reason justly. It is the ready victim of every plausible fallacy. To ignorant labor capital seems the tyrant, whose burdens it has borne through storm and blast with rags and hunger as its only recompense. Well may capital tremble when political power is in the hands of ignorant poverty. You cannot remove the power; you must destroy the class; you must enlighten labor. Enlightened labor can think rightly. It knows that capital is the motor of the age. It is ever changing places with capital — the incompetent heir with the able employee. Enlighten labor, and our ignorant class fades away like the memory of a troubled dream.

But whence the criminal and indigent? The victims of capital? Not so. Question statistics, and from the darkest page comes the answer: Our poor spend $1,000,000,000 every year for intoxicants. Labor, worth $1,000,000,000 more, is yearly incapacitated by intoxicants. Three-fifths of all poverty, nine-tenths of all crime, comes from intoxicants. Here is the efficient cause of poverty, vice, and distrust. This is more than sentiment; it is danger. The $2,000,000,000 yearly taken from labor must be saved — an economy which, almost alone, will eliminate the criminal and indigent classes.

But of itself it can not solve this problem. The great need of our business civilization is conscience. It alone can establish absolute confidence between labor and capital. Capital without conscience means tyranny; labor without conscience, anarchy. Out from the shades of Gethsemene, out from the riven tomb, He of the thorn-crowned head is walking down the troubled ages, lifting from bruised and staggering man the burden of his woes, speaking conscience to every soul; and here, where Christianity is the basis of society; here where childhood's first lispings learn at mother's knee and from mother's lips the story of that Ineffable One, we know that conscience may be a universal fact. Back of Christian faith lies conscience; back of conscience, confidence. The church must come to the rescue of our conscience, shipwrecked as it well-nigh is in the tempest of this century's struggle for gain. Capital must be humanized; labor must be Christianized. Christain labor is the sublimest force in history. It awoke to the morning cry of Paul Revere, and rallied on the green at Lexington; out from the yearning arms of home it marched into the flame of battle, and sent God's thunder-bolts smoking against our national sin — marched forth, not for itself, but for the slave; and to Christian labor our hope must be anchored in this conflict of to-day. But faithless labor; let that procession which yesterday marched through Chicago declaring robbery just; let the barricades of Paris; let these show the fury of labor without conscience, without God. Then let the song of Bethlehem's morning stars peal on, peal on, till its melody touches every troubled spirit; touches them in the vaults of greed, in the homes of the lowly, in the camps of sin — touches and soothes and wins. Let the bugles of conscience sound the truce of God through the whole world forever!

When the barriers to mutual trust have been leveled — and they will be; when we have a sober, an intelligent, and a Christian people — and we will have them — the sounds of this conflict will die away, as the distant thunders of a stormy night recede and die before the breaking of a summer's dawn. With confidence established right-relations will result, labor and capital will join hands, and this problem will be solved.

> "A glory shines before us
> Of what mankind shall be—
> Pure, generous, brave, and free:
> A dream of man and woman,
> Diviner still, but human,
> Solving the problem old,
> Shaping the age of gold.
> Ring bells, in unreared steeples,
> The joy of unborn peoples;
> Sound trumpets, far off blown,
> Your triumph is our own."

# SCHILLER AND GERMANY.

By VICTOR E. BENDER, of Knox College.

### BIOGRAPHICAL.

The subject of this sketch, Victor E. Bender, is of German parentage, born in Granville, Illinois, September, 1861. He received a common school education, graduating from the high school of that village at the age of sixteen, in 1878. For the next two years he taught school in a German settlement three miles from Granville, teaching the English branches half of the day, and the other half was given to instruction in German. During these two years the thought foremost in the mind of the young man was to acquire a college training, and to this end he secured a position as librarian in Illinois College, at Jacksonville. An accident prevented him from entering upon his duties at the time contemplated, and so he was compelled to surrender the position and continue to teach another year. In the fall of 1881 he entered the scientific department of Knox College, Galesburg, Illinois, with the intention of continuing until his finances were exhausted, and trusting to a vague providence for further resources. In his junior year he was appointed one of six students in a local contest in oratory, in which three juniors and three seniors participated! Mr. Bender secured the first prize, the subject of his oration being "Schiller and Germany." This subject was suggested by the speaker's close association with Germans and German literature. The winning of the first prize in this contest entitled him to twenty dollars and the privilege of representing the college at the inter-collegiate contest, which took place at Lincoln, Illinois, in 1884, and upon which occasion he won the prize of seventy-five dollars and the honor of representing Illinois at the inter-State contest. Upon the latter event he gained the second prize and such honors as are usually bestowed upon the victors in oratory. By request of the faculty of the college he delivered his oration on commencement day, a privilege which has been accorded to all orators who has represented Knox College abroad. The two years following Mr. Bender's graduation, in 1885, he spent as principal of the public schools of Abingdon, Illinois. In 1888 he was offered the chair of elocution in Knox College, which position he accepted, resigning at the expiration of one year to engage in newspaper work in Omaha, Nebraska. After doing the work of a reporter on the Omaha *Bee*, and later on the *Dispatch*, he became city editor of the *Republican* in the fall of 1889. In January, 1890, he purchased the Omaha *Mercury*, a paper devoted especially to the legal interests of the city, and is still editor and proprietor. June, 1889, Mr. Bender was married to Miss Alma B. Colville, of Galesburg, Illinois, who since his freshman year has shared in his numerous victories and occasional defeats.

## THE ORATION.

Delivered at the Inter-State Oratorical Contest, Columbus, Ohio, May, 1885, taking second prize. Judges: Rev. H. W. Bayliss, Hon. S. M. Clark, Hon. J. W. Hallsday, Gov. Hoadley, Dr. E. K. Young, Dr. J. Heckman.

History is a fabric woven of the threads of countless lives, interspersed with lines of deeper color and denser fibre. Every nation has its individual pattern, its peculiar shade—the bright or dark, the variegated or plain, prevails according as the influence and direction of individual lives may determine.

The history of Germany reveals a brilliant and distinctive double fibre, interlacing her fabric like beautiful threads of gold. It represents the lives of Schiller and Goethe—the patriarchs of German literature, the apostles of their country's intellectual freedom. Of the two, Schiller is pre-eminently the true German, embodying in his nature every essential attribute of German individuality, feeling and responding in every genuine sentiment of the German heart.

A hundred years previous to Schiller's advent in history, Germany lay prostrate under the desolating stroke of the Thirty Years' War. It was the Great Sahara of her history. Here and there, like feeble plants on a sterile soil, we see isolated intellects extending the feeble tendrils of their ideas, but the dire ravages of war had crushed out every element of growth and vigor, leaving industries, science, literature, church, nation, in a state of indifference and apathy. Oh for some quickening, reviving power that would arouse her lethargic faculties; that would invigorate and vitalize the exhausted forces of the nation! That power came. Toward the middle of the eighteenth century there is a perceptible thrill of life throughout the empire— Lessing had infused the life-giving current. The prostrate nation slowly rising to her feet; Goethe extends to her an aiding hand; and in the very midst of this reawakening, this alternation of light and darkness, this breaking of clouds, this promise of morning, there bursts the clear light of perfect day! As the midnight fires, kindled by the mercenary Robber Moor, broke from the plundered castle and set aglow the dark Thuringian forests, so the fiery passions that raged within that rugged creation, "The Robbers," burst upon the gloom of the nation's lingering woe. Friedrich von Schiller had completed the trinity that effected Germany's restoration. Lessing, Goethe, Schiller—the seed, the flower, the fruit, of her social and political reform.

But what were the more specific relations of Schiller to his native land? Hitherto the tendency of German thought had been toward the abstract, the metaphysical. Sentiment was chilled in cold philosophy, the heart yielded to the mind, spiritual impulse was put down by mental predominance. Lessing and Goethe, with their contemporaries, sought to dispel this prevailing mysticism of thought— to lead the German mind out of its labyrinths of speculation into the light of moral truth. Thus when Schiller appeared, the mental and moral elements of society were far from being homogeneous. It remained for him to reconcile mind to mind and heart to heart.

The drama of "The Robbers" at once revealed his genius and proclaimed his mission. In it were voiced the burning words that trembled on the lips of an oppressed nation; words that heaped upon the social condition of Germany the *onus* of popular condemnation; words that urged, advocated, demanded immediate and radical reform; and they were uttered with the authority and power of one supremely endowed.

The dramatic cast of Schiller's writings aided much in their dissemination and influence. Ideal creations were embodied and impersonated; pictures of the mind were made objective; fiction became real; reality, impressive. The stage proved the great medium between Schiller and his countrymen, interpreting to the masses the lofty conceptions of the poet-thinker. Not only as a dramatist, but as poet, historian, and philosopher, did Schiller enrich and adorn. His history of the Thirty Years' War, embellished with graceful expression, expanded by philosophical comment, illumined by the light of candor and truth, is a pillar of German literature. The philosophy of Kant, that stupendous structure of thought, rising, as it were, in a single night above the debris of shattered philosophies, received from Schiller permanence and beauty.

But Schiller's true sphere lay not in recording the conduct of war, nor yet in solving the problems of an abstruse philosophy. It lay rather in creating a higher ideal of individual duty; in producing and sustaining the genuine sentiment of fraternal love. His mind was ever filled with ideals of the possibilities of humanity. Freedom and patriotism were twin conceptions of his soul, and to establish the one and foster the other; to teach, to elevate, to perfect; this was the all-controlling purpose of his life. As an idealist and a reformer he saw and felt his country's greatest need, and under the inspiration of patriotic impulse he caught up the fallen standard, and proclaimed his mission and his service. "The public," he says, "is now *all* to me, my study, my confidant, my sovereign. Something majestic hovers over me as I determine now to wear no other fetters save the sentence of the world, to appeal to no other throne but the soul of man." And to this voluntary consecration he firmly adhered.

In a much wilder field, but with a less sympathetic nature, Goethe was at this time a noted figure in the work of the nation's reform. He recognized the genius and felt the influence of Schiller, but regarded him with a jealous apprehension, and every possibility of personal contact was avoided. Each was the sole representative of his respective province of thought, and in the higher atmosphere of their beings they figured against an open horizon, like the overtopping heights of two distinct and separate ranges. But circumstance casts the initial thread to many a close-knit friendship. Mutually repelled at first, chance brought them together, and their exalted natures yielded, touched, coalesced. In the reciprocal light of this spiritual exaltation, literature was enhanced in breadth and beauty, humanity became worthier, human destiny higher and nobler.

True friendship is a potent alchemy. From the mingled sentiments of kindred hearts is evolved the gold of character and worth. In the communion of these two men of transcendent genius there was a mutual awakening of yet latent powers; Schiller's fervor and intensity warmed the less passionate Goethe; while the calm, comprehensive mind of the latter modified the ideal creations of his friend, and reduced them to a more practical ideality, enabling him to grasp more completely and effectively the great problems of the human weal.

The Thirty Years' War, with the interests it involved, the issues to which it gave rise; with its innumerable phases of nature and character; with its motives, prejudices, hopes, and ambitions; replete with every shade and variety of human conduct, now offers Schiller the possibilities of a mighty drama —a means to develop thoughts and ideas of individual and national utility. And with a felicity of poetic and philosophic genius he embodied those ideas in the inimitable characters of "Wallenstein."

Towering above the field of French history he sees the sublime figure of the Maid of Orleans. Oh what scenes of thrilling action cluster about her! He sees her a peasant among her flocks, he sees her in the transport of inspiration, rushing to the field of conflict, now in the ranks, now in command, leading the charge, subduing, conquering, crowning; suspected, accused, condemned, burned. But above the ashes of this lowly shepherdess of Domremy there lingers the spirit of her consecrated life, beautified, exalted, perpetuated, by the transforming touch of the German poet.

But the fostering light which had burst so suddenly upon Germany and Europe, which had dissipated the mists of moral darkness, and now stood in the zenith of its splendor, was soon to be obscured. Clouds of mortal disease impede and withhold its rays; but as the curtain thickens and darkens there is a final struggle of the spirit, a rift in the clouds, a baptism of refulgent light, and it passes irrevocably into shadow and night. Need I say what *was* that last, that greatest, benison? Need I say how from the mystic depths of legendary lore he led the hero Tell? how he placed him in his native Alps and bade him redeem his olden glory? how he reawoke in forest and in valley the song of the Alpine hunter; and flecked the hills with flocks, the dales with happy homes? How Despotism clouded, then obscured their happiness; and how at last the clouds were dissipated, and Freedom smiled again? Ah! he baptised the land in the imagery and beauty of a poet's conception, and Switzerland stood transfigured. In this matchless representation of the old legend Germany recognized the genuine qualities of statehood. The patience, constancy, bravery, patriotism, of the primitive Switzer, reproduced in living, sentient characters, touched and moved the nation, and welded closer the bonds of sympathy and love. That priceless legacy lives in history and hearts. It was but yesterday that German rights were jeopardized and the nation affronted. Across the borders the aggressive Napoleon was marshaling his forces to the exhilarating notes of the "Marseillaise," but the sturdy German heart was swayed by an incitement stronger and deeper than that of martial music. Throughout the confederation, from Strasbourg to the Baltic, by imperial mandate, the theatres rang again with the voice of Wilhelm Tell, and modern Germany, catching the spirit of that grand old drama, rallied in defense of Fatherland. Know you a higher tribute that can be paid to genius? Know you a richer legacy that can be left a native land?

Thus as a dramatist we see him peopling the stage with the sublimest conceptions of character and art; in the garland of poesy he has woven the brightest flowers of song; from the field of civil strife he gathered lessons of human wisdom; into the dark recesses of philosophy he carried a torch of truth. Yet underlying all his intellectual powers was the character that gave them firmness and dignity; the heart that warmed them with feeling and sentiment; the soul that exalted and idealized. The great heart of humanity was the source of his every impulse, the pulse of national sentiment determined the vigor of his works. He was the center of a new social and political organism; the embodiment of sincerity and devotion; the type of a patriot, poet, and man.

Germany has had her scientists, poets, her statesmen and generals; her Humboldt and Heine, her Bismarck and Moltke. In every department of human knowledge she keeps pace with the prodigious strides of the age, but at no time has she so rallied her forces and asserted her intellectual and moral powers as at the close of the eighteenth century — when the germs implanted by Lessing, Herder, and Lavater, were in their fruitage; when Goethe wrote, and Richter puzzled and pleased; when the whole world could acclaim with Germany, *"Es lebe Friedrich von Schiller!"*

# CONSERVATISM, AN ESSENTIAL ELEMENT OF PROGRESS.

By E. C. RITSHER, of Beloit College.

### BIOGRAPHICAL.

The winner of the first prize in the oratorical contest of 1886, Mr. Edward Charles Ritsher, was born in Beloit, Wisconsin, September 8, 1864. After passing through the grammar schools of that city he entered the Beloit High School to prepare for college. In 1881 he was graduated with honor from the high school, and then began his life of more advanced study, to which the same term, "with honor," has always been applicable. Entering Beloit College in the fall of the same year the excellence of his work won for him the Waterman Prize, which is assigned to the graduate from any Illinois or Wisconsin high school passing the best entrance examination. At the close of the freshman year he was also awarded the Bridgeman Prize for excellence in declamation. During the Sophomore year he showed unusual ability in the work of the debating societies, being the leading speaker on the winning side in what is known as the Archæan Debate, a coveted honor; and also being successful in two joint debates of the principal literary societies. The following year spent in outdoor life brought the student back to the latter half of his college course with much improved health. At the old-time "junior ex." he was assigned a philosophical oration, and at the end of the year the scholarship of the class was awarded to him. The final year of college life was one of marked influence and prominence. Besides obtaining other college honors, Mr. Ritsher passed successfully through the home, State and inter-State oratorical contests. His oration is its own proof of excellence. Notwithstanding the incursions on time and strength in filling these appointments, the valedictory oration was assigned to Mr. Ritsher at

his graduation, and thus, in 1886, he completed his course with very distinguished success. It ought also to be added that he was repeatedly elected to journalistic honors, but always felt obliged to decline on account of doubtful health. In college he was also identified with Christian work. After leaving college he became the assistant principal in the Beloit High School. In 1887, deciding to study law, he became a student of Columbia Law School, New York City, and was graduated in 1889 with the degree of bachelor of law. A few days later he delivered the master's oration at Beloit College. In October, 1889, he was admitted to the Chicago bar, winning high commendation. Locating in Chicago he has been remarkably successful in his profession, and it takes no prophet's eye to predict for him a large and an influential future.

---

## THE ORATION.

Delivered at the Inter-State Oratorical Contest, Lawrence, Kansas, May, 1886, taking first prize. Judges: Pres. J. B. ANGELL, Judge J. B. CASSODAY, Hon. J. K. NASH, Hon. EUGENE WARE, Rev. Dr. THOMPSON, Hon. T. D. THACHER.

The nineteenth century has been a century of wonders. Prodigies have marked her onward course. The mechanical appliances of ages have been revolutionized. The most stubborn forces have yielded to the mind of man.

The present generation seeks new worlds to conquer. It penetrates the social and moral life of man, and there endeavors to rival the material world in startling revolutions. This invasion of unknown regions calls together men of energy and character, but it also gathers in reckless adventurers. Vandals have arisen in the very realms of thought, wielding the intellectual weapons with ruthless hands. They cry against those who counsel moderation. They declare war on what they call the bigotry of the past. To avoid conservatism they leap into fanaticism. Determined to reform society by a single stroke, they bid defiance to reason and produce their legitimate fruits Socialism, Nihilism, and Rebellion. Is there truth in their doctrines? Is there method in their madness? Let the horrors of the French Revolution be your answer!

If we pause to examine the facts in the case we find no truth in the cry of these Philistines. No yawning gulf separates the conservatives from the reformers. Their ultimate aim is the same. They differ only in their methods. The conservative people of the world are not bigots. They are not the enemies of progress. They grasp the truth with unerring mind. They strive for its success with loyal hearts. The difference between the conservative man and the would-be reformer is a difference not of heart but of brain. It is the difference between the practical man and the theoretical man.

The radical reformer acts in view of the ideal, rather than the actual world. He believes that a certain thing is right and that all else is wrong, and he says, "Give me the right or give me nothing." He believes that he is entitled to the whole loaf, and he proposes to have the whole loaf or starve. The smallest portion of truth suffices so to engage his attention that he forgets everything else, and becomes blind to all that is not comprised within the narrow horizon of his beliefs.

These men have an idea, a plan, a theory, and mounting the lofty platform of "principle," they defiantly proclaim their ideas, and proceed to attack the fixed institutions of centuries before they have secured the means of success. They do not consider that success in human affairs is not to be obtained by such absolute proceedings or by a mere appeal to philosophical argument. They do not consider that the human mind instinctively rebels against such treatment. They do not consider that they deliberately insult the intelligence and common sense of their fellow-men. It does take principle and it does take courage to pursue such a course, but we are placed in the world to accomplish something, not merely to make martyrs of themselves. And while we must admire the pluck of the so-called reformers we cannot but condemn their judgment. We cannot fail to see that their methods are futile and fraught with danger.

The truly conservative men, on the contrary, realize that man must be dealt with not as an ideal but as he is. They realize that tact must be exercised in human affairs. They appreciate the fact that the body politic, like the human body, must develop strength and energy by slow, sure processes; that all abnormally rapid growth is but the symbol of decay. These men take no narrow, visionary view of a subject, but grasping at once, and as a whole, the matter which comes to their notice, they so calculate, arrange, and combine the conflicting elements, that while the everlasting *principle* is placed boldly forward so as not to be mistaken, care is taken that it shall not be endangered by a negligent or rash estimate of the circumstances which oppose it.

Truly conservative men respect an honest foe. They realize that the principle for which they are contending is not the only one in the world, but that there are other doctrines, other facts, other interests, which demand recognition. They are willing even to take the crust if they cannot get the whole loaf. They are willing to make use of stepping-stones to reach the exalted position for which they strive. And they are none the less men of principle for so doing; they simply combine with their principle tact and common sense. They realize that yonder mountain height of achievement must be reached—not by a reckless and fanatical attempt to climb straight up its perpendicular sides, but rather by following the winding path of policy which with its gentle ascent leads ever onward ever upward to the glorious summit of success!

This is the only road to achievement. Step by step is the universal law of progress. The whole material world bows reverently to its sway. The wondrous power, which out of chaos produced the Universe—the earth, the air, the heavens with all their starry splendor—was a power working not by mighty revolutions, but slowly, silently, through infinite ages. The forces of violent action—the wind, the flood, the earthquake shock—are the forces of destruction. Wherever we turn our eyes the evidence of this law confronts us. All nature is under its domination. Is man so mighty a creature that he can safely defy the laws of the very power that gave him birth? History teaches the reverse.

The English nation escaped from a condition of servitude and tyranical oppression, not by violently throwing off the yoke, but by over a century of steady, systematic, and intelligent growth. The Magna Charta, the Petition of Right, the Bill of Rights—those three great documents which have been aptly termed the "Bible of the English Constitution"—were wrested from haughty kings not by a party of one idea, not by fanatics thoughtless of all else, but by men who considered the interests of all parties, and who for that very reason were able to develop a symmetrical and powerful public sentiment. As one of our ablest political philosophers well says, "The healthful development of the English Constitution was due to the fact that no particular principle ever obtained an exclusive influence. There was always a simultaneous development of the different forces and a sort of negotiation or compromise between their pretentions and interests."

Across the Channel, however, the case was different. The French people defied the law of progress, and as a consequence there arose in France certain factions with "Liberty" for their watchword—"Liberty though the Heavens fall." Revolution they considered the touch-stone of progress; one idea, the condition of success. Violating the very principle for which they fought they refused to consider other interests; they scorned to compromise with other factions; they listened not to the claims of monarchy, religion, or law. And those dark pages in the history of France, from the perusal of which the very demons turn in horror, are the record of their deeds.

Biography, too, adds its testimony to the immutability of the law of progress and bears witness to the success of those who recognize this law. Who is the man who has transformed Prussia from a mass of petty states to that great and glorious nation, second to none on the European continent? Bismarck; a man of iron will, a man of dogged persistence, and yet withal, a man of such consummate tact and policy that for twenty years and more he has held his position as chief man of the realm in spite of opposition, aye, even with the consent of his bitterest political enemies. German unification was not an idea original with him. Patriots and reformers for a century before had been longing to accomplish this very thing. Bismarck was the first to grapple with the subject as a statesman and not as an enthusiast. Others had sought to make a nation in a day; Bismarck was willing to give a lifetime for the work.

Who is the man who in England to-day wields a power and an influence which defeat and political overthrow have not been able to cripple? Gladstone; the Christian statesman, the man of principle, and yet, for the sake of the welfare of England, so conservative, that irrespective of party ties, he seeks for the symmetrical development of all English interests. His name is destined to become immortal, not as the leader of a party, not as a champion of one idea, but as a statesman who could be active without being partisan, conservative without being stationary, progressive without being fanatical.

Turn to our own history, to the name of one who will live forever in the memory and the heart of this nation, to Abraham Lincoln, the emancipator of the slaves, the savior of the Union. Coming into power when the nation was at a crisis, when as a people we were wholly absorbed in watching one great event, he never forgot for a moment the multiplicity of our interests as a nation; he never allowed his hatred for an evil institution to triumph over his reason; but amid the revilings of those fanatics who have plunged us into ruin, he boldly declared, "My paramount object is to save the Union, and not either save or destroy Slavery. What I do about Slavery and the colored race I do because I believe it helps to save the Union, and what I forbear, I forbear because I do not believe it would help to save the Union." And at that time when even among our Northern men conflicting opinions prevailed; when 50,000 of our troops were from the border slaves States; when the salvation of the Union demanded the earnest and unqualified support of every loyal citizen - at that time a policy less broad, a course less statesmanlike, a rallying cry less comprehensive, would have plunged us into irretrievable disaster and ruin. And I ask—and I voice the sentiments of men than whom there are none greater in this nation, than whom there are none more loyal — I ask if in 1856 the Garrisons, and the Phillipses of the North, and the Davises, and the Toombses of the South, had been replaced by men with the sagacity of Abraham Lincoln; if we had used more policy in our treatment of an institution morally wrong yet legally recognized; if we had considered all the interests of this nation — should we not have secured the emancipation of the negro without the cost of five billions of treasure, without devastating and beggaring one-half of our fair land, without the sacrifice of six hundred thousand human lives, without twenty-five years of sectional strife, without plunging the negro into a condition of political servitude more oppressive, if possible, than his former state?

There doubtless is a place in the world for radical reformers, and without question they perform a grand work by arousing to activity the public mind. But victory has rarely perched on their banners and their watchword has too often been changed from "principle" to "intolerance." The sands of time are red with the blood of their slaughtered victims; yet the result of their warfare has been extermination, not peace.

The *conservative* men are the doers of the world. What reformers could bring about by violence and revolution they accomplish by natural means. It is time to denounce the fanatical slander which is cast upon them. Malicious attack may dim the splendor of their successes, but it cannot effect the record of their achievements. Their eulogy is engraved on the imperishable tablets of time. As long as civilization advances, as long as Liberty endures, their fame is secure. And if in the dim ages of the future their forces ever should be outnumbered, and the legions of wreck and ruin run riot, the tradition of a former civilization will yet remain a glorious monument to the memory of conservative men.

# MOB AND LAW.

### By H. H. Russell, of Oberlin College.

## BIOGRAPHICAL.

Howard H. Russell is a typical westerner, full of push, pluck and energy. He was born in Minnesota, in 1855, but spent the greater part of his life in Iowa. He prepared himself for college in Griswold Institution, Davenport, Iowa, where his father was a professor. In 1875 he began the study of law, and graduated at the Des Moines Law School in 1878. For six years he was an active and successful practitioner, and won for himself a name and place as one of the most promising young men at the Iowa bar. In 1880 Mr. Russell was happily married to Miss Lillian Davis, of Corning, Iowa, a daughter of the senior partner of his law firm, and a woman of singular sweetness and beauty of character, and to her is due more than to any other human agency the turning points in his life, for in 1883 he became an active and earnest Christian worker rather than a successful man of the world. He spent the next five years in Oberlin College, Oberlin, Ohio. In addition to pursuing his collegiate and theological studies he carried on successful pastorates at North Amherst and Berea, Ohio. Upon his graduation at Oberlin in 1888, he was invited by the Congregational Union of Kansas City, Missouri, to establish a city mission enterprise, and immediately began work in a large tent in Southwest Kansas City. His organizing talent, personal magnetism, and winning manners, his sympathy and interest in the masses, are attested by the phenomenal growth of the Southwest Tabernacle Church. In less than three years he built up a strong, aggressive young church in the face of many obstacles. Mr. Russell has recently accepted a call to the Armour Mission in Chicago, the largest and most important city evangelistic enterprise in the West. He is a leader of men and a force in whatever community he resides. Following is his excellent oration.

## THE ORATION.

Delivered at the Inter-State Oratorical Contest, Lawrence, Kansas, May, 1886, taking second prize. Judges: Pres. J. B. ANGELL, Judge J. B. CASSODAY, Hon. J. K. NASH, Hon. EUGENE WARE, Rev. Dr. THOMPSON, Hon. T. D. THACHER.

The scene is in a manufacturing city. Five thousand strikers have gathered to discuss their wrongs. They have been out of the shops more than a week. Yesterday they forced their way into a factory, stopped the engines, and drove out the men who were still at work. To-day they made a riotous assault upon a mill, but were repulsed by the police. To-night they come with scowling faces and vindictive threats to listen to the incendiary doctrines of socialism. A professional anarchist, summoned from a distant city, feeds the flames of malice by the following harangue:

[ANARCHIST.] "Comrades— I rejoice with you to-night that the hosts of degraded toil are mustering for war. We battle for the destruction of the system of wage-slaving. It is a fight for liberty, a fight for wife and child, a fight for bread. What is this monstrous wrong that in a land of gold dispenses lavish favors to the lazy few, and binds the millions of honest toilers with chains of penury and want? It is the curse of Private Property. Property is theft, because it enables him who has not produced to consume the fruits of other people's toil.

"In the past twenty years the wealth of this country has increased over twenty billions of dollars; every cent derived from the labor of the working class. Into whose hands has this wealth found its way? Have you any of it? ('No,' says a voice in the crowd, 'but we helped to produce it.') I'll tell you where it is. In the three cities, New York, Boston, and Philadelphia, are twenty men who hold, as private property, over $750,000,000. In twenty years these aristocratic pickpockets have fleeced the people of that enormous sum, and only three cities and twenty robbers heard from. This is why, in a land of plenty, tramps and starvelings multiply their dismal hordes. This is the glorious land of millionaires and tramps. Your wages are reduced to the starvation point, and you are told the trouble is over-production. You produce too many shoes, therefore you must go barefooted. You produce too much clothing, therefore you must go naked. You produce too much grain, therefore you must starve. Men of toil, how long will you basely cringe, while the lash of avarice lays welts upon your backs? Do not hope for relief from the government. The law-givers are the hired hands of the property-class. They make laws only for Goulds and Vanderbilts. Then capital goes to court and buys judge and jury. The whole machinery of law is geared for oppression. The government must be overthrown. Anarchy, the only law of liberty, must take its place.

"Comrades, the time for revolution has come. Our weapons —torch, pistol, dynamite. Assert your rights at once, or you are cowards. Look at these great factories and massive blocks. Capital has stolen them from you. See the gilded palaces of luxury. You have built them for idlers, while your own families are houseless. Lift up your starving children. Let them look upon the tables of the rich heaped with viands snatched from their hungry mouths. Go forth to-night; take back your stolen property. If you set afire the dwelling of the capitalist, or blow up his mill or factory, no matter; it is yours. You have earned it; he has taken it from you. You have the right to burn what is your own. And if you chance to take a life or two, no matter; it is not murder to kill the pirate or the highway robber. In his greed he kills those dear to you. You strike for your rights. Your wife and children go cold and hungry. Sickness follows. No money for medicine or doctor. And so death comes. I knew such a man; only yesterday for lack of money to hire the hearse he carried the rough coffin of his murdered child upon his shoulder to the grave; and on the street he met his heartless employer, with liveried lackeys, riding at his ease. Workingmen, awake! Away with such infamy! The tocsin of war has sounded—death to the capitalist! (A voice: 'Down with the millionaires! Kill them to a man!') Let robbers and pirates meet the fate they deserve—death. Come up from the hovels of serfs, and take the torch for vengeance! Come out of the treadmills of despair, and sweep your slave drivers to destruction! Burn and kill! Hurl the plundering syndicate of capital to perdition!

'To arms, to arms, ye brave! The avenging sword unsheathe!
March on, march on, all hearts resolved on liberty or death.'

"The red flag points the way. Fall in with your thousands, shoulder to shoulder. We have nothing to lose but our shackles; we have a world to win! Forward! Liberty or death!"

Who can depict the terrors of an angry mob, lashed into madness by the tongue of hate? The profane howl of pandemonium rises on the affrighted air. Blood-red eyes are glaring with rage. Dirk-knives and pistols flash. Great clubs are swung aloft in grimy hands. A brawling, bloodthirsty mob waiting only a signal of the red ensign of blood to surge forth to burn and kill.

It is the hour for a hero.

There are moments when the weal or woe of many homes, when the safety of the nation hangs on the word and action of one brave man. Such a moment is this. There is a movement in the crowd, and there comes forth a man of giant frame. A working-man, and yet 't is plain to see a man who thinks. In hours of respite from his furnace forge he has studied the burning problems of the age. He is a man of conscience, with cool brain, clear eye, steady nerve. He is well known among his fellows. As he bares his brow to speak, the clubs are lowered and the knives are sheathed; the curse half muttered dies away, and intense silence rests upon the multitude as he thus addresses them:

[WORKINGMAN.] "I do not come before you to enlarge the story of our wrongs. That we are victims of an unjust social system has been ably shown. It is a fact that the idle few amass great fortunes by the strain of muscle and sweat of brow of other men. It is true that we who produce the wealth are not permitted to enjoy its fruits. All this is more than plain.

"Let us look this matter in the face. We have been wronged. Is that any reason why we should rush into destruction? We seek justice for our homes. Shall we gain our end by making widows and orphans of our wives and children? We have come to-night, men, where the ways divide. The question is: Which way does wisdom lead? Will you at the bidding of a stranger turn yourselves into a pack of thieves and murderers? Or shall we seek redress by lawful means?

"This movement to secure living wages began last week. We protested against reduction. This was right. We struck. This was our privilege. We persuaded other men to join us in the strike. This was lawful. At that time we had the sympathy of almost the entire city. But when violent hands were laid upon those who refused to strike, and some attempted to destroy the mill to secure our ends, we lost the good-will and gained the condemnation of our friends. Shall we make another and more fatal blunder? Has labor ever won success by its defiance of the State? What do Pittsburg, Chicago, and the Hocking Valley teach? What has always been the cost of violence? Millions of gold and torrents of blood. What the result? Failure. Shall we plunge again into this crimson sea of blood and fire?

"This vigorous orator, who makes speeches but never marches with the crowd, has tried to spur you to action by calling you cowards if you refuse to break the laws and put your lives in peril. 'T is always braver to do right than wrong. In this case, it is safer, too. I heard once of a shrewd Yankee who refused to fight a duel. His friends said he would be called a coward, and this was his reply: 'I would rather be called a coward all my life than be a corpse for five minutes.' ('His head was level,' exclaims a man in front, and applause resounds in all directions.) No, brothers, let us not stain our hands with blood; let us commit no deeds of violence, and public opinion will again call for our rights.

"Who is it talks to-night of anarchy and treason? Who counsels robbery and murder? An exile from his own country, for his country's good. A hireling, just as ready to start a strike at capital's request as to help the cause of labor. A blatant instigator who orders the red flag forward, then skulks in safety while his poor dupes rush madly on to ruin. Will you choose his counsel? I tell you that for turning wrong to right this is the best government in all the world. It is left for you and me to pass what laws we please. Eighty per cent. of all the voters are workingmen. Look at the lawful rights already gained for labor: Imprisonment for debt abolished; the common school established; the homestead granted free of cost; a mechanic's lien to secure our pay; our homes exempt from penalty for debt. These are but a fraction of the poor man's rights. The humane laws we have are pledges for the future. They guarantee a peaceful settlement of our strife with capital.

"Let us, then, stand united in this strife; but let us also be firm as the rock in support of the laws of our land. Let us be true to our manhood, our homes, and the State. Let us seek relief, not with the bullet but the ballot. Not revolution but arbitration be our watchword, and the air will yet ring with cheers of victory!"

The hush in the assembly, the sobered looks upon the faces of those rough men, show that the manly words of their fellow-toiler have won the full assent of their better judgment. Quietly by twos and threes they disperse to their homes.

What is the lesson, my friends, taught by scenes like this? These are serious times. Days of riot, plunder, torch, and murder. In February, London pillaged; in March, Belgium drenched with blood; in April, our own Fort Worth and East St. Louis ravaged by death and terror. Flower-crowned May has come, and to-night the hospitals of Chicago are filled with the dying victims of anarchy. What is the duty of the hour? Manifestly this: Obedience to the law must be enforced; peace and order must be maintained. If need be let the bugles blow, and a million men be mustered into line. Dislodge the law-breaker whether he hides behind bludgeons or money-bags. While statesmen and philanthropists are hastening toward a better social system, capital and labor both must stand submissive to such statutes as we have. Law, though imperfect, must be supreme.

In Cuba, in 1867, an American citizen was wrongfully arrested by the Spanish authorities and condemned to die. He was led out to be shot. As he sat on his coffin waiting for the volley, the American Consul, hastily alighting from his carriage, wrapped around him the stars and stripes. "Fire upon that flag if you dare!" he said. They dared not fire, and his life was saved. Round the rights of labor and the rights of capital an invincible government has wrapped the sacred mantle of protecting law. If the hand of avarice dare assault the one or the torch of malice the other, let retribution fall swift and dreadful as the thunderbolt.

Thus shall be ushered in that better day, in whose kindly light shall thrive not greed but right, not *Mob* but *Law*.

# JOHN BROWN.

By J. H. FINLEY, of Knox College.

### BIOGRAPHICAL.

John Huston Findley was born at Grand Ridge, Illinois. He was a graduate from Ottawa Illinois High School, June, 1881, and valedictorian of his class. He then remained out of school the following two years, at the end of which period he entered Knox College, Galesburg, Illinois, and graduated from this institution, June, 1887. He received the essay prize in his freshman year on the subject, "The Jew in Modern Politics;" and won the oratorical prizes at Knox College contest, the inter-collegiate contest, and the inter-State contest. The title of his production on these three occasions was "John Brown," and it was a very vivid and earnest appeal for a little kind feeling for the memory of poor John Brown. As soon as the telegram announcing Mr. Finley's victory was received the bells of Galesburg rang out in quick succession, and it is stated how a bold "prep" broke through the doors, and crawled through the dark passages to the college roof, broke a piece from the old bell with an axe, so drunk was he with glee. At the reception and banquet tendered Mr. Finley, a beautiful memento of the occasion presented was a piece of metal finely polished, laid in in a plush case, bearing the inscription, "Knox College Bell. Broken for Finley, May 5, 1887." In the fall of 1887 he entered upon the post-graduate course of Johns Hopkins University, Baltimore, Maryland, remaining in this institution until February, 1889, when he accepted the position of secretary of the New York State Charities Aid Association, which position he fills with entire satisfaction. In June, 1890, on invitation, he delivered the master's oration on the subject, "A New Science." Mr. Finley is a young man about twenty-five years old, and for so young a man he has made an excellent showing.

## THE ORATION.

Delivered at the Inter-State Oratorical Contest, at Bloomington, Illinois, May, 1887, taking first prize. Judges: Hon. PITMAN SMITH, Hon. JOHNSON BRIGHAM, Hon. J. H. ROWELL, Gov. J. B. FORAKER, Rev. PHILIP BROOKS, Senator J. R. HAWLEY.

Far up the wooded slope of one of the Adirondacks there is a lone grave. It is marked by no tall monument, and but for its very remoteness and seclusion there in the wildness of those enchanted hills, it might be passed unnoticed. An old mossy tombstone resting against a huge rock marks it. There are several inscriptions upon the stone. One faintly records the death of a Revolutionary patriot. Beneath it another, a strange companion for the former, reads: "John Brown, executed at Charlestown, Va., December 2d, 1859." At these words the bleak and cold Adirondacks vanish. The summits of the Blue Ridge appear in the distance. The Shenandoah winds dreamily through its fertile valley. Northward the heights along the Potomac are seen; and nearer, the village of Charlestown. And see! beyond the village spires a gibbet arises against the blue sky, and from the gloomy prison an old man with flowing beard and hoary head, like a prophet of old, is led out to die — John Brown, the traitor or the patriot, the murderer or the martyr — which?

One generation makes history, the next records it. It is ours to collect the memorials of our Civil War. Every hamlet cherishes them; every city builds them in marble or bronze, but more universal than these is that dearer memorial of the heart which enshrines the heroes of that war. Time will erase all these, and the coming centuries will know but two characters as representatives of this period — Lincoln the Emancipator, and Grant the Soldier. Yet there is another, who, from his peculiar part in the struggle, cannot be soon forgotten — the grim, gray herald of the conflict. Before him we pause in doubt. His only monument is a gibbet, his epitaph, "traitor;" yet we seem to hear the war-cry of the Union armies marching to victory, led by that soul whose body lay moldering on the distant mountain.

The striking singularity of his life has made its outlines familiar. It seems taken from the chronicles of another page. It has no counterpart in American history. An old man, Brown left his wild home on the Adirondacks to take part in the slavery struggle in Kansas. Impatient of the peaceful submission of the Free-State settlers, he at once resisted the depredations and outrages of the pro-slavery men, and began retaliatory measures. With a small band of men, among them his sons, he committed that deed known as the Pottawatomie murders, dragging from their homes at midnight five unarmed pro-slavery men and killing them in cold blood. In the border warfare thus begun he took so prominent a part that the very name of "Old John Brown" was a source of terror to his enemies. When the struggle ended, he left Kansas and conveyed a number of slaves from Missouri to Canada. A few months later he made his startling appearance at Harper's Ferry; seized the national arsenal, held it for two days. Finally captured, he was tried, convicted, hanged.

Such is the brief story of his life as the world knows it; yet little of the man is revealed in these bare facts. Lives are measured by motives and results. His life was noble or base, great or insignificant, according as the motives inspiring it were noble or base, the influence exerted by it great or mean.

Many judge him wholly by these facts. To them his deeds are the plottings of a heart burning for revenge. He entered Kansas to avenge the wrongs of his sons, to fight Missouri, to incite war between the North and South. Urged by his blind insanity and frenzied hate he made the foolish and criminal attack upon Harper's Ferry, and was rightly adjudged murderer, insurrectionist, traitor. True, in the midst of his murderous deeds he avowedly sought the freedom of the slave. But assassins of presidents have pleaded the good of the country; and the anarchist, as he hurls his bomb, shouts for the liberty of the oppressed. Is Brown, then, for this the less a traitor, the more a patriot? If a crazed fanatic, under the pretext of a worthy end, may thus take the law into his own hands and execute it after his own insane idea, where is our protection against the outlaw and the mob? We were at that time in a critical position. But for this mad act the sectional chasm, by a few more delicately arranged compromises, would have been successfully bridged, thousands of lives and millions of dollars saved, and slavery quietly and peacefully removed. Others hold that his influence in bringing on the war was infinitesimal. Like other fanatics, he leaped beyond the defensive ramparts of common prudence, and falling, the conservative, the sensible men, were left to defend the principle and secure the object for which he foolishly and futilely became a martyr.

If, then, we measure his deeds by the standard of human law; if we view his life in its rugged exterior alone; if we estimate his influence by the unsuccessful end of his designs his character must be denounced, his life be termed a failure, and his whole public career be utterly condemned.

As great worlds course nightly through the skies unseen do they not reflect the light of a hidden sun? So the life of John Brown would long since have gone out in darkness did it not shine with the light of eternal right and moral heroism. The purpose which inspired his life was the emancipation of the slave, and behind that purpose was compassion for the oppressed — a purpose born of the "Puritan idea" of freedom and justice, by his direct descent. Note the steps: His ancestors fled from Europe to America for individual liberty; his grandfather died in the war of the Revolution for the liberty of his countrymen; he was executed for the liberty of a despised race.

With a Puritan sternness he had more than a Puritan tenderness. See him as he sits watching through the long winter night by the bedside of that sick child. Note the kindness with which he always treated his prisoners; the gentleness with which, when on trial, he met the curses of his foes, the rebukes of his friends; or see him as on his way to the gallows he stoops to kiss that negro child. Can you believe that revenge could live in that heart? Ah! no. It was the wail of a race in bondage ever ringing in his soul that led him on.

The black night of Pottawatomie is past. Through the trees that border the creek the morning sun shines upon the mutilated and bloody faces of five stark bodies. Where is the murderer? A short distance up the stream in the cover of the forest a little band of roughly clad men are seated around a rude table. They are silent as one of their number, an old man with long, white beard, in low broken tones asks a morning blessing. There are blood stains on his folded hands. What a scene is this! Hypocrite? No. Here is the true man consistent with himself. He saw that dark deed necessary, and he did it. Without the shedding of blood there was no remission of this sin. Slavery was not to be talked, preached, or educated out of existence. Men had talked, but the slave ships only increased their loads. The slave territory was widening. With Kansas, more would be seized. What other means would answer? "Providence," said he, "has made me an actor, and slavery an outlaw." He took the law into his own hands, but for no personal interest. He struck, during a national crisis, upon the solid ground of real principle, in a cause not personal, not local, not even national, but human.

Fanatic, madman, fool, if you please; such have been the world's great reformers — men who stake their lives on a principle. "Wise men argue questions; fools decide them." Our legislators had discussed and enacted compromises for forty years. They had now removed that old landmark — the Missouri Compromise — and the western territory, once secure, was again with the reach of slavery. With the foresight of a statesman, Brown saw, and said, that slavery and the Union could not exist together; but wiser and more truly patriotic than the statesman who cried, "The Union, slavery or no slavery," he said, "Down with slavery." Upon that conviction he raised his arm in Kansas. The ruffians halted; the Free-State men took courage; the territory was won for freedom.

We are not surprised, then, to find him in that last heroic scene of his life, daring, with a handful of men, to meet a nation; facing an ignominious death, and, what is worse, an all but universal execration for a race which had no rights white men were bound to respect. Mad as his attempt may appear, it has glorious parallels in history. Leonidas at Thermopylæ, Schamyl on the borders of Russia, Toussaint L'Ouverture in St. Domingo, failed as did he. Had we stood beside him in Charlestown prison on the evening of his capture, we might have said, "Yes, he failed;" but to-day we say, "He did not fail." His death made all men either the friends or foes of slavery. Between the North and the South stood John Brown's gibbet. Henceforth it was slavery or Union. Compromise was no longer possible. Had he succeeded, he must have failed. His failure was his success.

"For humanity sweeps onward; where to-day the martyr stands
On the morrow crouches Judas with the silver in his hands;
Far in front the cross stands ready and the crackling fagots burn,
While the hooting mob of yesterday in silent awe return
To glean up the scattered ashes into History's golden urn."

Fearlessly, heroically, he met his fate. Hear him as he stands before the Virginia court to say why sentence should not be pronounced upon him: "I see a book kissed here which I suppose to be the Bible. That book teaches me that all things 'whatsoever I would that men should do unto me I should do even so to them.' I have endeavored to act upon that instruction. I believe that to have interfered as I have in behalf of His despised poor was not wrong, but right. Had I so interfered in behalf of the rich, the powerful, the so-called great, every man in this court would have deemed it an act worthy of reward rather than punishment. Now, if it is judged necessary that I should forfeit my life for the furtherance of the ends of justice, and mingle my blood further with the blood of my children and with the blood of millions in this slave country whose rights are disregarded by wicked and unjust enactments, I submit." Byron dying amid the marshes of Missolonghi, La Fayette bleeding at Brandywine, and shall I say Washington at Valley Forge, showed not such disinterested bravery, such generous devotion. Traitor? Then were the brave who fell at Lexington traitors. They taught us this, "that we may resist with arms a law which violates the principles of natural justice." Emmet did it in Ireland; Wallace, in Scotland; Garibaldi, in Italy, and we honor them; John Brown did it in America, the land of the free, and we hanged him.

Is this his fitting and final reward? The soaring shaft that stands by Potomac's stream answers, No. The monuments, which a grateful people have erected to the memory of those who died for the slave, say, No. The gratitude of millions freed from bondage says, No. And the day will come when even the mountains of Virginia will echo back the answer, No.

# THE MAN AND THE STATE.

By PARKE DANIELS, of Wabash College.

### BIOGRAPHICAL.

Parke Daniels was born in Rockville, Parke County, Indiana, on the 4th day of October, 1865. He was graduated from the Rockville public schools in May, 1882, and on the 16th of the following September entered the senior department of the preparatory school of Wabash College, Crawfordsville, Indiana, graduating at the close of the year with the honor of first-prize man in declamation. In the fall of 1883 he entered college proper, and soon developed a strong liking for the work of the literary society. He soon took rank as a debater, and throughout his college course maintained the reputation of being a superior writer and speaker. His share of honors won in college for excellence with the pen and on the platform was large. As the representative of his college in the State oratorical contest he won the privilege of representing the "Hoosier State" in the inter-State contest. His style of delivery was said to be easy and effective, receiving the highest mark of the nine discourses. It is impartial to add that but for the marking on thought by Governor Foraker he would have taken first prize. How strange that Mr. Daniels should have written so much democracy in his speech being an earnest Republican. In later years he has won a good reputation as a political speaker. In September, 1887, he entered the law office of McDonald, Butler & Snow, Indianapolis, as student and clerk, which position he held over three years. Business has called Mr. Daniels into the South, and he is now temporarily located in Mississippi as superintendent of manufacturing. It is his purpose, however, soon to return to the law, in which profession he is destined to be successful.

## THE ORATION.

Delivered at the Inter-State Oratorical Contest, at Bloomington, Illinois, May, 1887, taking second prize. Judges: Hon. PITMAN SMITH, Hon. JOHNSON BRIGHAM, Hon. J. H. ROWELL, Gov. J. B. FORAKER, Rev. PHILIP BROOKS, Senator J. R. HAWLEY.

"The worth of a State, in the long run," wrote John Stuart Mill, "is the worth of the individuals composing it." "We put too much faith in systems and look too little to men," was the opinion of Lord Beaconsfield; and a late German writer of our century holds it to be an unhealthy state of affairs "when the man is sacrificed to the citizen."

In these varying phases is found the expression of a hidden half-truth that has been the battle-ground of the ages. Men have been slow to learn and declare the fact of their intrinsic superiority over States. While the few may have recognized the true sovereignty — the individual man — it has been the superstition of the many to accept the principle of State omnipotence and bend the knee to the efficacy of law.

This form of superstition is not a thing entirely of the past. During the period of our country's life it has experienced an emphatic decay and a pronounced revival as well. Amid the scenes that marked the dawn of the nineteenth century, that epoch memorable in the history of liberty as the birth-period of the "common man," the old belief that States could do all and should be all went down, but could not be forgotten. Once more, to-day, the tide of political thought is setting back toward the idea of a "paternal" policy of government. A century of free thought and free discussion has bred among the rank and file a high degree of political self-consciousness. The people are rising to a knowledge of their power as law-makers and rulers, and demand a trial of their own law. The "labor candidate" is abroad in the land; the "farmer candidate" is formidable, and the liquor interests, alas! so unprotected in our day and generation, are clamoring for protection in their "rights." Every class, every section, every interest, is demanding recognition and legislation. Thus is democracy put upon its test. Many ask, "Will it endure?" Wherefore returns the old superstition, firm, enduring throughout the ages, to urge as the only safeguard of democratic institutions — *the wide extension of State control.*

It is suggested that our modern civilization, rapidly advancing, intensely practical in its character, bringing in its deep complication the most minute divisions of labor, demands not less but more government. In the marvelous achievements of private enterprise are seen monopoly and oppression. On all sides arise the evidences of a vast disproportion existing between the different parts of our social structure. While one passes his life in an atmosphere of poverty and destitution, not daring to claim one foot of the earth which God has made for all men, another enjoys wealth and luxury and comfort; he has acres numbered by thousands—he is lord paramount; the other is vassal.

All this we know to be radically wrong. Though poverty's lament is the threadbare theme of the ages, we cannot close our eyes and hearts to the cause of humanity—

> "Nor hear with a disdainful smile
> The short and simple annals of the poor."

But whence and how shall the remedy come? Manifestly it must come from society which owes it. But through what agency shall society apply its remedy? Once more the answer is caught up, resurrected from the tomb of heathen civilization: "By the intervention of that power through which alone society as an abstract personality can act—the State. Let the State abolish the right of property in land. Let the State buy and control the railroad and the telegraph. Suppress the middle-men who stand between production and consumption. Let the State be banker, merchant, landlord, teacher, parent, to us all for our mighty civilization demands a form of government which shall be more responsible to the individual for his welfare, and more potent to satisfy his ever-increasing desires."

Thus reasoning we are enabled to establish and verify a theory of government which is well called "paternalism." Plausible, indeed, are these arguments, but are they adequate? Do they comprehend in their scope the matter of price that must be paid the State for its services? Do they cover the phase of the question that is not seen as well as the phase that is seen? Look just beyond this frost-work of theory. Is it an exalted standard of individual character, a free and vigorous people, an advancing civilization, that you see? Not so. Rather it is likely that amid a grand confusion of princip!es and privileges you will see national degeneracy and individual dependency—a tyrant, as it were, sitting upon a throne; it is the rule of despotism most terrible, and through and in it all you read the motto of a departed civilization: "Men made only for the State."

But is the man made for the State? The chief sophism of the ancient law-giver, and of the modern theorist as well, consists in confounding the idea of society with the idea of the State, by attributing to these organisms the same end and destiny. Were the hypothesis true the action of the State might be extended illimitably. But it is false. Society is a grand aggregate of human character, a federation of men, "veritable beings endowed with immortality," who "have a different destiny from that of States." The social pulse throbs with the energy of individual life. Social forces are dynamical and active; government is all mechanical, inert, passive. Government has no being, it is but form, and perishable. States and governments are born but to die. And yet, as mankind moves onward in the march of civilization, keeping time with the everlasting refrain of "freedom," the heavy ordnance of government must lumber on as well; its forms must yield to that "increasing purpose," which through the ages runs—there must be improvement in the sphere of authority. And there has been progress here. How is it shown. One machine is better than another of the same kind, because it better accomplishes the purpose for which both were made. One form of government surpasses another only in so far as it conforms more perfectly to the idea of personal rights, and gives better expression to the individual citizen's worth. Men speak of the "paternal care," and "solicitude" of the State and of the "benefits of government." These are false and delusive phrases. What more is the State that an index of sheer power? "Government began in tyranny and force," and has continued in that character from the dawn of society to the present time—a conservative, restraining influence. What power has given to the past what of beauty and good and worth it contains? Not the State. What power sends the spirit of energy and industry and life coursing through the great arteries of the present? What power is building the structure of civilization ever and to-day? Not the State, but the man; the unit is doing all this. It is the character of the State to stand as a grim sentinel on every path of achievement, challenging all innovation, impeding all progress. It speaks the words of ill-omen and death, "Thus far and no farther shalt thou go." But the individual says, "I am free; I am progressive; I will climb loftier heights of achievement." And thus it is by the force and energy of individual character that the world is pushed along.

The State is made for the man. The question which nations must answer, and answer for their weal or woe, is: Where shall State function stop and individual action begin?

Says one, "the State is the moral being organized in society for the preservation of rights and justice." The immediate function of government is protection, the spirit of all its laws should be justice. But government is not bound, in duty or obligation, to secure to the individual his due measure of happiness. The chief obstacle which stands between the desire for happiness and its attainment is not the fact of the interference of other men, but the frailty of human nature. When, therefore, we say that because it is the function of government to protect men in their rights, it should secure to them that measure of happiness they are entitled to enjoy, we must say that government should protect men against their own greed, their own lust, their own improvidence; in a word, that government should protect men against themselves. Such a theory is false in conception and would be fatal in practice. Man has free will, and he has the right to liberty, higher and antecedent to that of happiness. Underlying the structure of society is the law of equal freedom. Every man has the right, God-given and supreme, to the fullest exercise of all his powers compatible with the same right in others. To secure this right, to enforce this law, is the first and supreme function of government. Let the State over-step this line of duty and it is apt to become, no longer a protector, but an aggressor. Rightly enough the State is clothed with certain duties pertinent to the general welfare and the conduct of public business. It carries the mail, it educates the poor, it wields the strong arm of the "police power" preserving order, protecting life, health, and social comfort. But it will not do to say that because the State does all these things well it can and should do more. Whither does this process of reasoning tend? Read the answer in the experience of nations. Turn to the Europe of to-day. What nations are the freest, yet withal, the most enterprising and happy? They are those whose laws encroach least upon the domain of personal activity; where individuality has the broadest scope where the power of the government is least felt.

Take France. Her history is a history of bloodshed and revolution; but at last France uplifts her head among the proudest and freest nations of the earth, to declare with them the great truth, that "within limits of right all human transactions should flow from the voluntary action of man."

But how stands the case in Germany, the land of Luther and Schiller. Germany leads the world in learned thought; her armament is unsurpassed, here government is strong and pure, but above all it is "paternal," and concealed in that element of paternalism is one of the most arrant despotisms that exist in all Europe or the world. How fares the cause of liberty there? What of the German citizen? A veritable slave, so firmly held within the restraints of the law that he has become a mere chattel in the hands of an iron-willed prince. And it is well that Bismarck should now draw tighter the bands of the law, thereby to increase the power and fortify the strength of the German Empire; for if the time ever comes, and it may be near at hand, when again the war-cry of France shall ring out for him to hear, his armament must needs be strong to avail against the storm that will follow. When again the inspiring strains of the Marseillaise shall echo among the vine-clad hills and across the waters of the German Rhine let Prince Bismarck beware, for he will be destined to meet an army of *men*, strong in the spirit of freedom, and imbued with that true love of country which is born alone of a free government and whose power is well-nigh invincible.

But go elsewhere. Search the history of the far past or scan the horizon of the contemporary world. Wherever there is a paternal government, one that assumes to discharge those functions which by the laws of nature are assigned to the sphere of personal effort, there will be found a degenerating people, a stagnant civilization. It is the sternest teaching of all history that a paternal government cannot but degrade the manhood and dwarf in its development the character of the people it rules.

As far as may be practicable let the people care for themselves. Such is the verdict of experience. It is not to the principle of paternalism that we must look for the protection and perpetuity of democratic institutions, nor yet to the opposite and equally dangerous extreme of individualism. Between these opposing principles lies the vantage ground of American politics. Upon the wholesome mean rests the solvent of hostile ideas, and out of it grows the scheme of our political salvation. Self-help generates stability; personal responsibility begets manhood. The American people are, above all else, thoroughly individualized, thoroughly independent, and wholly capable of governing themselves. What has brought about this result? It is the principle of individual responsibility, in the family, in the community, in the State and nation; it is this idea, put into practice, that has brought to the history of the American people a halo of glory; and it is this idea, handed down to us in the memory of Lexington and Valley Forge, enshrined in the immortal deeds of those who fought away their lives that men might enjoy it—this must be our rock, the hope of our future.

Yet, there is withal a charm that lingers about the ideal of strong government. It is natural for men to echo in their hearts the poet's longing:

> "Oh for a man with head, heart, hand,
> One strong, still man in a blatant land,
> Aristocrat, autocrat, democrat—one,
> Who can rule and dare not lie."

But may this blind worship of government die out from the hearts of men, until it be lost in the fervid glory of a new and better *regime*. Away with the belief that the State can make us "o'er all the ills of life victorious." Let reformer and statesman alike reject the principle of State omnipotence and strive to imbue the individual man with a consciousness of his own power; and when both shall be actuated, not by greed of gain or glory, but by that broad and wise philanthropy which is grounded in common sense and which rises above sentimentality, then will right relations exist between the man and the State; liberty and authority will meet on common ground, recognizing their union in a common cause—that cause the exaltation of human character, for this is "the end of Nature, to reach unto the coronation of her king."

# PRINCIPLES OF POLITICAL PARTIES.

By R. G. Johnson, of DePauw University.

### BIOGRAPHICAL.

Robert Grant Johnson, winner of the inter-State oratorical contest, at Greencastle, Indiana, in 1888, was born near Crawfordsville, Indiana, in 1865. His parents belong to the thrifty farming class of this State. In the district school where Mr. Johnson acquired his early education he was particularly distinguished by studious habits and a remarkable faculty of memorizing. He was always a favorite at the Friday "dress parades" in the school-room, and at school exhibitions. He took great interest in history and books of travel, and at an early age was master of Dickens's Child's History of England. At the age of sixteen he became restless and dissatisfied with the farm. While toiling under the hot sun in the fields his mind was off to the city dwelling upon other vocations. His cousins from college came to visit him, and he began to form ideas of college life, and finally told his father of his determination to leave the farm. Being an only son of sensible parents he met with the most substantial encouragement. In the fall of 1883 Mr. Johnson entered DePauw University, at Greencastle, and showed his capacity by making two years of preparatory work in one. In his freshman year he became a member of the Delta Kappa Epsilon College fraternity, in which he took an active part; he also turned his attention to speaking, winning the first prize in declamation over the sophomores and juniors, and was thenceforward recognized as a formidable contestant and debater. Gifted with a voice of remarkable richness and strength, which he assiduously cultivated, an earnest and direct style of speaking, he always made a good impression. At the inter-State contest Mr. Johnson delivered a speech on "Principles of Political Parties," which was peculiarly adapted

to the political outlook of Indiana at that time. After graduating he engaged in the campaign of 1888, making speeches for the Republican party, with marked success. As soon as election was over he went to Chicago, and found employment as a newspaper reporter, but in a few months entered the law office of Sheldon & Sheldon. In the fall of 1889 he entered the senior class of the Chicago College of Law, graduating in June, winning the first prize of fifty dollars for the best essay. He is now admitted to the bar, and holds the position of managing clerk for Sheldon & Sheldon.

## THE ORATION.

Delivered at the Inter-State Oratorical Contest, at Greencastle, Indiana, May, 1888, taking first prize. Judges: Gov. J. B. FORAKER, Judge FRAKE, Rev. STEWART, Prof. WAREY, Messrs. WINSTEIN and MITCHENER.

### ANALYSIS.

I. Logical ground for existence of parties.
II. Necessity of two parties.
III. Derivation of principles underlying political parties.
IV. The principles traced in political history.
V. Outcome of attempts of independent parties, based upon narrow issues, to subvert dominant parties, e. g., Abolition, Free-soil, etc., Labor, Socialistic, and Prohibition parties considered.
VI. Errors of third partyism.
VII. Power of public sentiment to secure reform through existing parties.
VIII. Conclusion.

We live under a government of majorities. Through party organization alone can the will of the majority be ascertained. If there were no parties, no principles enunciated, no tickets nominated, each citizen must write his own ballot, and, from the multiplicity of interests, the conflict of desires, endless confusion would result. Parties represent ideas, convictions, concerning the rights of men in government. To secure majorities parties must be organized upon the broadest political principles. As the principle is narrowed the number of followers is correspondingly decreased. Parties representing narrow issues can no more secure majorities than can a religious denomination representing details in worship include a majority of Christians. Without organization upon the broadest principles majorities are impossible. Two fundamental principles give two parties.

Whence are these principles derived? They are found in the universal law of action and reaction. This law exists in the nature of all matter, of all force. Consider a shooting star, a sweeping hurricane, a political revolution, a religious reformation: they are but manifestations of an universal conflict between two forces — one tending to produce change, the other to resist it. Progress, social or political, is the resultant of this conflict. This law, inherent in mind and matter, divides men into radicals and conservatives, and upon this division are established political parties around whose principles the people gather and cluster as bits of steel about the poles of a magnet. What is all political history but the record of the action and reaction of radical and conservative ideas crystalized about contending principles of government.

The conflict has always been between the ideas of strong central and local self-government — a constant struggle to maintain an equilibrium of these forces. The dagger of Brutus sought not so much to stab the body of Cæsar as to destroy the tendency toward centralization. The ruins of rich cities upon the Rhine stand solemn monuments of the reaction against that declaration of absolutism, "I am the State." In Russia, in Austria, in Germany, this conflict prevails. The last seven centuries of Irish history is but a desperate struggle between these same antagonistic forces. The principles of the Whig party in England, "that all positive institutions exist for the general good," stood arrayed against the Tory principle of "the divine right of kings." It flamed like the motto of Constantine, an inspiration to the Commons; it fired with dauntless courage Hampden and Pym and Cromwell and Milton. Constantly resisted by the conservative idea that "the king can do no wrong," it steadily gained the vantage ground, securing self-government for the Englishman at home, rising victorious in New England, winning the day at Lexington, at Bunker Hill, and Yorktown, until we behold its legitimate fruit in the fundamental principle of our government, that "the people are the true source of all political power."

At the formation of our Constitution, these ever-active and opposing principles were at work, contending for the shaping of the Republic's destiny and creating the two great parties that must ever control it — one advocating strong central, the other, local self-government. But did the acceptance of the Federal principle in the Constitution destroy the logic by which Hamilton urged a strong central government, or that by which Jefferson contended for the opposing principle of State's sovereignty? By no means. These same parties, actuated by the same persistent principles, divided upon the interpretation of that Constitution and have passed down the century in unbroken parallel lines. Whatever their name they have never lost identity: whether denominated Federalist or anti-Federalist, Republican or Democrat, one has been the liberal, the other the strict constructionist in the interpretation of the Constitution, and because of this, one has always desired more, the other less, legislation on measures of national reform and progress. Hamilton's tariff policy, internal improvements, the disposition of the public lands, Calhoun's nullification resolutions — all involved the question of the relative functions of State and national government. It was thus when Webster met, in matchless eloquence, the champion of the South; the same conflict when our fathers shouldered muskets and marched to the fields of death. Back of the lines of steel at Gettysburg and Appomattox, aiming every bayonet, loading every cannon, inspiring every charge, sublime in the smoke of conflict, stood colossal the opposing principles of State and nation. Ah! there was more than a social and moral issue in that contest. Our Lincolns, our Sumners, our Grants, met the Davises, the Stephenses, the Lees, not on the moral issue of slavery only — they fought for a broader idea, a political principle. They fought for the integrity of the nation.

The war wrote in characters of blood, "Each State is subordinate to the nation;" but it left human nature unchanged, and the silent conflict of centralization and local self-government, agitated by new issues, goes on.

An era of good feeling, as during Monroe's administration, may prevail, hiding, temporarily, these differentiating principles from public view; nevertheless, they exist. They are the criteria to which every political issue is referred. Because one believes that the national government should foster home industries by protection, the other that the function of government ceases with securing "tariff for revenue only," the two great parties are divided upon the tariff question. Opposition to the inter-State commerce, the government postal telegraph, and the Blair educational bills, is based upon the fundamental idea that such legislation is an invasion of the rights reserved to the States.

Both from necessity and expediency two great parties exist. By mutual criticism both are held within the bounds of reason. As the suspension of one physical force would disperse the myriad planets into chaos, or the suspension of the other bring them to a dead center, so the removal of the motive force underlying one party would bring despotism as the suspension of the other would drive us to anarchy and confusion.

When these great principles are in abeyance, minor parties, based upon social and moral issues, spring into existence. Such parties fail because they involve no political principle broad enough to subvert that of a dominant party. Did the Abolition party enact the fourteenth and fifteenth amendments? The Liberal party, the Free-soilers, the anti-Masons, the Greenbackers, all have folded their tents and sleep in peace, while the two parties representing principles of government ever prevail. Does not the failure of these portend the same fate for the Labor and Socialistic parties of to-day?

The error of outside party reformers is a misconception of the essential nature of parties and their relation to the people. All problems of law and politics have a real and an ideal side. Neglecting the real, idealists evolve abstract theories, fanatics attempt to put them into practice. Having but one idea, they consider it of supreme importance, and viewing it alone, and not in its relation to the other necessary ideas of government, they have a distorted view of all. Their theories presuppose an ideal state of mankind, unattainable so long as human nature is the basis of society. In practice, the third partyist accomplishes the opposite of his theory. Under the theory of emancipating the slaves third partyism defeated Clay and elected Polk, precipitating the Mexican war and the further extension of slavery. It elevated to the presidency that tool of the slave power, Buchanan, well-nigh wrecking the Union. But what of the Independent Prohibition party? Shall six million temperance men forsake the parties of Hamilton and Jefferson, of Jackson and Clay—parties established upon principles of government—for a party based upon a social and moral issue?

What superior intelligence or force of reason entitles one third partyist to dictate to twenty sincere temperance men of a dominant party just how prohibition shall come? He points to no laws enacted by assemblies of his political faith, to no triumph at the polls. In New York, Massachusetts, Indiana, Ohio, Michigan, third party tickets have defeated temperance legislation, and whenever it fails to co-operate with a dominant party its effect is to put the temperance cause into the hands of its enemies. Five States have already demonstrated the inability of the Prohibition party to accomplish any good results through its own strength, and it only remains for the other thirty-three to consign it to oblivion. Every temperance enactment has come through dominant parties; every attempt at reform through a third party has resulted in disaster.

A political party is not called into existence to serve a transient issue, then pass away forever. The causes of real political difference are opinions with respect to principles of government; these causes are permanent, inherent in the nature of man. Social and moral issues do not, cannot originate or sustain a political party; for when these issues are thrust into politics they involve the principles underlying the parties which of necessity already exist, and upon these basal principles must every political issue be finally settled.

Back of every reform and every statute stands public sentiment, which rests not on parties, statutes or creeds, but upon the perception of right and wrong implanted in the bosom of man. Public sentiment is the omnipotent power that enacts, enforces, enthrones, dethrones. What is your statute, your penalty, unless behind it stands a living public sentiment? The man is a hero who violates the law. What statute will ever stigmatize John Brown as a murderer, or write the name of Benedict Arnold alongside that of "the Father of His Country?" Public sentiment rules a political party with inexorable decree. It said to the Democratic party, "Put Boss Tweed behind prison bars," and it was obeyed. It spoke again, and grayhaired Jacob Sharp passed to his grave through the same cell. Not third party, but public sentiment dictated that sentence in the Republican platform, "Iowa has no compromise to make with the saloon." Public sentiment sustained the mayor of an Irish-American city who decreed that only the stars and stripes should float from the flag-staff of the City Hall. It pronounced against a third term. It said to the hero of Appomattox, in whose presence the crowned heads of Europe had stood uncovered, and whose praises had been echoed in every tongue of the civilized world, "Thus far and no farther," and the most distinguished citizen of the world retired to the shades of private life. Without public sentiment nothing can succeed; with it nothing can fail. Temperance reform will come, not by reason of third party, but in spite of it. It will come because the sublimest forces of a Christian civilization are at work creating a public sentiment before which evil will flee as from the avenging angel of God. Statesmen must adopt the will of their constituents or fall before the flood-tide of popular opinion. Political parties based upon essential principles of government, and commanding majorities, alone wield sufficient power to enforce the dictates of public opinion.

These outside movements are but ripples upon the great sea of political thought; they can never change the direction of resistless ocean currents. Identified with permanent parties are the rich legacies of patriotic statesmen; the mystic chords of memory, stretching from a thousand battle-fields where sleep heroic dead, bind men to these parties with ties that can not be severed by transient issues. The feeling of loyalty, inspired by father's sword, hallowed by mother's tears, throws a halo of glory around their principles that can never be extinguished by the will-o'-the-wisp of independent parties. Issues come and issues go, but political parties, based upon inherent tendencies of human nature, dignified by brilliant intellects, cemented by the blood of brave men, go on forever. Abstract theorists may battle against nature, cultured independents may seek to degrade their principles, but the parties representing them will stand—they will stand

> "As some tall cliff that lifts its awful form,
>   Swells from the vale and midway leaves the storm;
>   Though round its breast the rolling clouds are spread
>   Eternal sunshine settles on its head."

# THE DEFENDER OF THE CONSTITUTION.

By HARRY M. HYDE, of Beloit College.

### BIOGRAPHICAL.

Harry Morrow Hyde, the second-prize orator of 1888, was born at Freeport, Illinois, October 6, 1869. After he graduated from the Freeport High School he became a student of Beloit College, Beloit, Wisconsin, in September, 1888. Upon the inter-State contest occasion he chose as his subject, "The Defender of the Constitution," and, with a rich, sonorous voice, was master of his subject. Mr. Hyde is a polished speaker, and an enterprising young man. He is engaged as city editor of the Dubuque (Iowa) *Daily Times*.

### THE ORATION.

Delivered at the Inter-State Oratorical Contest, at Greencastle, Indiana, May, 1888, taking second prize. Judges: Gov. J. B. FORAKER, Judge FRAKE, Rev. STEWART, Prof. WAREY, Messrs. WINSTEIN and MITCHENER.

While the press and the orator are busy discussing the great social and political evils which threaten our republic, we must not forget that it is upon the legislator — the law-maker — that the final solution of these problems depends. For after discussion must come legislation, and law is supreme. Reform, to be effective, must begin in the halls of our legislatures.

This, then, is my excuse for telling over again to-night the story of a man who united in himself many of the traits of the ideal representative. It is an old story. The lesson of his life is a simple one, but it is a story that can never be told too often. It is a lesson which the people of these States can never learn too well.

The United States nominally became a nation in 1776. But it was not until many years afterward that the Union was firmly cemented. For a while the feeling of a common weakness and of a common danger bound the States together. For a while, too, the great spirits of the Revolution kept the Ship of State from going to pieces on the rock of Disunion.

But the sparsely settled territory of the United States was scattered along the whole Atlantic coast. The interests of the different sections were varying and often hostile. The Congressional delegations of the several States came together rather as the ambassadors of foreign powers than as the Congress of a common country.

Even before the beginning of this century two of the Southern States had passed ordinances of nullification. They had declared that no State is bound to obey the supreme law of the land. Nor let us lay the whole blame of this disaffection upon the South. Let us remember that during the war of 1812 even staunch old New England threatened to secede. In fact, during some period of our history, nearly every section of the country has been affected by the virus of disunion. This, then, is the great problem which our fathers had to solve.

The question has been settled now with the pen and with the sword. And while we give due credit to the soldier, and to the writer, let us not forget the man who fought out the great battle in the forum of Congress. In the face of odds, against an hitherto invincible opponent he fought, and he saved the Union.

When slavery began to press for a solution, its advocates seized upon this old and hitherto unsettled question of nullification and State rights.

In 1828 Calhoun published his first book on the subject, and thereafter the apostle of secession, in Congress and out of it, lost no time in spreading the seed of his doctrine. He is in the Senate now, triumphant, dictatorial. The men in the North cringe before his sarcasm, his tempestuous eloquence. They can not unravel the subtilities of his crafty argument. Where is the man who shall meet this giant spirit of disunion? Who shall save the charter of our liberties from the hand of disloyalty? The crisis has come and God has made ready the man for the crisis.

Now he is a boy and there falls into his hands a handkerchief on which is printed the Constitution. The boy reads it, his imagination is aroused, he ponders it well. Now through discouragement, through poverty, he is at college, and he delivers a Fourth of July address. There are a few sentences in which contain the prophecy of his life-work. "There is not a single government in Europe," he said, "which is not based on usurpation and established, if established at all, by the sacrifice of thousands. But in the adoption of our present system of jurisprudence we see the powers necessary for government voluntarily flowing from the people, their only proper origin and directed to the public good, their only proper object." Here is embalmed the spirit of the mission which he came into the world to perform. A clear sense of national unity and of the only means by which the United States can remain a nation.

And now Webster is a lawyer, an eloquent, successful lawyer, the first jurist in New England. Massachusetts, the State of his adoption, whom he loved so well, calls him from the bar and sends him to represent her in the councils of the nation. His practice, income, and professional reputation, are immense, but he lays them all down, and obedient to the call goes to Washington. A second and third time he is sent back to Congress, where the echo of his oratory fills the ear of the nation. And now the old "Bay State," grown proud of the son of her adoption and his achievements, envelopes him in the nobler mantle of Senator.

Daniel Webster is now forty-eight years old, in the full flush and vigor of his transcendent powers. He is ready now to speak the last word of his great message, to fulfill his mission to the people of these States. Here then is the man whom God has made ready for the first great crisis of disloyalty, and now his opportunity has come.

One day he walked from the Supreme Court into the Senate Chamber, and heard there Colonel Hayne heaping taunts upon the New England of his love, and weaving into a glittering and delusive fabric the doctrine of disunion and disloyalty.

The next day Daniel Webster obtained the floor to deliver his reply to Hayne. The South was triumphant and scornful; the North anxious, half expectant and half afraid. And well it might fear. For in the speech of Hayne reason and eloquence had conspired together. But the hour came, and when thousands had gathered to listen, while the Union trembled and disloyalty laughed in its sleeve, the glorious old Titan lifted himself to speak. He was tranquil, dignified, colossal, bearing himself with an ominous calm. For under the great forehead his dark eyes were burning with a dangerous fire. The people looked; they listened; they were moved; they melted before the glowing thought and the stern logic of the orator. "Mr. President, I shall enter upon no encomium of Massachusetts. She needs none. There is her history—the world knows it by heart. The past at least is secure. There is Boston, and Lexington, and Concord, and Bunker Hill—and there they will remain forever." And in remembrance of that hour the grand old commonwealth has ever poured out upon Daniel Webster the choicest vials of her love.

Then he turned to the attack upon the Constitution. What he said lives in the memory of us all. The supreme importance of the Constitution as the bond of national unity was fully demonstrated, and the great speech closed with that wonderful period, "Liberty and Union, now and forever—one and inseparable."

And with those words the life-work of Daniel Webster is accomplished. The great service which he was born to render to his country is achieved. They mark the topmost summit of his eloquence, and thus much is certain: That of all the victories gained by Union forces in the rebellion these two are the most important: The debate with Hayne, and the battle of Gettysburg.

Nor did the effect of that great speech die with the orator and with the hour. Eloquence gave it life and wings. And with the lips of every school boy, and in every hamlet of our nation, Webster has repeated his message to the people of these States until the idea of national unity has become the very center and core of the national character.

Daniel Webster, whom nature endowed with a trumpet voice and the forefront of a lion, spent all his life in preparing for that debate. His early study of the Constitution, the sharp training of his legal battles, the exhaustive studies and the victories of the constitutional lawyer, the eloquence and the statecraft of the Congressman, all these looked forward with a single eye to that day. And so it was that out of the North came forth this champion, who, with a logic as irresistible as the granite of his native hills, should meet and overthrow the fiery eloquence and delusive sophistry of the South. What man has poured upon the altar of his country a nobler offering?

We know there are those who call Webster ambitious; who forget the great things of which we have been telling, and reserve for him all the reproach, all the scorn, they can heap into that one word—ambitious. But if to the defender of the Constitution, to the savior of the Union, be denied "that last infirmity of noble minds," what man may aspire? On what could worthy ambition be better based?

We know, too, that the private character of Webster had many faults. But we can afford to let the shadow of his noble deeds fall over them and hide them from our sight.

In 1852, at his country home, again under the shadow of the great mountains and within sound of the great sea, the monumental life of Daniel Webster was ended. When William Pitt, the foremost orator of the British Parliament, passed away, England took him home to her heart in the grand old Abbey of Westminster. She raised over his tomb the tribute of a loving nation at once a memorial and an inspiration to all the future. But we—

> "We have no high cathedral for his rest,
> Dim with proud banners and the dust of years,
> All we can give him is New England's breast
> To lay his head on—and ten thousand tears."

But oh! thou mighty spirit of eloquence, teach us still the lesson of thy life. Teach us to reverence high resolve, and resolute endeavor, and noble achievement. Teach our lawyers to plead for justice and for truth. Give to our statesmen a steadfast incorruptibility, a far-seeing vision, and an eye single to the interest of the State. Help us all, each in his own sphere, to labor for the welfare of our country and the advancement of humanity.

# THE PHILOSOPHY OF INEQUALITY.

By ED. H. HUGHES, of Wesleyan University.

## INTRODUCTORY.

Ed. H. Hughes was the champion orator of 1889. His oratorical style partakes somewhat of the ministerial order. His delivery was in striking harmony with the thought of his oration, and his self-possession before the audience was acquired by a year's work in the ministry. He is a graduate of the Wesleyan University, Delaware, Ohio, and a member of the college society, Delta Tau Delta. Mr. Hughes is now attending the Boston Theological School to more thoroughly prepare himself for his life-work as minister in the Methodist denomination.

## THE ORATION.

Delivered at the Inter-State Oratorical Contest, at Grinnell, Iowa, May, 1889, taking first prize. Judges: Gov. J. B. FORAKER, Pres. CHAMBERLAIN, Prof. S. G. BARNES, Judge J. T. PHILLIPS, Gen. J. C. COWIN, Hon. W. N. HORNER.

Society is regulated by two laws. One is inherent; the other, adopted. One is immutable; the other, variable. One is self-executive; the other must be executed by chosen means. Inherent law establishes the fact; adopted law supplies the conditions. The one says, "Man must think;" the other, "Man must proclaim thoughts that prove loyalty to government." The mutual relation of these laws often leads to a false classification. Inherent law has been declared legalized custom and captious minds have clamored for its annulment. Futile are all endeavors to make better what Omniscience has made best. Reformers propose a visionary scheme of government as a substitute for the plan inaugurated of God. Prominent among their attempts is the one whose object is the repeal of the law of inequality.

Social conditions are the prolific source of rebellion against impurity. Widows' homes, orphans' asylums, and almshouses, stand contrasted with unbroken households, cheerful nurseries, and brown-stone fronts. Men look indignantly upon this picture of social life. Suffering Lazarus excites their deepest sympathy. Purple-clad Dives bears the odium of existing conditions. Pity overpowers reason, and dictates the cry, "Inequality is a product of custom, not of necessity. Custom must be brought into harmony with justice." Influenced by this thought our enthusiast gives free rein to daring fancy, and becomes an apostle of the gospel of inequality.

Is general inequality avoidable? Nature, in the language of analogy, answers, "No," and makes earnest protest against universal equality. "To him who holds communion with her visible forms she speaks a various language." Variety is her law. The relations among her products are expressed by the sign of inequality. Shrubs, trees; hills, mountains; rivers, oceans; islands, continents — all speak of inequality in the earth's structure. Anemone and oak grow in the same soil and derive vitality from the same elements. But nature is none the less beautiful because of her lack of uniformity. Her variety, rather, is her charm. She is none the less useful because here she rises into lofty mountains and there extends herself into rolling prairies. Thus society's analogue declares inequality to be an inherent law of human relations.

Imagination builds lofty castles; experience levels them to the ground. Test the theory of universal equality by the results of its operation. Its advocates speak eloquently of this Utopia, and, considering their system only in its inauguration, fancy that their dream may become a reality. Not candid, not truly philosophical, they study introduction apart from conclusion. A factitious sentiment results, leading to the advocacy of an impartial division of all material wealth. Like all other false doctrines this one includes only sufficient truth to render it plausible. An inspection of human character and environment betrays the fallacy. This man is shrewd and industrious; that man, stupid and thriftless. This man is deterred from labor by disease and accident; that man is advanced to riches by health and good fortune. This man maintains a large and expensive family; that one supports himself alone. This man develops and utilizes all his powers; that one wastes his life in indolence and sloth. Condition will eventually respond to character and culture; for inequality of ability produces inequality of attainment. Furthermore, the theory is impracticable, because not all occupations are equal either in duties exacted or interests involved. The difficulty and general utility of any employment determine the remuneration of its followers. An innate sense of justice claims premium for superiority.

But a doctrine declared false by history, and by reason, demands fertility in expedients. The charm in the discovery of this Elysium must not be broken by the cold logic of facts. Seeing that their empire of equality is not yet established, the upholders of this theory suggest an annual redistribution. This plan would destroy all incentive to labor. No man would distribute the fruits of his honest toil among the idle and vicious. Ardor of enterprise would no longer characterize our commercial system; for commerce admits of but one equality —that of honest competition. Human nature presents an insuperable barrier to the progress of this reform. Is it eagerness to uplift humanity that has led to this idea of a division of wealth? Is it the fancied ignominy of poverty that has stirred hearts to their depths and incited the promulgation of this view? Or is it malicious envy that has overcome the instincts of the nobler self and demanded wealth that has been gained by the sweat of other's brows? Whatever the motive, the result is invariably the same. Although these pretended reforms have been rendered attractive by rhetorical beauty; although powers of vivid description have presented the moral and social advantages of this glittering empire; yet common sense, the preventive of continual revolution, has overcome its flashy rival, and fancy has surrendered to practical truth. The deceptive currents of imagination have whirled men into this channel "of appearance where naught but fallacy reigneth." Enthusiasm, unfounded and unbounded, has caused bold statement, reckless conspiracy, and desperate attack against existing institutions. The scaffold and the guillotine have changed imaginary into real ignominy; centuries will not obliterate the sad memorials of man's folly. The hopeless experiment has merely displayed the monumental ignorance of those who detest, denounce, defy, the Providential order. The tempest of impulse is at last stilled under the calming influence of cool judgment. He who properly respects himself, now asks nothing more than a hearty recognition of his manhood. Men wisely conclude that a ship with a nobler device upon her streaming banner will never plough the waves of the dark and dreary social sea.

We study mankind by comparison and by contrast. We begin by discovering resemblances and end by contemplating diversities of character. This fact is conspicuously illustrated in our own America. The profound German, the vivacious Frenchman, the strong-minded Englishman, the witty Irishman, and the honest Scotchman—all have contributed to the composition of the national character. Every American audience is a world in miniature. Often in the veins of one person flows mingled the blood of the five great races. The qualities that distinguish nations and men combine to produce inequality in human endowments and acquirements. This inequality is as prophetic as it is historic. In one there burns fires of sparkling imagination; in another there surges powers of resistless argumentation. In one there glows the genius for music or art; in another, the genius for invention or handicraft. Whence arises this state of inequality? Equalize conditions, it is said, and you will equalize character. The answer is, condition is rather the product of character. The true, divine philosophy of inequality is found in the fact that the varieties of opportunity for individual activity and the interaction of diversified talents supply the only condition under which human progress is possible. Behold now the results of that innovation which establishes equality among men. Let a capable power issue this decree, "All men shall be equal." There shall be no poor, no rich; no weak, no strong; no ignorant, no learned. What would result? The outcome would be the creation of individual independence. No one can be dependent upon his equal. In fact, the extent of our dependence upon any one is determined by his relation to us and by his superior power and means. Our dependence upon the Infinite is, therefore, absolute. Interdependence among men gives rise to universal brotherhood. Establish equality and you sweep away influence, the grandest agency in the world's amelioration. Influence implies inferiority. One cannot influence him who is in all respects his equal. Upon this condition friendship's foundation is laid. Love is the result of the soul's influence. Not even this divine principle could exist under the dominion of equality. Ordain independence and you destroy sympathy. There could be no excitant of sympathy if there were no inequality of suffering and hardship. The breaking of this golden band would mark the dawn of an era of supreme selfishness and stoicism. Equality would expel from the minds of men all thought of laudable enterprise, for under its reign there could be no greatness. No name would shine with the lustre of renown. No heart would thrill under the commanding influence of any historic character. Providence being merely general, there could be no men whose marked genius and splendid service in times of emergency seem to indicate providential dealing. The *regime* of equality would annihilate many practical moral virtues, for the possibility of evil gives to righteousness the coronal glory. If there were no penury, no pain, what would become of fortitude, patience, resignation? If there were no greatness, no wealth, what would become of benevolence, charity, human pity? If there were no luxury what would become of temperance? If there were no power what would become of justice? Under the proposed system hearts could never prove their sterling coinage. The withering breeze of selfishness would blast forever pure generosity, noble self-denial, and heroic devotion. Under the present system the surface of character may seem chilled by worldly cares, or etiquette may cultivate the art of pleasing, yet the warmth of human sympathy lives in the depths of the coldest heart, and at times the dormant fires blaze forth and betray the sympathetic nature.

The perversion of the principle of inequality arouses opposition to the principle itself. It may be said that inequality necessitates power and that power is often misapplied. True it is that "man's inhumanity to man makes countless thousands mourn." But equally true it is that gravitation ceases not her operation even when life is imperilled.

"When the weak mountain trembles from on high,
Shall gravitation cease if you go by?"

Ah! True it is that power is not always indicative of merit. True it is that misguided power has baffled reform, prevented education, neutralized morality, stifled conscience, silenced the pleading tones of religion and given fearful force to ignorance and vice. Yet let it be remembered that power, although the father, is yet the conqueror of persecution. For when the legions of evil have been routed and the emblems of victory have graced the banners of right, then have been aroused the energies of strong souls, and power has become the ally of truth.

What, then, is the proper deduction from the existence of inequality? Not that any man should be enslaved, but rather that all men should be free to exercise those "inalienable rights" to which nature entitles them. Plato may write of the model "Republic;" Moore may find in "Utopia" a political and social paradise; Bacon may describe a "New Atlantis," but society will never be regenerated until the dawn of the joyous morn when the heralds of peace shall proclaim the universal equality, not of accident, nor of artificial conditions, but of moral privilege and of enlightened conscience, and shall announce as the criterion of every man's conduct—

>"To thine own self be true,
>And it must follow as the night the day,
>**Thou canst not then be false to any man."**

# RIOT AND REVOLUTION.

By J. A. BLAISDELL, of Beloit College.

## BIOGRAPHICAL.

James Arnold Blaisdell was born at Beloit, Wisconsin, December 15, 1867. Named for his father, the distinguished Dr. James J. Blaisdell, of Beloit College, and the honored Dr. Arnold, of Rugby, the subject of this sketch has thus far amply justified the hopes engendered by his baptismal appellations. Mr. Blaisdell received his early education in the grammar schools of his native city, and later spent three years in the Beloit High School. His final year of preparation for college was passed in the Beloit Academy, and in the fall of 1885 he entered collegiate life. Early in his course he evinced marked ability both as a scholar and a writer, and at the close of his freshman year carried off the Bridgman Prize for excellence in declamation, and the German Essay Prize, in which thought and style were the deciding elements. In his sophomore year he was chosen to lead his society in the public debate of the Archæan Union, and won in a contest of unusual brilliancy. At the close of the same year he was a second time awarded the German Essay Prize, notwithstanding the fact that competition was open to all the college classes. In his junior year he won the Burke Essay Prize and also the Rice Extempore Prize, winning the latter in a spirited public contest in which he evinced in a marked degree the "ability to think on one's feet." After this contest his victory in the approaching home oratorical contest was conceded as a foregone conclusion, and he entered the inter-State arena with an oration generally believed to be one of the best ever sent from Beloit College. This belief was justified by the outcome of the contest, Mr. Blaisdell being ranked first in thought and composition by two judges, and ranked second by the third.

Throughout his college coure he was the authorized correspondent for several of the leading newspapers in Chicago, Minneapolis, and St. Paul. He filled successively every position on the board of editors of the *Round Table*. Until his senior year he was undecided whether he should enter upon journalism or the ministry, but he ultimately chose the latter field, entering Hartford Theological Seminary in the fall of 1889, and at the close of his first year was awarded the Scholarship Prize of two hundred dollars. Mr. Blaisdell possesses the generous impulses and manly qualities of heart and character which go to make up a symmetrical manhood. His past record promises such a wise use and preservation of his powers that one may fairly believe his success and usefulness have but just begun.

## THE ORATION.

Delivered at the Inter-State Oratorical Contest, at Grinnell, Iowa, May, 1889, taking second prize. Judges: Gov. J. B. FORAKER, Pres. CHAMBERLAIN, Prof. S. G. BARNES, Judge J. T. PHILLIPS, Gen. J. C. COWIN, Hon. W. N. HORNER.

It is said that Louis the Sixteenth was sleeping one night in his palace at Versailles when a courier suddenly burst through the door shouting: "Sire, the Bastile is stormed!" "It is a revolt," said the king, turning to rest again. "Sire," said the messenger, "it is not revolt; it is revolution!" When Louis woke the Reign of Terror had begun.

Louis sleeps again, and the Reign of Terror is done; yet the history of the world is in the story of that midnight messenger. One day the Pope sits supreme in the Vatican dictating the infallible decrees; the next, the theses on the church at Wittenberg have challenged Pope and Prelate, and started the fires of German reformation. One night the stars shine peacefully through an Italian sky; at dawn the flag of Garibaldi's Thousand is on the heights above Palermo. In the silence of the darkness the same question is forming as that which the messenger brought to Louis. Are the theses and the flag but the signals of riot? Or have they behind them principles which, though defeated on many fields, will some day triumph as revolution? It is no child's conundrum; it is the momentous dilemma of statesmen. At the midnight the messenger comes;

and the world, like the Bourbon monarch at Versailles startled from slumber, and with whirling brain, reads the theses, marks the war-flag amid the rattle of drums and gathering of legions, and, in that solemn, awful moment of decision there in the darkness, would throw its very kingdom at the footstool of a prophet.

So every age has cried: "Tell us, oh seer, the signs of revolution." The world called Socrates and Plato rioters; in a Roman court Paul met the same charge. Ah! could that world have known its error, Truth need not have traveled the road of martyrdom through so many dreary centuries!

Let history be our seer to-night. Let the reformers of the past guide the reformers of to-day. Call back, then, those great reformers of history; the murdered Gracchi from the Roman forum, Luther from his sleep at Wittenberg, Knox from the shadow of the Parliament House at Edinburgh, William of Orange from a martyr's grave, Gustavus Adolphus from a warrior's death at Lutzen, the elect of our age —Wilberforce from Exeter Hall, Garrison from his Boston prison, Phillips from the broadcloth riot in Faneuil Hall, Lovejoy from sentinel-guard upon the Mississippi. When you have called the long roll, ask what was the center aim of each revolution. The Gracchi will answer, "Our's was liberty for the poor;" Luther will reply, "Liberty of thought:" William of Orange, "Liberty for the nation;" Gustavus Adolphus, "Liberty in creed;" while these latest reformers give answer, "We fought for the liberty of mankind."

If, then, this history means anything, it means that no revolution can be successful which does not promise wider liberty to men. We need go back only to the days of '62 for a clear example of the power of liberty as a principle of revolution. For two years the North had given of her bravest and her best. Army after army of the boys in blue had marched away in eclat only to join a silent soldiery. For every fireside in the North there was a new-made grave beneath the Southern sun. And still the days grew darker. England seemed to espouse the cause of disunion. The nation seemed walking the way of darkness and despair. Above the storm at last there rose a statesman's voice: "I do not wonder at the want of sympathy on the part of England with us. The South says, 'I am fighting for slavery;' the North says, 'I am not fighting against it.' I would have government announce to the world what she has not yet done. I would have her send her proclamation down to the gulf: 'Freedom to every man beneath the stars.'" The nation heard and profited. It promised emancipation to the slaves; and the civilized world came back to the Northern standards as they swept onward to their triumph.

But, while no movement can become a revolution without liberty as its essence, it is evident that liberty is not the only requisite to its success. The bloodiest pages in the history of riots have been instigated by the spirit of liberalism. The traveler may still find the spot where Madame Roland was guillotined. From the palmier days of wealth she was led to the dungeon and to death. Is it strange that, as she climbed the scaffold stairs and saw the mocking statue of Liberty before her, she uttered that cry which pierces the sternest heart with the wildness of its agony: "Oh liberty, liberty; how many crimes are wrought in thy name!"

What, then, besides liberty, is essential in revolution? Let us call again our court of reformers. When the Genoans came to Cavour to complain of the tyranny of Charles Albert in the days when Italy was struggling for federation, did he advise arms, bombs, firebrands? He said: "Gentlemen, I propose that we demand a Constitution;" and sixty days later Charles had granted one. When the American colonies arraigned George the Third, the first four indictments were, "He has refused us laws." Find a single revolution that has not had its dogmatic Knox and its strict Calvin, as well as its Luther and Garrison. History does not mention one. Here, then, is a crucial distinction between a movement that is destined to end in mere riot and one destined to become a revolution. As the guarantee of liberty, the one seeks liberty, the other seeks law.

Yet the reformer who has grasped only the truth that every successful revolution must have for its war cry:"Wider *liberty under better law,*" knows only a part of the secret of triumph. There is another significant picture of French riot. It is of a band of fearless men marching to the guillotine. They hurry along as if in the wild enthusiasm of victory, while the "terrible chorus" of the Marseillaise rings to the very stars. History has called them the Girondists. Why did they succeed only in creating a riot—these wild singers? They believed, mark you, in *liberty* and in *law*. They were the best citizens France had. They sought a republic as their goal; they found death! Thus they prove merely rioters, and, standing in the center of the greatest catastrophe of the eighteenth century, they are witnesses that a man may not safely throw his life into a cause if it is the champion merely of *liberty* and of *law*. The secret lies farther and deeper than that. It is the greatest English statesman who says: "No greater calamity can happen to a people than that it should break utterly with the past." Reform is a growth. The Girondists had sworn to annihilate the kingdom. They would not brook delay: "To-day or never!" Not so do reformers work. They have the source of their power back in the mighty mountain centuries of the past. They are willing to educate and wait. Like fire-keepers on Persian mountains, they watch through dreary centuries for the man and the hour.

So has it ever been in the story of progress. Notice this truth in history. Rome! Carthage! Liberty was the watchword of each; for the defense of that liberty the one gave law to the North, the other, to the South. Between such nations a contest must be desperate. The Mediterranean is white with the sails of the African queen. Hers is the wealth of the world; hers the glory of the past. She lays the pathway of her conquest through eternal snows and along the Alpine heights which have never heard a footfall since the hand of the Creator left them in their silence. Carthage meets Rome; Hannibal, Fabius; brilliance, the patience of *growth*; and Carthage is blotted from the earth.

For *liberty*, under *law*, through *growth*—these are the three vitalizing principles which give to revolution its conquering power. They are the historic criteria by which every man may judge of any struggle to which he is asked to give his life.

Yet there are some men to which the voice of the past can speak with still more explicit guidance. Sounding down the ages comes the voice of any ancient seer who read, in tragic letters on a palace wall, of a God in history; and on the morrow the glory of Chaldea was trampled in the dust. Now and then great souls have caught the very battle hymn of an army that moves to revolution without the flash of burnished spear or or blood-red banner. /The hundred thousand exiles who have halted at the border-pillar of Siberia, to pluck for the last time a grass blade from the soil of Russia, or, once for all, to catch the sunshine of a face through a storm of tears; the slave singing at midnight the songs of the better days that are coming — think you that they never heard a chorus wilder than the Marseillaise?

> "Right forever on the scaffold; wrong forever on the throne;
> Yet that scaffold sways the future, and behind the dim unknown
> Standeth God within the shadow keeping watch above His own."

Yes, *liberty, law, growth,* these three; but let this God-watching within the shadow be also in the movement, and that movement becomes invincible. The world need not question then whether it will end in riot or in revolution. It is born to triumph. Yes, this Christ, who is the captain of all growth, never leads his army to failure. Do you think me extreme? Then read of the singing soldiers of Adolphus who conquered a peace for Protestantism; the praying soldiers of Cromwell who started the march of Puritanism round the world. Let Mirabeau speak: "God is as necessary as liberty to the French people." Nay, let all history speak. Mark the advance toward Christianity as the sun-worship of the East gives way to the one spiritual God of Mohammedanism. Mark, then, the conquering progress of the Moslems, because of the Christian principle they had, till Mohammedanism holds its dominion from the Caspian to Gibraltar and the Pyranees. Its blood is boiling; it will cross the mountains. Rome will admit its sway; Europe shall kneel before the crescent. Luckless day for Mohammedanism! For behind the mountains was the cross, and the cross was conqueror. Search still farther the progress of pure Christianity as men have become strong enough to bear its full light, and when at last you have followed the "Mayflower" through its storms you will find "no Doubting Castle by the side of Plymouth Rock."

*Liberty, law, growth;* embracing these under the banner of the pure faith in Christ, a revolution is born. So it was in the very dawn of history. Lashed in the bondage of Egypt, a nation consecrated themselves to strike for liberty. |Under the thunders of Sinai they learned their laws. Through two centuries and a half they had grown into nationality. Above them was their God; Him only would they serve. What wonder that the sea held back the army of its waters. The skies gave them food. The desert gave them drink. For them the night banished its darkness. Peoples melted at their coming. Behind them were chariot-wheels that were broken and crowns of centuries in the dust. So, invincible as destiny, the cloud rolled on its way.

In the years that are coming other Israels will leave their bondage; other clouds roll Canaanward; other men must give their lives. Not in vain will any soldier fall if he falls wearing the colors of liberty and law, in an army where pulses the blood of patient growth, and for whom the sign of the cross is the oriflamme of war.

# THE PURITAN AND THE CAVALIER IN OUR NATIONAL LIFE.

By S. W. NAYLOR, of Washburn College.

### BIOGRAPHICAL.

Samuel W. Naylor, the first successful Kansas orator, was born January 7, 1864, three and a half miles east of Topeka. A branch of his ancestral tree sailed up the James River with the famous Smith. In the spring of 1854 his parents joined the colony for Kansas, and settled in Tecumseh Township a few miles east of Topeka. Ten years thence, in the fall of 1864, his father was taken prisoner by Price's forces, but shortly afterward escaped and returned home and died from exposure and cruel treatment received while a prisoner. The care of a large farm and four small children now devolved upon his mother. In the fall of 1870 she removed her family to Topeka for the sake of educating her children, remained four years, and returned to the old homestead. Our subject's early education was obtained in a country school. When nineteen years old he entered Washburn College. He found employment to sustain him through a seven years' course in this institution as steward of the boarding club, business manager of the *Argo*, secretary of Gov. Osborn's committee in the State Senate, etc. He was president of the college Y. M. C. A. for four years, an active member of the Republican club, and a participant in college athletics. In the spring of 1889, under the influence of Mr. Robt. P. Wilder, he volunteered for foreign missions, and through Mr. Naylor's influence no less than one hundred and twenty-five students in Kansas have taken the volunteer pledge. His graduating day was shrouded in gloom. His mother, while on her way to hear his graduating exercises, was thrown from the buggy on a hard paving, inflicting injuries from which she died July 6, 1890. Mr. Naylor is now taking a course in the Boston School of Theology, after which he will sail for some part of the foreign field. Few young men have come to wield so wide an influence in Kansas as Mr. Naylor.

## THE ORATION.

**Delivered at the Inter-State Oratorical Contest, at Lincoln, Nebraska, May, 1890, taking first prize. Judges: Judge A. YAPLE, NOBLE L. PRENTIS, Rev. D. H. SNOWDEN, Prof. F. B. RAFTER, PAUL H. HANNUS, T. M. MARQUETT.**

The Puritan and the Cavalier colliding formed modern England; uniting, established our Republic. The Cavalier sprang from chivalry, the flower of feudalism, a chivalry fostered by caste and maintained by princes. He defended the king against usurpation of power by party or sect; he upheld the royal prerogative. The Puritan was born of freedom of thought and of action. His awakened conscience revolted against caste in Church or State; he combined religious independence with civil liberty. Law incarnate in royalty was the embodiment of Cavalierism; law and liberty, the basis of Puritanism.

While the Cavalier was reinstating the monarchy overthrown by Cromwell, the Puritan was founding our Republic. Later, however, the Cavalier imprinted his vigor and statesmanship upon our Constitution and Declaration of Rights. His lofty principles of liberty were accompanied by irrepressible buoyancy and knightly gallantry. "He knew how to live gracefully, fight stoutly, and die honorably." With austere face and uncharitable mien, the Puritan of New England stands upon the canvas of history a sombre, ungraceful figure, void of the delicate colorings of gentleness and the forms of politeness. He was simple, rugged, genuine manhood. His doctrine read: "Faith in God, faith in man, faith in works," a creed ample for this life and that which is to come. Threatened by a common enemy, the chivalrous Cavalier of Virginia stood side by side with the stalwart Puritan of New England: Washington, Jefferson, Lee and Patrick Henry; Hancock, Green, Putnam and Adams. Such were the characters—refined by the Roman, the French, and the Norman; tempered by the Angle, the Saxon, and the Briton—that established our Republic.

Pointing to the Revolutionary soldier, the world exclaimed, "An American!" No; the American was not yet. The Puritan and the Cavalier were not amalgamated by the issue of the Revolution. Adhering to hereditary traits and inclinations, they effected distinctive developments. The Cavalier founded his civilization upon caste. Property was for the few, education for the few, labor for the negro. Slavery dulled the conscience, impoverished the masses, and made every planter a feudal despot. The Puritan, attracted to a climate congenial to his sterling energies, founded his civilization upon the cottage home. Look at the sturdy commonwealths which his spirit of progress permeates: see the foundries and factories; churches, common schools and colleges — monuments of material development and intellectual freedom. Virginia branded the South with the mark of retrogression; Massachusetts stamped the North with the elements of progress. Caste sovereignty and bonded labor produced Hayne and Calhoun; the excessive animus of slavery brought forth Quantrell's band, the Younger Brothers, and John Wilkes Booth. Free labor and free thought developed Garrison, Phillips, and — will you deny it? — John Brown, who, his great soul bursting with sympathy for the bondman, dared a nation, and fell — traitor or patriot — a martyr to his convictions.

The Puritan and the Cavalier were politically partisan, opposed the one to the other. It is well; opposition and antagonism underlie progress; we recognize greatness by comparison. Superiority is worthy of pride in the degree that rivals are mutually worthy of respect. The party which achieves the greatest good is paramount, not necessarily that which dominates. The tendencies of the North and the South produced different interpretations of the Constitution. Individuality developed; interests widened; thought diverged; opinion ripened into argument, which culminated in the matchless debate of 1830. With elegance of rhetoric and ardor worthy of a more righteous cause, Robert Hayne sets forth the precepts of Southern chivalry, State rights and caste sovereignty — the mutterings of the great rebellion. The reply comes like a thunderbolt. Daniel Webster, with loftier genius, more convincing logic, and a holier cause, addresses the Senate while a nation listens. The occasion grows upon him. His great arm rises and falls with a deep cadence of his voice. His ponderous sentences glow with the idea of federal unity. He strips from iniquity the splendid garb of chivalry and shatters the fallacies of State rights. Then clank the shackles of four million slaves; then freedom's shout rings round the world; then the deep, solemn vow of the great North goes up to heaven, "This Union shall be preserved."

Partisanship had now become sectionalism. Under the former a republic is capable of the highest development; under the latter there remains but a step to disunion. In the light of history the question is not, "Why should there have been war?" but "How was war so long averted?" The North and the South, fortified alike by logic and eloquence, would make no concessions, accept no compromise. The only arbiter was war. War confirmed the principles of the Puritan, revolutionized the civilization of the Cavalier, and vindicated, once for all, our free institutions. It did more: it broke down partition walls; facilitated communication between the North and the South; unified commercial interests. It smoothed the way for Northern industry and individuality to permeate the South, and for the genial temperament and warm-hearted hospitality of the South to enter Northern society. It softened prejudices; it quickened the pulse of civilization; it enlightened. It was good. The Civil War was the consecration of our Republic; for it cut the nerves of sectionalism and bound the North and the South together with the cords of peace. It made possible the ultimate fusion of Puritan and Cavalier tendencies into the full-rounded American character. The American has not yet come to the citizen masses, but the type has appeared. It is found in him — a Cavalier by birth, a Puritan by education — whose ungainly form environed a character which combined the sturdy dignity of the North with the buoyant gallantry of the South. Yes, "from the union of the Puritan and the Cavalier, slow perfecting through a century, from the straightening of their purposes and the crossing of their blood, came one who stands as the first typical American, who first comprehended within himself all the strength and gentleness, all the majesty and grace, of this Republic — Abraham Lincoln. He was greater than Puritan, greater than Cavalier; for in his ardent nature were fused the virtues of both, and in the depths of his great soul the faults of both were lost." In this type, the ideal, we may conceive the real.

The influence which the Puritan-Cavalier principles have had in the world's progress is of vital significance in the estimation of our national life. To a world ruled by caste and sect the declaration that all men are created equal was a glittering absurdity. The discovery of the paradox therein contained has revolutionized the world and shaped the progress of the nineteenth century. The spirit of Western liberty breathes upon France and the French Revolution prepares the way for the republic. The cry of "Liberty and Equality" nerves the sinewy frame of the slave of San Domingo; he springs into the full stature of a man, asserts his sovereign rights and forges the Haytian republics. Democracies rise in Mexico, in South America, in Africa, in the islands of the sea. Greece throws off the yoke of Ottoman despotism. The wonder of to-day is Brazil, transformed in a night. Portugal wavers. The masses of Europe, with "muscles and sinews hardening and knotting for the struggle,

"Wait for the dawning of a brighter day,
To snap the chain the moment when you may."

The world voices the once asserted, now demonstrated truth, all men are created equal.

The formative element is superior to the revolutionary in civilization. Frenzy and fanaticism may rebel and overthrow, as Robespierre in the French Revolution; but sagacity and statesmanship form and reform, as the Puritan and the Cavalier in the creation and development of the United States. Our principles are so deeply rooted in the perpetual that two centuries of unrestricted immigration have not perceptibly changed them. The European toiler, dwarfed in faculties and soul, gropes in the new-found freedom, and often confounds liberty with license; but he is plastic. Restrained by law, enlightened by precept, he readily yields to formative influences and enters into the spirit of our national life. Why should he not? Does our national emblem speak a meaningless language? Associate the brilliant red with the chivalrous Cavalier, the unassuming blue with the stanch integrity of the Puritan, the purity of white with the freedom of enlightened conscience, and you conceive the embodiment of the noblest qualities of all nationalities; not merely the flag of a nation, but the emblem of liberty, the ensign of progress. The annual assimilation of a vast foreign element is a living witness that the energies of our ancestors have ever been the vital forces of our progress. With such inherent energies stimulating it, public sentiment is not content merely to preserve, but seeks reformation and perfection in continued development. Significant is the national sorrow at the untimely death of Georgia's eloquent son. The head-lines read, "Henry W. Grady Dead," but back of the candid, loyal-hearted brother the North sees the New South. That New South, pausing over the grave of her brilliant, devoted son, is conscious of her resources, her possibilities, her privileges and duties, herself an important factor of our nation. The New South is wiser than the old. The inspiration of Northern industry courses through her veins. The hum of factories and the whirl of machinery rise like a New England hymn. "There was a South of slavery and secession; that South is dead. There is a South of union and freedom; that South is living, breathing, growing every hour."

What of Puritan and Cavalier? Do we incorporate their virtues? Do we preserve and transmit their embodied truths? A living principle, a deep conviction of life, enables the present to gather and keep the richness of the past. The Puritan, echoing Plymouth Rock, upheld the divine right of man, as man. The Cavalier, reflecting Jamestown, stood for the constitutional right of caste. Both were actuated by one basal principle, an intense conviction of what each apprehended as truth. Nor are the energies and virtues of the Puritan and the Cavalier dead. Dead! They are but straightened and strengthened by exertion in antagonism. They are woven and knit into the fabric of our commonwealth. They permeate the secret bonds of society; throb in every pulse of our national life; charge it with the tremendous meaning of an ideal republic. We stand upon the vantage-ground of incomparable achievements. Courageously facing the future, we move forward in the path of reform, conscious that our national life must be perfected by interior development and progress.

# OUR ENGLISH LANGUAGE.

By A. C. Douglass, of Monmouth College.

BIOGRAPHICAL.

Alonzo C. Douglass was born near St. Joseph, Missouri. At an early age he entered the district school in the neighborhood where his parents resided. When he was ten years of age his parents removed to Kansas, and settled on a farm in the vicinity of Cedar, now Denison. His first summer in Kansas was spent herding three hundred head of cattle, learning something of the life of a cow-boy; although too young to mount a horse, and often, being in the midst of a large prairie, where there was neither rock, stump or fence, he would mount this difficulty by taking advantage of his horse while eating grass and jump astride its head; immediately being elevated he would slide down its neck to the saddle, seat himself, and be ready for duty. When sixteen years old he was enrolled as a student in the Campbell Normal University, Holton, Kansas, taking a commercial and teacher's course. In September, 1885, he entered the sub-freshman class of Monmouth College, Monmouth, Illinois, graduating June 12, 1890, and receiving the degree of bachelor of arts. He was a member of the Philadelphian Society of Monmouth College. Two years he was a member of the Philo-Eccritean Lecture Association. His chief distinction in college was his success as an orator. Winning the local contest, March, 1889, he represented Monmouth College at the inter-collegiate contest of Illinois in October of the same year, where he received first honors. At the inter-State contest of 1890 he won second prize on the subject, "Our English Language." Mr. Douglass intends to devote his talents and his life to the ministry of the gospel. Having been received as a student of theology by the Kansas City presbytery of the United Presbyterian Church, he entered the Seminary at Xenia, Ohio, in September, 1890, where he will take a three years' course.

## THE ORATION.

Delivered at the Inter-State Oratorical Contest, at Lincoln, Nebraska, May, 1890, taking second prize. Judges: Judge A. Yaple, Noble L. Prentis, Rev. D. H. Snowden, Prof. F. B. Rafter, Paul H. Hannus, T. M. Marquett.

From a rugged rock-bound hill-side there bubbles a silver stream. Winding out through a landscape of beauty, its rippling waters flash diamonds from their sunlit surface. The murmuring music of the wavelets makes sweet harmony with warbling birds. Many a tributary separates the banks. But the stream rushes on, leaping over rocks, plowing through meadows, wandering into deep forests, ever increasing in grandeur, until a mighty river it marks the boundaries of empires, bears on its bosom their stately fleets, and rolls on in majesty to the great ocean.

Such is our English language. Starting from its obscure source, this stream has flowed down through fifteen hundred years of history. It has been beautified by the teachings of Nature, broadened by the ceaseless flow of linguistic tributaries, and deepened by the profoundest thoughts of the human intellect, until it appears to-day an accumulation of the learning of ages — the glory of the Anglo-Saxon race, the inspiration of the civilized world.

Fifteen centuries ago, when an avalanche of savage hordes from the North was sweeping over Europe; when the tottering walls of the Western Empire were falling and the glory of the Cæsars was departing; when that total eclipse of ancient civilization was coming on, leaving vice and violence to rule the dark night; when philosophy was dead, art forsaken, and literature forgotten, our ancestors — fit types of the age — left their homes amid the gloomy wastes and the low-lying marshes of Holland, launched their pirate boats on the North Sea, and steered for the white cliffs of Albion. Their manners were rude, their character savage, and their religion false. Their speech was a mongrel dialect, yet it contained the germs of a language marvelous in power, infinite in influence, divine in mission. The history of this language is the history of the Anglo-Saxon people. Its mechanism contains a truer picture of race-vicissitudes than is found in the pen-paintings of Hume or Macaulay. The vice and virtue of each succeeding age is stamped upon it. Words that mark the ebb and flow of the tide of humanity tell of the ages of superstition and ignorance. They portray the degradation of man and the awful depths of his fall. In them, also, truth is seen emerging from a cloud of blind fanaticism. Right and might are crowned on a common throne, while despotism and oppression crouch at the feet of liberty. The clanking chains fall from the limbs of the captive. The darkness of paganism clears away for the light of Christianity. Barbarian becomes civilized. The hand of God is seen guiding the affairs of men; and banners of love, light, and liberty, float as the ensigns of united peoples.

But history, written in chronicles or preserved in the structure of a language, is often a record of that which man would fain forget. Evil excludes the good; blood stains every page; inhumanity marks every epoch. The English language, though fraught with lessons from human history, has yet greater fields for research, a grander mission of intelligence. Advancing civilization has made it heir to the most illustrious languages of mankind. The Greek, with its symmetry, purity, and grandeur; the Latin, combining vigor, grace, and dignity—both representing the highest types of ancient culture and refinement—have given their place to the English, the modern representative of Christian civilization. Grecian beauty and Roman strength have united to make ours the language of the sublimest age of history.

Alas, that Greece should have perished! That such architecture as the Parthenon, crowning the Acropolis of Athens, should crumble to dust, or that the statuary, carved on pillar and pediment, should be the shattered relics of such imperial splendor! Oh, Empire of Rome—heir of Grecian culture magnificent in the luxury of beautiful gardens and peaceful villas, that thou, too, shouldst be as a dream of the fancy! The mist of centuries envelopes these majestic ruins; their time-tarnished domes fall into decay; but the glory of the age which they represent is preserved in their languages. Time may wear away the Parthenon and the Coliseum, but the beauty and power of the Greek and Roman tongues will remain unchanged.

These were the prevalent languages when Christianity was introduced, and thus they became the "vehicles of the truths of revelation." But the spirit of the age was skeptical, cruel. Noble languages could not save pagan institutions. The fourth and fifth centuries, with their social and political upheavals, saw a second Babel. Each petty kingdom of mutilated Europe formed its dialect. The Bible, proclaiming peace and good will to men, was lost amid the ruin of crumbling empires. The needy multitudes knew not its teachings, felt not its influence. Then Gregory, touched with sympathy for the blue-eyed Angles on the streets of Rome, thought to teach them of the humble Nazarene, and struck the key-note to the pæan of modern civilization. To a promising race he gave Christianity. This faith has been the guiding influence through the mightiest conflicts of centuries. It was the power that broke from the Anglo-Saxon the shackles of ignorance and superstition, and that wrought this crude speech into a noble language and literature.

From this time forward the power and influence of our language increased slowly but grandly. Seven centuries passed in preparation for a literature. The Norman conquest came and with it a higher type of refinement. For a time the Englishman seemed forgotten. The court, learning, and art, spurned his speech. His rich legendary lore promised to be unsung, his conquests and valor, untold. Feudal lords bound him to the earth. The fountain of fame was to him as the water of Tantalus. But it was not to be always thus. The feudal system of the Norman was a greater evil than his culture was a blessing. The Englishman hated civilization which did not civilize. A new era was dawning. Feudalism and chivalry —noblest institutions of a blinded age—could not suppress the growing influence of that divinely-taught principle, the universal brotherhood of man. Through common interests a common speech was adopted, and the problem of equality was solved. The heart of the serf thrilled as he heard his language ringing through palace halls, enriched by the cultured sentiment of a courtly nobility. Thus the river, silently flowing beneath the rough surface of society, broke forth in singular sublimity. English literature found a beginning. Chaucer became the father of English poetry, Wyclif translated the Bible, and our language began its mission to the world.

Anglo-Saxon civilization is unparalleled in its material growth, its broad learning, and its social, moral and political development. Men come and go, and the immortal products of their genius are their bequests to the world. The accumulations of art and science make the contributing ages appear like the range of mountain-peaks—each towering high above its predecessor in Alpine magnificence. We behold and wonder what influences could have produced such grand results. Did inventive genius alone make the greatness of America? Has mere strength of arms carried England's flag into every habitable part of earth? Does Saxon valor, Saxon ambition, and Saxon firmness, account entirely for the civil and religious liberty of one-half the globe? No. Transcending all these powerful agencies, the English language stands out the exponent of modern civilization. It is the embodiment of progressive thought, the matchless attainment of a progressive age. In its store-house of words are the gems of the classics and the pearls of modern tongues. It is the key-stone in the arch of commerce to-day. In every battle against tyranny it has furnished the countersigns of freedom. Magna Chartas, Declarations of Independence, and Emancipation Proclamations, are its products. It is the "language of Bunyan and the Bible" —an argument for the Christian religion. Would you know its influence to-day—destroy its literature, blot out the results of its existence, and think what would be the condition of the world. Where would be our glorious institutions, our resplendent civilization, our blood-bought liberties?

Our literature seems boundless like a summer landscape; we approach the apparent limit, while Nature keeps unrolling her scroll of beauty. English libraries testify to an elegance of expression, a vividness of description, a terseness in narration, not to be found elsewhere. Note the stately prose of Macaulay, the picturesque delineations of Scott, the rugged energy of Carlyle; but these are only of thousands who have made our language shine with sunlit brilliancy. English literature bears the impress of every advance of education and morals. Science has given it a vocabulary abreast with her phenomenal development. Christian philosophy has placed therein truths never dreamed of by a Plato or an Aristotle. Here, no less than in society, the progress of morals has witnessed evolution. The sensual odes and Bacchanalian songs, rehearsed at the midnight revels and chanted around the altars of the gods, departed with the civilization that gave them birth. The pure character, the virtuous teaching, the ennobling sentiment are now the demands of literary merit and culture.

Grand principles and momentous questions have aroused the sleeping art of the ancients, and oratory has burst forth in this new language. Here it has found its true mission and achieved its greatest victories. The halls of parliament and of congress have been fit substitutes for the bema and the forum. The burning eloquence of Burke and Chatham, Henry and Webster, pleading for freedom, justice, and equality, was never surpassed by the "Orator of Athens" inveighing against Philip, or the Roman senator thundering against Catiline.

Is the poetry of our language excelled by any other? Did ancient bard ever picture human nature like Shakespeare? Is the "Fall of Troy" to be compared with the "Fall of Man?" Were Achilles and Æneas sublimer heroes than the fallen Archangel? Ah! gifted poets have sung and proved that—

> "From Saxon lips Anacreon's numbers glide,
> As once they melted on the Teian tide;
> And fresh transfused, the Iliad thrills again
> From Albion's cliffs as o'er Achaia's plain!"

As Napoleon marshaled his armed hosts before the pyramids of Egypt, he said, "Soldiers, forty centuries look down upon you." We, to-day, from a height of truth and liberty, say: Forty centuries look up to us. The crisis of nations finds our race leading a mightier and a more glorious civilization than forty centuries have seen. Yet after all this advancement, this attainment of power, our language seems only to have begun its mission. The rivulet that gushed from its fountain has swelled into a great river, and all its usefulness seems yet before it. Greater fields of thought are to be fertilized; ships of State are to float serenely, sublimely, on its majestic current; it is to broaden into a mighty ocean and wash every shore of humanity.

To-day the civilized world looks to the Anglo-Saxon, with his linguistic inheritance, for the solution of every question of moral reform; Christendom recognizes him as her defender; heathedom sends forth wails of distress for his sympathy.

This eminence is his because of his eloquence and song in the triumphant march of human freedom. Thus, as "through the ages one increasing purpose run," we may see in a veiled but certain future the destiny of our race, dedicated to truth and to God; and we may hear reverberating through the centuries the glad anthem of that "varied music from an hundred tongues," our English language.

# ORATORS AND ORATORY,

AND

# PLAGIARISM.

# ORATORS AND ORATORY.

### By Prof. George W. Hoss, A. M., LL. D.

Nothing brings heart within touching distance of heart like the tongue. Hence, speaking seems nature's ordained means of informing and moving men. While this is true generally, in no country is it more specifically true than in ours. This fact grows out of the nature of our institutions. Here all men are free — free to think, believe, and utter what they will. The humblest farmer or craftsman has the same right to utter his thoughts that a governor or president has. This is not so in monarchies or despotisms. Moreover, public opinion, especially in political matters, is largely formed by means of public speaking. Our laws are largely made and applied by this same means, hence he who cannot speak, often cannot rise in these departments. Hence in a government by the people the tongue is a power.

Second, in the preaching of the gospel this is more markedly true. This rises in importance and sacredness above law-making. When Christ said, "Go preach," He hallowed public speaking above any act or utterance ever made by man. He ordained it as a means for the accomplishment of the greatest work known to humanity, namely, the salvation of the race. He enforced this command by his own example; he wrote no words, but spake, and never as man spake. Here is a marvel, a kingdom to be established, and not a statute or a line written by the law-giver. This command and this example still stand as law and guide, as they did eighteen hundred years ago. Viewed, therefore, from either the sacred or secular side of the facts, the plea for public speaking becomes strong.

Viewed intellectually the orator stands midway between the poet and the philosopher; oratory, between poetry and philosophy. 'T is a legitimate child of this holy wedlock, an heir apparent to the throne in this royal household. One side of oratory addresses the understanding, and seeks to convince — this is philosophy; the other side addresses the imagination and sensibilities, and seeks to please, to move — this is poetry, at least poetic. Therefore high oratory, eloquence, is a composite of philosophy and poetry, addressing the understanding, the imagination, and the sensibilities, and binding these three in one, sweeps on to the will, and compassing the whole man in its purpose, bears him on, right on to the highest sphere of life, namely, action; noble, heroic, and at times sublime, awe-inspiring action.

Oratory is therefore a happy blending of the didactic, argumentative, passional, and the ornate; a kind of philosophic poetry, a poetic philosophy, and these often on fire.

From the above, as a basis, we may divide oratory into four general classes, which for the sake of method we will call the

### DIVISIONS OF ORATORY.

Of these we notice:

I. THE ORATORY OF REASON.

The matter of this is fact, truth, principle; its form argument. It is clear, cold, logical, condensed. Its principal aim is information, conviction; hence in the main it avoids both imagination and feeling, especially in the body of the discourse.

This style is found in the lawyer's argument addressed to the judge; in the judge's charge to the jury; in pleading before cabinets; in State papers and the like. The Declaration of Independence is a good specimen: "We hold these truths to be self-evident: that all men are created equal; that they are endowed by their Creator with certain inalienable rights; that among these are life, liberty, and the pursuit of happiness. To secure these rights governments are instituted among men, deriving their just powers from the consent of the governed." The Bible furnishes fine specimens: "In the beginning was the Word, and the Word was with God, and the Word was God. The same was in the beginning with God. All things were made by him, and without him was not anything made that was made. In him was life, and the life was the light of men." John, I.

This style finds its highest expression in mathematics, in geometry. This last is pure reason; no feeling, hence no gesture, no declamation, no attitudes.

Of this class of oratory Webster and Morton, of this country, and Lord Lyndhurst, of England, are good representatives. Their matter was chiefly argument, hence their manner unimpassioned. Lyndhurst, says Webster, would at times make an entire address without raising his hand in gesture. Morton gestured but little, Webster more, but much less than Clay.

This style of oratory relies but little on delivery, but almost wholly on matter, hence not so popular; often called dry, especially by the young and the unlearned.

II. ORATORY OF THE IMAGINATION.

This is ornate, artistic. It is elegant in language and rich in imagery. This is the field of the esthetic. Thought is robed in a garb of beauty that pleases, charms, captivates. Figures of rhetoric, classic allusions, harmonious sentences, rich and varied imagery, unfold before you like the ever-changing scenes in a panorama, Imagination rules the hour persuading you that the ideal is real, that the real is ideal, "giving to airy nothings a local habitation and a name." If possessed of bolder pinion, it ascends into the sublime where it awes while it attracts. The orator has in a good degree become the poet, and, like the poet, gathering his singing robes about him, and ascending the mount of vision, touches his harp and passes in music and beauty out of sight.

Of this style of oratory Everett and Burke are at times good representatives. In Everett the artistic and ornate are prominent, sometimes in excess. In Burke the reasoning is sometimes obscured by ornament, the fruit is hid by excess of leaf and flower. This class of oratory is sometimes characterized as oriental, pleasing rather than convincing, showy rather than strong; a kind of Bird of Paradise with more wing and feathers than body. We gaze upon it as upon a picture, and listen to it as to an opera—pleased, delighted, yet seldom moved. The fruit of high eloquence is wanting. There is but little resolve and less action. The esthetic reigns here, hence nearer kin to fine arts than any other style of oratory.

III. ORATORY OF FEELING, PASSION.

Here the heart rules. Here words come warm with feeling, often aglow with passion. They breathe, they burn. Men speak as if a divinity stirred within, not by form or rule, but as of old, when moved by the Holy Ghost. This form of oratory has its birth in great occasions, when mobs are to be quelled, revolutions to be guided, or country to be saved; when "men's lives and fortunes hang on the decision of the hour;" as when Jonah cried in hot haste, "Yet forty days and Ninevah shall be destroyed;" or when Peter ejaculated his prayer, "Lord, save, or I perish." In this last the whole man was in his speech; his soul flew on winged words to the ear of the Master.

A remarkable instance is found in modern times in the case of Patrick Henry, the mouth-piece of the revolution, when he shouted, "Give me liberty, or give me death!" and a nation springing to its feet, shouted to the tyrant across the sea, "*Liberty or death!*" This is eloquence—great thoughts, strong feeling, and impressive delivery. Coupled with great virtues it inspires, awes, conquers. It crowns the orator king, while the multitude bows in ready submission to his will, or rises in its might to do his bidding.

Feeling, passion, is the conquering agent. The law of its power is, *passion is catching;* the tear begets a tear; joy, joy; fear, fear; courage, courage; heroism, heroism, as certainly as fire kindles fire. Hence the law: *The speaker who wishes his audience to feel, must feel first.* This is the law of eloquence, universal, unvarying. So the world has judged in all ages, and so judges to-day. Hence all who have been great in eloquence have been great in passional power; as Demosthenes, Chatham, Fox, Mirabeau, Henry, Otis, Clay, Whitefield, Simpson, and hosts of others. So the great preachers of other days in this and other countries. They burned as well as argued their way into men's souls.

This true, it is inevitable that the man who can't feel deeply and express himself strongly, may justly despair of high eloquence. These feelings must be broad, lasting, and strong, burning like fire in the bones, like lava beds in heart, blood and brain. These are a power; they crown their possessor victor.

IV. ORATORY OF DELIVERY.

This is the field of elocution, and is what the ancients called action. When Demosthenes was asked what was the first principle of eloquence, he answered, "*action;*" the second, "*action;*" the third, "*action.*" Cicero said, "all the parts of oratory succeed as they are delivered." "Delivery," says he further, "has the supreme power in oratory. Without it a speaker of the greatest mental, power cannot be held in any esteem, while with it one of moderate ability may surpass those of greatest talents." Quintilian held much the same view, saying 't is not of so much importance what are ones thoughts, as it is in what manner they are delivered. These statements are strong, too strong for our age, but we can abate a large per cent. and still have a strong plea for delivery. A more intellectual age puts a lower price on delivery.

Speakers strong in feeling are usually impressive in delivery, so we find the same representatives as in the last division. One of the ablest ever known in this department was the great field preacher, George Whitefield. His powers were simply marvelous. His voice, says his biographer, could be heard distinctly by thirty thousand people. It is said he could pronounce a single word with such pathos as to throw an audience into tears. Garrick said he would give a hundred guineas if he could pronounce the single letter O as Whitefield could. His preaching moved the practical Franklin, and so impressed the cold and skeptical Hume as to say, "I would go twenty miles any day to hear him." His power was largely in delivery, his printed sermons showing neither great power of thought nor wide range of scholarship. Such men should not have their speeches printed unless the speaker can be printed with them. Their speeches should be heard, not read.

EXAMPLES: Henry Clay won largely through delivery. His clarion voice, flashing eye, and dilating figure moved senates almost at will. It is said a single exclamation from him would bring an audience to almost breathless silence. In delivery, Lord Brougham was king. In sarcasm and invective, attack and defense, he was terrific. He was the gladiator of Parliament. Fierce, vengeful, irresistible, you more than saw his glare and heard his roar—you felt them. He seemed a mixture of man and lion—the lion often in front. This is the victory of physical courage and physical force. These have won with many; as Fox, Chatham, Mirabeau, Luther, and others. These were the men to contend with popes and kings, men who, as Luther says of himself, were born to "fight whirlwinds and devils." Such men are for great crises, times that try men's souls, when blood touches blood, and victory is born of death. The oratory of such men like themselves is powerful in passion and action, hence powerful in delivery.

From the above survey it is obvious that the problem of oratory becomes in a good degree the problem of metaphysics. He who would control mind must know mind. He must know how to address the understanding to the exclusion of the imagination and feelings, and *vice versa*. He must know how to build a solid masonry of argument, strong as a military fortress, and if need be, as rough and cold; and when built, he must know whether to leave it thus, or to soften its rugged outline by flinging over it a drapery of sunshine and flowers. He must know whether reason rules alone, or whether reason blended with the imagination, or feeling, or both.

At other times he may wish the imagination to rule, weaving a web as light as gossamer or gorgeous as the Orient. At another time it is passion, when the soul becomes a furnace, and speech a mixture of whirlwind and fire. In a word, he must know, and that clearly, whether his aim is to *please*, to *instruct, to convince, to move*, or *to storm*. His aim known, he will know his instruments, whether logic, rhetoric, delivery, singly or combined. Here as everywhere aim or end must determine means.

# PLAGIARISM.

By Prof. Stephen G. Barnes, Ph. D.

The editor of this volume of oratory has honored me by a request to contribute, on the subject of plagiarism, a chapter that shall be "general and brief." The gentle reader is therefore and hereby warned that no ponderous polemics, no sensational details, are to be expected; only a "swallow flight, that dips its wings and skims away."

The plagiarist is a literary pickpocket; he lives in the region of dishonesties that are small and mean. But he is also an ostentatious fop, and is therefore compelled to be audacious with his stolen "shreds and patches." No offender against moral law is more sure to be found out, and to be counted a knave for his thievery, and a fool for his display. This no one will deny. So long as we stick to generalities, and confine ourselves to the abstract plagiarist, there is no special difficulty. It is when a concrete case arises, and one is asked "Did X plagiarize?" that the rub comes. In morals, as in statecraft, the application of the law is what taxes the vision and strength of humanity.

Let us look for a little at *meum* and *tuum*, at the problem of production and reproduction. It seems clear, to begin with, that without receiving there can be no giving; there will be nothing to give. The man in "Joe Miller" who never reads books, because he is too busy writing them, is droll, because he is in such utter incongruity with the conditions of literary production. When the Amazon can dispense with all its tributaries, then may an author ignore all other authors. And not only material but skill comes from contact with other minds; iron sharpeneth iron. The literary apprentice puts himself to school; he studies the methods used in literature; he translates, imitates, selects, varies, adapts. Having something to say is not enough; he must know how to say it. If he wishes to be heard as a German, he must have command of the German language; if he wishes to reach men through the channels of literature, he must learn where those channels run, and at what places in the great blank wall that faces the young aspirant his stream will be admitted. And most important of all is the inspiration that comes from great writers and orators, men whose powers are utterly beyond our reach, but whose splendid thoughts and noble achievements arouse in us energies undreamed of before, and raise to a furnace heat all the fusible materials of the soul. Only by such excitation of his various capacities can man find what is in him, and what is strongest in him, and thus discover his real self. No man has been original, in any high and supreme sense, who has not first been imitative.

The value of all this process, however, depends on its steady movement toward the goal. To put it in Hegelian phrase, "self-realization" must be its purpose and its vindication. To be filled passively with material from outside is no high attainment, even though it is better than absolute emptiness. The mind that makes itself real, selects; it begins by selecting its authorities, it goes on by selecting from its chosen authority that which most commends itself for assimilation. Then its growing wealth demands arrangement, and system begins; logical relations are discerned and followed, and in the course of time the mind has its own convictions and philosophy. Just so is it with methods. So long as one uses the method of another as the method of another he is a mere copyist; not until he begins to decide what he can do best, and what devices he can best employ, is there any real beginning to his life as an artist. From that time forth the materials of others are simply foods that nourish and expand his individuality; the methods of others are but exercises by which he trains his powers for independent work.

He who would produce, therefore, must first reproduce; he who would have a *meum* must begin by liberal use of the *tuum*. And by such use "the party of the second part" is most highly honored; the measure of such appropriation is precisely the measure of his influence. But it is to be noted that appropriation and exploitation are not identical. Thought is not an ornament that can be appended externally; no one really makes it his own who does not "chew and digest" it, incorporating it thus with the body of his thinking. A man may have a trick of verbal memory which will enable him to recall passage after passage from literature, and yet they may be as helpless as withered seeds scattered over an iron soil. He may absolutely forget word and phrase, just as he may forget entirely a cooling draught of water, yet the strength and joy of it may enter into all his subsequent work.

"Ye shall be original" is the tempter's lure to this plagiaristic tree, and we need to see that here as in Eden we get the knowledge of good by losing it, and of evil by incurring it. Plagiarism is in direct contradiction of those habits of mind which will make a man really original. It is the folly of a green peach that would fain have itself painted with poisonous red, so as to make men think it ripe. Especially should the young speaker have patience with himself, and confidence in the good nature and good sense of his audience. He is still and necessarily in his 'prentice period, still gathering his materials, still testing his powers, still engaged in that most fascinating search for the true self, whose expression will be his service to his generation. Under such circumstances it is sheer folly to seek originality in the ordinary and superficial sense. He will merely rake over the remote corners of his mind for some unused and forgotten remnants of former acquisitions, whose very disuse proves their ineptness. Or he will seek some author or thinker whose views are singular, and will slavishly repeat his statements in a kind of theatrical imitation of real fire. Still more cheap and tawdry is the method of contrariness, of saying things that are startling because negative, in which attitude the would-be original is no more admirable than a baulky mule. At the foot of this slippery plane is the man who seeks some presumedly unknown production, really exhibiting qualities he is anxious to display, and who "conveys" his speech bodily, with such alternations and mutilations as may suffice in his mind to bring it down to the suppositional level on which the audience may be led to believe his own powers disport themselves.

In sharp contrast with all this folly and fever is the simple and effective rule of genuineness. Let a man give his own, and give his best, taking a theme in which he is thoroughly interested, and saying the things that he fully believes. It makes no difference if they have been said thousands of times before: that is true of all the things best worth saying. Freshness, individuality, will invest with an infallible charm the most familiar thoughts. Life is the secret, not superficial strangeness. Life everywhere makes its own place, and furnishes its own justification.

What then shall be our attitude towards the words and phrases of another? First of all is needed a protest against the use of quotations as mere ornament; it is in the taste of the savage who pierces his upper lip for gold rings, not because they have any fitness there, but because he conceives them to be pretty. Beauty must be subordinate, or it becomes unmeaning and offensive. When quotations are made, they should be clearly indicated. In the olden time a man took his materials wherever he could find them; Shakespeare, Milton, borrowed by the wholesale, for that was the universal spirit of literary work. The poet was no more obliged to originate his figures than the green-grocer to offer nothing but what he raised in his own garden; the public asked no question beyond the quality of the goods. Wisely and unwisely all this is now changed. A man is understood to claim as his own all that is not distinctly labeled otherwise; and the unacknowledged spoliation of happy phrase and sonorous period has therefore become an inexcusable dishonesty. In writing, quotation marks should show every borrowed passage, used because better than our own and therefore by no means to be presented as our own. In speaking, since quotation marks do not appeal to the ear, special care should be taken, not only to show where the borrowing begins but where it ends. Such frankness automatically prevents excessive quotation; the lack of it usually suffices to "kill" a speech, for nothing is more damaging than a growing suspicion in the audience that the speaker is a daw parading in peacock's feathers.

If we were to dip into the history of plagiarism, pages could be filled with famous cases, and their arguments *pro* and *con*. The charge has often been rash and ridiculous, based upon the slightest of resemblance, or neglectful of the fact that literature is by its nature a highway for thousands of feet. No one can be asked to read everything on his subject, so as to be sure he says nothing that anybody else has said. Many offenders have been more or less exonerated by the plea of unconscious recollection. Some minds have a tenacious sense of verbal form, and with them the recollection of a thought, and of its words, are one and the same thing. But with our present literary standards such a man ought to watch his memory as closely as he would his hand if he knew himself to have tendencies toward kleptomania; the memory should be trained a little further so as to include not only the words but the name of the man who wrote them. The author must be above suspicion. It is vastly better to err on the side of openness than of silence. The first stirring of unwillingness to state frankly where borrowed material was obtained should reveal the man to his own conscience as not far from the kingdom of thieves. For him who willfully filches and brazenly parades his fine periods no drumming out of the camp with the rogue's march can be too severe. The cases that have occurred in the history of these oratorical contests show that society still has a duty of instruction by means of vigorous penalties. Let us hope the time is not far distant when audiences will be reasonable in all their demands, and speakers thoroughly honest and gladly generous in all their dealings with the great world of thought into which it is their and our magnificent privilege to be born.

www.ingramcontent.com/pod-product-compliance
Lightning Source LLC
Chambersburg PA
CBHW021954220426
43663CB00007B/813